VENTURE CAPITAL IN EMERGING MARKETS

VENTURE CAPITAL IN EMERGING MARKETS

LESSONS FROM INDONESIA'S DIGITAL DECADE

**ADRIAN LI AND
LEIGHTON COSSEBOOM**

WILEY

Copyright © 2025 by John Wiley & Sons. All rights reserved.

Published by John Wiley & Sons, Inc., Hoboken, New Jersey.
Published simultaneously in Canada.

No part of this publication may be reproduced, stored in a retrieval system, or transmitted in any form or by any means, electronic, mechanical, photocopying, recording, scanning, or otherwise, except as permitted under Section 107 or 108 of the 1976 United States Copyright Act, without either the prior written permission of the Publisher, or authorization through payment of the appropriate per-copy fee to the Copyright Clearance Center, Inc., 222 Rosewood Drive, Danvers, MA 01923, (978) 750-8400, fax (978) 750-4470, or on the web at www.copyright.com. Requests to the Publisher for permission should be addressed to the Permissions Department, John Wiley & Sons, Inc., 111 River Street, Hoboken, NJ 07030, (201) 748-6011, fax (201) 748-6008, or online at http://www.wiley.com/go/permission.

Trademarks: Wiley and the Wiley logo are trademarks or registered trademarks of John Wiley & Sons, Inc. and/or its affiliates in the United States and other countries and may not be used without written permission. All other trademarks are the property of their respective owners. John Wiley & Sons, Inc. is not associated with any product or vendor mentioned in this book.

Limit of Liability/Disclaimer of Warranty: While the publisher and author have used their best efforts in preparing this book, they make no representations or warranties with respect to the accuracy or completeness of the contents of this book and specifically disclaim any implied warranties of merchantability or fitness for a particular purpose. No warranty may be created or extended by sales representatives or written sales materials. The advice and strategies contained herein may not be suitable for your situation. You should consult with a professional where appropriate. Further, readers should be aware that websites listed in this work may have changed or disappeared between when this work was written and when it is read. Neither the publisher nor authors shall be liable for any loss of profit or any other commercial damages, including but not limited to special, incidental, consequential, or other damages.

For general information on our other products and services or for technical support, please contact our Customer Care Department within the United States at (800) 762-2974, outside the United States at (317) 572-3993 or fax (317) 572-4002.

Wiley also publishes its books in a variety of electronic formats. Some content that appears in print may not be available in electronic formats. For more information about Wiley products, visit our web site at www.wiley.com.

Library of Congress Cataloging-in-Publication Data Applied for:

Print ISBN: 9781394313655
ePDF ISBN: 9781394313662
epub ISBN: 9781394313679

Cover Image: © ChonnieArtwork/stock.adobe.com
Cover Design: Jon Boylan

Printed and bound by CPI Group (UK) Ltd, Croydon, CR0 4YY

C9781394313655_170425

The manufacturer's authorized representative according to the EU General Product Safety Regulation is Wiley-VCH GmbH, Boschstr. 12, 69469 Weinheim, Germany, e-mail: Product_Safety@wiley.com.

To Pandu Sjahrir, Michael Soerijadji, and Helen Wong, your visionary leadership, rooted in discipline, wisdom, and fortitude, has been the driving force behind our firm's progress to date, serving as a beacon for entrepreneurs across the region. Your courage and conviction in furthering Indonesia's digital ecosystem have made a profound impact on both the economy and society, and will continue to do so for years to come. It is a privilege to partner with you on this journey, and I offer my heartfelt gratitude.

— *Adrian*

To Annisa Bella Syana. S., your imaginative ideas and relentless focus inspire me every day, fueling my optimism about the next generation of creative minds. It is an honor to know you and to do this work with you.

To Aditya Hadi Pratama, thank you for helping to make this book possible through our fascinating coffee chats.

— *Leighton*

ABOUT THE AUTHORS

Adrian Li is a seasoned entrepreneur and investor in Southeast Asia's tech sector with more than 20 years of experience. Since establishing one of Indonesia's earliest venture capital firms in 2014, he has backed more than 80 companies to date, including some of the most renowned names in the region such as Stockbit, Xendit, Julo, Carsome, and others. With entrepreneurial roots in China and Indonesia, his first startup in China was in online English training which was acquired in 2010. He later created new ventures with Rocket Internet in China and Southeast Asia before laying the foundation for what would ultimately become one of Indonesia's leading venture and growth equity firms AC Ventures in 2019. Adrian completed his undergraduate education at Cambridge University and his MBA at Stanford GSB. He is a Kauffman Fellow, Class of 2021, and a long-standing YPO member.

With more than 15 years of experience in Asia as a media and marketing entrepreneur, **Leighton Cosseboom** founded Southeast Asia's leading tech PR firm Content Collision, with a deep roster of Fortune 500 clients like Alibaba, Western Digital, and Expedia Group. His ventures serve a variety of global blue-chip clients such as Cision, Axel Springer, South China Morning Post, and Boston Consulting Group. Leighton was a senior editor

ABOUT THE AUTHORS

for Tech in Asia, where he broke stories on Indonesia's first mega-rounds of funding and became known as the market's top tech reporter. He double-majored in journalism and advertising at the University of Oregon, in recent years, he served as a senior leader at AC Ventures, overseeing owned and earned media programs and providing hands-on support to more than 120 portfolio companies. He is now the founder of Mission Media, a strategic marketing consultancy in Asia.

CONTENTS

GLOSSARY — xi

KEY INDONESIAN CONGLOMERATES IN TECH — xiii

ABOUT AC VENTURES — xv

FOREWORD — xvii

PREFACE — xxi

CHAPTER ONE
  E-COMMERCE EMERGES IN THE WILD — 1

CHAPTER TWO
  A GERMAN ROCKET SHIP ARRIVES — 15

CHAPTER THREE
  THE EARLY ERA OF E-COMMERCE BATTLES — 39

CHAPTER FOUR
  PAYMENTS, LOGISTICS, AND POLICY SCRAMBLE TO KEEP PACE — 55

CONTENTS

CHAPTER FIVE
    GOJEK, GRAB, AND THE WAR FOR TWO-WHEELED DOMINANCE   73

CHAPTER SIX
    INDONESIA'S VENTURE OPPORTUNITY, HIDDEN IN PLAIN SIGHT   91

CHAPTER SEVEN
    THE EVOLUTION OF FINTECH IN INDONESIA   103

CHAPTER EIGHT
    COVID-19 BRINGS DIGITAL ADOPTION FORWARD BY 10 YEARS   119

CHAPTER NINE
    IMPACT IN THE TIME OF DIGITIZED MICRO-BUSINESS   137

CHAPTER TEN
    THE NEXT 10 YEARS: INDONESIA'S DIGITAL DECADE   149

REFERENCES   159
INDEX   199

GLOSSARY

API	Application programming interface
B2B	Business-to-business
B2C	Business-to-consumer
B2B2C	Business-to-business-to-consumer
BNPL	Buy-now-pay-later
BRI	Bank Rakyat Indonesia
C2C	Consumer-to-consumer
CAGR	Compound annual growth rate
COD	Cash-on-delivery
ESG	Environmental, social, and governance
GDP	Gross domestic product
GMV	Gross merchandise value
halal	Arabic for "permissible," used in relation to *sharia* law, often with regard to the ingredients of foods, cosmetics, and other consumer products
IPO	Initial public offering
KPI	Key performance indicator

GLOSSARY

KYC	Know-your-customer
Mbps	Megabits per second
MSMEs	Micro, small, and medium enterprises
O2O	Online-to-offline
ojek	Indonesian word for motorbike taxis that are the transportation lifeblood of traffic-jammed Jakarta
OJK	*Otoritas Jasa Keuangan,* Indonesia's financial services authority
R&D	Research and development
sharia	Islamic religious law that governs aspects of day-to-day life for Muslims in addition to religious rituals
SME	Small to medium enterprise
VC	Venture capital
LP	Limited partner (and investor that put money into VC funds)
warung	Indonesian term for mom-and-pop shops and outdoor food stalls found throughout the archipelago

KEY INDONESIAN CONGLOMERATES IN TECH

All Included in Forbes Top 50 Richest People and Companies in Indonesia (Note: Table is not exhaustive)

Company	Description	Key People	Tech Investments
Astra International	Southeast Asia's largest independent automotive group	Budi, Arya, and Ardi Setiadharma	Gojek, Presetia Dwidharma, OLX Indonesia
Djarum Group	One of Indonesia's first *kretek* (clove cigarette) manufacturers; now highly diversified in banking, technology, retail, etc.	R. Budi, Michael and Martin Hartono	GDP Venture, Blibli, Gojek
Emtek Group	Technology, media, and telecommunications	Eddy, Alvin, and Adi Sariaatmadja	Grab, Bukalapak, Carro, Nium, Vidio
Kompas Gramedia Group	Mass media, hospitality, manufacturing, event organizing	Lilik and Geraldine Oetama	Skystar Capital
Lippo Group	Property development, retail, banking, hospitality, etc	Mochtar, James, and John Riady	Venturra Capital, Matahari Mall, OVO
Mayapada Group	Financial services, healthcare, media, property development, retail, etc.	Ang Tjoen Ming, Grace Tahir, and family	IDN Media, Medico
Salim Group	FMCG, retail, property development, etc.	Anthoni and Axton Salim	Rocket Internet via PLDT

(Continued)

(Continued)

Company	Description	Key People	Tech Investments
Sinar Mas Group	Paper and pulp, agribusiness, financial services, property development, energy, infrastructure, healthcare, etc.	Eka Tjipta Widjaja and family	Sinar Mas Digital Ventures, DANA, Living Lab Ventures

ABOUT AC VENTURES

AC Ventures is a leading venture and growth equity investing in tech-enabled businesses focused on Indonesia and Southeast Asia. The firm's mission is to partner with and empower entrepreneurs with more than capital to build valuable and enduring companies. It combines operational experience, industry knowledge, deep local networks, and resources to create value for startups. The firm's vision is to be a generational partner to entrepreneurs driving positive societal change and economic impact in Indonesia and beyond.

AC Ventures leverages the Upright Project from Helsinki for ESG and impact measurement in accordance with Northern European standards. It uses a "net impact ratio" to assess impact across four dimensions, scoring an above-average +37%, compared to the Nasdaq Small Cap Index's +29%.

To date, the firm has positively impacted more than 7.5 million lives and businesses in the region, including the improvement of lives for more than 4 million low and middle-income earners and MSMEs. Sixty-one percent of its companies are present in second- and third-tier cities, creating more than 200,000 jobs in the region.

Indonesia's MSMEs represent 98% of all businesses in the nation, which contribute more than 61% to the market's US$1.38 trillion economy. Estimates suggest that more than half of these are, in fact, women-owned. AC Ventures champions diversity and inclusion with women holding 50% of its in-house senior leadership roles. Across its portfolio, this figure comes in at 41%. It is an official signatory of the UN's Women's Empowerment Principles, the IFC's Invest2Equal program, and the UN's Principles for Responsible Investing.

ABOUT AC VENTURES

AC Ventures currently has more than US$500 million in assets under management, invested across five funds. Since 2012, the firm's partners have invested in more than 120 technology companies in the region, including some of the most iconic names in the ASEAN digital ecosystem. The firm's partners Adrian Li, Michael Soerijadji, Helen Wong, and Pandu Sjahrir lead a team of more than 40 professionals with offices in Jakarta and Singapore.

FOREWORD

A STORY OF DIGITAL EMPOWERMENT AND ECONOMIC AGILITY

This book comes at a pivotal moment, as we stand at the crossroads of unprecedented global challenges and a transformative era in Indonesia's digital landscape. Currently valued at US$82 billion, Indonesia's digital economy remains on track to reach US$360 billion by 2030.

The past few years have been marked by significant international challenges that have reshaped the global economy. The Middle East conflict, the ongoing Ukraine–Russia war, the decoupling of US–China relations, and the repercussions of rising interest rates and inflation have all created uncertainty at the time of writing. These global dynamics have had far-reaching effects, influencing markets and investment climates worldwide.

Yet, amidst this turbulence, Indonesia has shown remarkable resilience. Our nation has managed to maintain strong economic growth, along with manageable inflation and low government debt, distinguishing itself as an emerging market leader.

FOREWORD

Indonesia is experiencing rapid economic growth, primarily attributed to its favorable demographic composition, with over 70% of its 277 million inhabitants being between the ages of 15 and 64. This scenario, widely recognized as the "demographic dividend," presents a significant opportunity for the nation to enhance its financial position on the world stage.

To fully capitalize on this advantage, Indonesia must concentrate on elevating the average income of its citizens. This endeavor transcends mere financial gain; it is a critical imperative for the nation's future prosperity and stability.

Human capital development stands at the forefront of this growth trajectory. Our focus on improving human capital through technology, particularly in education and R&D, is integral. By leveraging technology, we can enhance the overall quality of local education and create a workforce ready for the global challenges of the digital age. The comparative data on international assessment scores show a pressing need to elevate our educational standards to global levels.

In terms of the economy at large, education, healthcare, and the environment emerge as critical areas for investment and growth. Digital transformation in these sectors is not just a matter of economic progress but also a commitment to the well-being and sustainability of our society.

The importance of technology and innovation cannot be overstated in driving Indonesia's economic growth. Tech-enabled companies have become the backbone of our economy, propelling us into a new era. This is where our focus on nurturing a vibrant ecosystem for startups and innovation becomes pivotal. Investment in healthcare, including R&D, has the potential to revolutionize the sector, providing better services and improving overall public health.

Environmental commitments, particularly our dedication to decarbonization and reducing greenhouse gas emissions, reflect Indonesia's role as a responsible global actor. It is an acknowledgment that economic growth should not come at the expense of our environment.

For the corporate sector, the message is clear: agility, cost-efficiency, and digital adaptability are key to navigating market uncertainties. The pandemic has underscored the need for businesses to be flexible and technologically equipped to face unexpected challenges.

The investment landscape, especially in the realm of mergers and acquisitions, offers vast opportunities, particularly for companies with strong cash positions. VC deal value in Indonesia has remained relatively stable year-over-year, with a keen focus on early-stage investments.

Indonesia's attractiveness as an investment destination is multifaceted. Factors like geopolitical shifts, the burgeoning e-commerce sector, and supportive government policies, play a significant role in shaping this landscape. Though fragmented, the investment space has seen a growing interest in early-stage deals, indicative of the confidence in Indonesia's long-term growth potential.

Our market, while still nascent, has shown promising signs of maturity, with exits via both trade sales and IPOs. This maturation is driven by sectors like e-commerce, mobility, and fintech, all of which have produced unicorns in recent years.

Indonesia's long-term prospects as a venture capital investment destination remain promising. Strong market fundamentals, coupled with a maturing investor base, indicate a bright future for the local digital economy.

"Venture Capital in Emerging Markets" is not just a narrative of the past and present; it is a roadmap for the future. It encapsulates the journey of a nation that is rapidly adapting to digital transformation while navigating global economic challenges. As you digest this book, I invite you to explore the variety of opportunities and challenges ahead for Indonesia in this exciting time.

—Pandu Sjahrir
Chief Investment Officer
Danantara

PREFACE

Over a decade ago, Indonesia's digital ecosystem was an emerging vision, with internet penetration hovering around 23% and e-commerce sales barely touching US$1 billion. Fast forward to today and internet penetration has surged to more than 65%, with e-commerce sales projected to surpass US$55 billion. The sheer magnitude of this transformation is astonishing, and as I look across the rapidly changing skyline of Jakarta Metro's megalopolis of more than 20 million people, I feel an overwhelming sense of déjà vu, reminiscent of my earlier days in China.

While the landscapes are different, the vibrancy and entrepreneurial spirit are undeniably present. Indonesia has not only embarked on a transformative journey but also one that will create a new generation of entrepreneurs, bringing about broader social and economic impacts than previously possible. I have had the privilege of witnessing and participating in this metamorphosis firsthand as an entrepreneur and investor. I hope to capture in this book the nuances of its digital narrative from its emergence in 2010.

This book is a testament to that journey, diving deep into the heart of Indonesia's digital transformation over the past decade. Through firsthand experiences and on-ground insights, we explore the key sectors that have come to define the nation's digital narrative.

The book begins with the nascent days of online retail when young startups were venturing into uncharted territories. The subsequent arrival of Rocket Internet shook up the landscape, introducing new dynamics and challenges.

PREFACE

The evolution continues, chronicling the fierce battles that marked the early era of e-commerce in Indonesia. Payments, logistics, and policies, pivotal aspects of the ecosystem, scrambled to keep pace, setting the stage for further development.

We then dive into the intertwined story of the rivalry between titans—Gojek and Grab—their strategies, innovations, and the impact of their two-wheeled takeover on Indonesia's streets. This narrative serves as a precursor to where we uncover the hidden opportunities for global venture investors in the archipelago that many had previously overlooked.

We then zoom in on the evolution of fintech, revealing its growth trajectory and pivotal role in Indonesia's digital journey. The seismic events of the COVID-19 pandemic spotlight how a crisis expedited digital adoption and altered consumer behavior dramatically.

Transitioning to the grassroots level, we emphasize the growing significance of micro-businesses in a digitized era and the impact of these enterprises on the economy at large. The book concludes with a vision of the next 10 years, setting the stage for what may be Indonesia's most transformative decade yet.

Throughout these chapters, we've woven in personal narratives, insights, and observations. Drawing from our experiences both within and outside the country, the heart of this story remains deeply Indonesian.

In sharing these experiences, I hope to offer a window into the world of digital development in a rapidly emerging market: its challenges, opportunities, and above all, its transformative power. May this book serve as both an inspiration and a guide for those keen to be part of the next chapter of Indonesia's digital story as the country moves boldly on to become the world's fourth-largest economy in the next 25 years.

Here's to the entrepreneurs, investors, and stakeholders leading Indonesia's digital transformation in the years to come.

Adrian Li
Founder and Managing Partner
AC Ventures

This book is about the emergence of Indonesia's digital ecosystem. While its roots can be traced back more than a single decade, the true essence of these pages is about the present and the foreseeable future.

We use the term "Venture Capital in Emerging Markets" in the context of the next 10 years, an exciting future brimming with the promise of revolutionary advancements in areas like climate tech, renewable energy, the dynamic shift of economic empowerment favoring the nation's burgeoning middle class, and beyond.

As a former tech journalist, I had the fortuitous timing of covering the local VC space just a few months before Indonesia's first mega-round of startup funding. This unique positioning allowed me to not only document but also actively participate in and influence the defining moments of an industry undergoing a seismic shift.

In crafting this narrative, I've strived to amalgamate the hard facts and key events that shaped the industry's trajectory. Yet, to offer a holistic and intimate portrayal, I have also done my best to channel the perspectives and insights of Adrian, providing a bird's-eye view from the investor's vantage point. When you come across first-person anecdotes in this book, they are shown through his eyes.

It is our combined aspiration that this book establishes itself as a useful guide for global investors casting their gaze toward emerging markets in Asia. The narrative is a record of the past, but also a compass pointing toward untapped opportunities.

After reading it, I urge you to share your thoughts, reflections, and critiques. Indonesia's digital story is still evolving, and your voice is an integral part of it.

Leighton Cosseboom
Founder
Mission Media

CHAPTER ONE

E-COMMERCE EMERGES IN THE WILD

As ASEAN's single largest market, Indonesia has long held incredible economic potential, underpinned by powerful demographic fundamentals, such as a young and growing population of more than 280 million people.[1]

In less than 10 years, Indonesia's digital economy has grown from its infancy to a forecast of US$360 billion by 2030.[2] This value creation has happened across many industries: commerce, finance, MSMEs (micro, small, and medium enterprises), climate technology, and more. But one thing they all have in common is that they were created by visionary founders who persisted through the many challenges faced on the entrepreneurial journey.

In the early stages of internet adoption, startups in Indonesia encountered not only external challenges like limited internet penetration but also significant issues with payment systems and logistics. These foundational hurdles were compounded by a scarcity of capital for startups and hence funding to create robust, scalable businesses.

This chapter examines the emergence of Indonesia's digital economy, highlighting influential individuals, pivotal companies, and defining events that catalyzed its growth. The narrative begins with the early internet forums that linked Indonesian diaspora communities and progresses to the establishment of the nation's first major e-commerce platforms. It recounts how Indonesia's digital landscape was meticulously crafted by pioneering entities like Kaskus, Tokobagus, Tokopedia, and Bukalapak amidst a backdrop of cultural, economic, and technological transformations.

As we examine the rise of Indonesia's first unicorns and the impact of foreign investors and returning diaspora, this chapter shows the forces behind the country's digital boom. Indonesia's e-commerce evolution testifies to the power of entrepreneurial spirit and the transformative potential of technology in shaping the future of a nation.

BEGINNINGS

To fully understand the birth and evolution of Indonesia's digital economy, we need to look back to the turn of the millennium.

By the start of 2001, some 150 licensed internet service providers were offering 150 Mbps of bandwidth—certainly not insignificant for a country that first connected to the internet in 1994.[3] The majority of users were using dial-up to check their email, chat, or catch up on news, so it was only a matter of time before the transition to e-commerce took place.

However, that transition might have taken longer had there not been a few key players already on the move and a couple of foreign serial entrepreneurs to pave the way. In late 1999, six years before Reddit was founded, three Indonesian students in Seattle, Washington, came up with Kaskus (short for "*kasak kusuk*" or gossip news in Indonesian), an informal forum for the large Indonesian student diaspora.[4]

An early social media progenitor, Kaskus was a strong community builder for the many Indonesians to stay in touch with developments back home while making English news accessible by translating it into Bahasa Indonesia. Kaskus cofounders Andrew Darwis, Ronald Stephanus, and Budi Darmawan also recognized the potential of the nascent web advertising sales market, as local news site Detik.com boasted 6.42 million visits in 1999.

However, battling Detik proved too expensive, leading Andrew's two cofounders to drop out of the project. In 2000, Andrew transformed Kaskus into its forum-like iteration, moving away from journalism into user-generated content.

That same year, Indonesia's famous tourist island of Bali became home to BaliCamp, the nation's first startup incubator, and a haven for software developers.

THE MARKETING DUTCHMEN

It was against this backdrop that Tokobagus (now called OLX Indonesia) launched in Bali in 2005. Combining the Indonesian words for "shop" (*toko*) and "great" (*bagus*), the e-classifieds site was the brainchild of Remco Lupker and Arnold Egg, two young entrepreneurs from the Netherlands who had discovered Bali's internet cafes on holiday and saw Indonesia's incredible e-commerce potential.[5]

Two decades ago, Indonesia had barely any startup infrastructure, so Remco and Arnold quickly learned Bahasa Indonesia and found that this opened doors when introducing e-commerce to the government and local business partners.

In those early days, the task of introducing Tokobagus to consumers was formidable. Trust was in short supply all around, and brand recognition was essentially nonexistent for the company at that point. As such, Remco thought of a simple solution to the problem: bring Tokobagus and e-commerce straight into Indonesians' living rooms.

In October 2005, Tokobagus launched the first of its many nationwide television campaigns.[6] This was followed quickly by online and out-of-home advertising. Soon enough, Tokobagus was in homes, in elevators, on billboards, and visible via Google and Facebook. The all-out advertising strategy paid off, as page views and unique visits soared.

As Tokobagus slowly increased its foothold in the C2C (consumer-to-consumer) space, Andrew continued building out Kaskus while studying in the United States. In 2008, armed with a new investor and CEO in Ken Dean Lawadinata, Andrew and Ken returned to Indonesia to give Kaskus a branding overhaul, resulting in Kaskus ending the year with 350,000 registered members generating 2.4 million page views daily.[7] Not only were Indonesians increasingly online, but they were also online for longer periods.

In 2011, Kaskus accepted its first investment from GDP Venture, a digital investment subsidiary of Djarum Group, a diversified conglomerate owned by the influential and wealthy Hartono family.[8] The investment allowed Kaskus to transform itself into a place where people could formally buy and sell from one another via a C2C e-commerce model. It was a natural progression, as many Kaskus users were already doing this informally.

The rising tide of C2C e-commerce served as an accelerant. By mid-2011, Tokobagus was recording 160 million monthly page views and growing by 100% year over year.[9] Tokobagus was also quick to embrace mobile, encouraging sales via its Blackberry app in May 2011.[10]

Even after Remco and Arnold exited the company to pursue other business opportunities (via an acquisition by South African conglomerate Naspers in 2012), the site continued to grow, hitting 1 billion page views by the end of 2013.[11] By then, Tokobagus was acknowledged as the front-runner of Indonesian e-commerce.

Both Remco and Arnold remained active in the Indonesian venture space after exiting Tokobagus, separately founding new ventures, investing in startups, and coaching young entrepreneurs. Remco has since passed away, but Arnold is still active in the venture capital (VC) space. He became an Indonesian citizen in 2013, and now spearheads a venture builder tied to Wright Partners and digital consultancy firm Sprout Digital Labs.[12]

ENTER THE UNICORN FOALS

Though Tokobagus had become part of a larger conglomerate with both its founders having moved on, their efforts to introduce e-commerce to Indonesian consumers, policymakers, and the business community paved the way for the first batch of homegrown e-commerce companies in the archipelago.

While many new e-commerce entrants ultimately died off, the trend did lead to the formation of two of Indonesia's earliest unicorns: Tokopedia and Bukalapak.

THE INTERNET CAFE GRADUATE

From 1999 until 2003, William Tanuwijaya was pursuing his degree at Binus University—a private college in Jakarta—when his father fell ill and was unable to continue supporting him financially.[13] As a result, William started to pull the graveyard shift at internet cafes to cover his tuition.

It was during those nights that he came up with the idea for Tokopedia, an all-encompassing marketplace that would bring e-commerce to MSMEs across Indonesia's more than 17,000 islands—a major reason why logistics costs in Indonesia account for a significant portion of the country's economy.

William and his cofounder, Leontinus Alpha Edison, believed their C2C marketplace would democratize commerce through technology. The goal was to ensure that consumers across Indonesia could clearly see and understand the prices of a wide range of goods. Tokopedia aimed to offer them the ability to safely buy these products online from any location in the country.

Before Tokopedia's arrival, consumers were paying different prices for the same goods depending on where they lived. Meanwhile, merchants in smaller cities had to overcome higher capital barriers to get their businesses off the ground and gain access to the larger national market.

The two cofounders began toying with their venture idea in 2007, deciding that combining "*toko*" (store) with "encyclopedia" would result in a winning name. At the time, they could not have imagined how big of a winning idea it was, as Tokopedia went on to become Indonesia's very first e-marketplace.

"At that time, there was no proper online marketplace in Indonesia. Instead, everyone used websites like online forums, social networking sites, and even blogs as platforms to buy and sell things online. Those websites then became what is known as a classified-ads e-commerce model in Indonesia," William recounted in an interview.[14]

There were two barriers to e-commerce growth back in 2007: a lack of scalability for sellers and a lack of trust in payment security for buyers. Tokopedia's solution for the scalability gap was to enable order and inventory management for merchants, while at the same time introducing the concept of escrow for payments. Tokopedia would hold a buyer's payment and only release money to sellers upon successful order delivery.

This was a smart move, as Indonesian shoppers wanted reassurance that they would get the goods that they paid for. Meanwhile, sellers had the reassurance that they need not spend too much extra to add another sales channel into their mix.

THE JAPANESE CONNECTION

Even though the brand's establishment proved to be an important milestone in Indonesia's e-commerce growth journey, it still took several years to bring the idea to fruition. William and Leontinus spent two years pitching investors on Tokopedia—and failing. William, a self-proclaimed "internet cafe graduate," would find himself stuck at the very first hurdle due to investor bias.

"They'd ask about my background," he said in an interview. "They wanted to know which university I studied at. I did not come from the Ivy League."

Another hurdle? Investors were skeptical about a homegrown Indonesian founder replicating the Amazon or Alibaba model and surviving for the long-term against competition from these big, established names.

In February 2009, the Tokopedia duo raised seed funding from PT Indonusa Dwitama, the holding company founded and led by angel investor Victor Fungkong.[15] At that time, William worked for a content provider owned by Victor, so trust was already in place.

Indonusa Dwitama was primarily a mining and energy services company, and William and Leontinus's idea was so compelling that Tokopedia became Victor's first investment in the tech sector. The pair was given office space at Victor's property in Central Jakarta.

With capital in hand, William went back to his alma mater, Binus University, to hire his first employees at a student job fair. For two days, not a single student signed up at the Tokopedia booth. Local talent did not see startups as viable employers, and it took William sharing his experiences in small group settings on campus and a good two years before anyone joined Tokopedia.

Victor's initial capital of Rp2.5 billion (~US$265,000) was instrumental in the launch of Tokopedia six months later on August 17, 2009—Indonesia's Independence Day.[16] Upon launching, William and Leontinus only had two employees: one engineer and one customer care representative.

At the time, Jakarta was reeling from terrorist bombings in July, a month earlier. Apparel sellers on Tokopedia began producing shirts to support the ongoing netizen campaigns with the hashtag #WeAreNotAfraid (#KamiTidakTakut), and thanks to the magic of search engine optimization, the buzz spread, and Tokopedia was off to a good start.

By 2010, Indonesia's e-commerce secret was out: it was the next likely gold mine for global investors. Japanese internet company Rakuten entered Indonesia via a joint venture with Indonesia's largest media group at the time, Global Mediacom.[17] Yahoo! bought Koprol, a social network for mobile users, the Indonesian equivalent of Foursquare.[18]

William had multiple meetings with American investors but continued to be passed over, likely due to his less-than-fluent English. He had better luck with Japanese and South Korean investors, which then led to Tokopedia's second investor coming on board in 2010: Indonesia-focused VC firm East Ventures.[19]

East Ventures was launched in 2009 by Willson Cuaca and Batara Eto.[20] Batara, who was born in Indonesia, had previously cofounded the Japanese social networking site Mixi, which went public in 2006 at a valuation of US$1.6 billion. East Ventures' vote of confidence in Tokopedia soon led to interest from other Japanese investors: CyberAgent Ventures, the venture arm of internet advertising company CyberAgent in 2011, and e-commerce company Netprice in 2012.

In February 2011, less than two years after its launch, Tokopedia boasted 7,800 active shops, 75,000 registered members, and up to 800,000 unique visitors monthly accounting for transactions of approximately

Rp2.6 billion (US$291,200)—a vindication for William, whose only "flaw" was that he wasn't a graduate of a big-name business school.[21]

THE SERIAL ENTREPRENEUR

Around the same time that Tokopedia launched in 2009, serial entrepreneur and fresh graduate Achmad Zaky started a web development business and eventually made enough money to support his own C2C marketplace, which he named Bukalapak (Indonesian for "open stall").

Unlike the Tokopedia team, Achmad and his cofounders Fajrin Rasyid and Nugroho Herucahyono did not have to wait long for funding. It turned out Japan had no shortage of e-commerce veterans who were keen on investing in Indonesia's burgeoning scene. By July 2011, the newly launched Batavia Incubator—a joint venture between Japan-based Rebright Partners and Indonesian finance firm Corfina Group—announced Bukalapak as its first incubate.[22]

Takeshi Ebihara, CEO of Rebright Partners, had been in the VC business for more than 15 years and was also a serial entrepreneur himself before becoming an investor. Takeshi's coaching proved instrumental. By 2013, Bukalapak had onboarded 60,000 merchants and was charting about 1 million daily page views.[23]

Bukalapak's biggest challenge, however, was the market. In the company's early years, Achmad and his cofounders noticed a lot of Indonesians calling merchants on the phone and placing orders.

He said in a 2013 interview, "We want to move the market away from this model and get them all to directly transact online. The payments market is not yet mature here. Ensuring that the transaction model is secure and convenient is what we want to do. Our vision is to be the biggest platform for individuals and MSMEs who want to sell online."[24]

THE FAMILY-OWNED CONGLOMERATE

With local funding in short supply before Indonesia's e-commerce boom, some startups chose to bootstrap and exit quickly, while others were not startups per se but rather subsidiaries of large, wealthy conglomerates.

Family offices in search of new investment opportunities initially were a key source of funding in Southeast Asia. But back in 2011, one of Indonesia's wealthiest families decided to go to market directly and launch its own e-commerce startup instead.

Djarum Group—run by the Hartono family—owes its fortune to the *kretek* (clove cigarette) business, but it has since diversified into real estate, banking, and more. Fresh from its digital experience with Kaskus, the conglomerate took the unorthodox move of establishing business-to-consumer (B2C) marketplace Blibli, an online shopping mall that became the first local e-commerce platform to offer a 0% installment program for buyers, as well as a midnight delivery service.[25]

Blibli's entry into the B2C space—where it was functioning as a digital shopping mall with official branded stores—was a stark contrast to the C2C pro-MSME model favored by Tokopedia and Bukalapak. By virtue of its corporate backing, Blibli did not need any further injection of capital.

THE BOOTSTRAPPER

Moving beyond physical goods, online travel agency startup Tiket launched in November 2011.[26] With a bootstrapping mindset, it was able to generate revenue from an initial US$1 million angel round and US$25,000 in prize money won from a startup competition. Cofounded by Natali Ardianto,

Wenas Agusetiawan, Dimas Surya Yaputra, and Mikhael Gaery Undarsa, Tiket grew quickly in its early days.

Natali was a serial entrepreneur searching for the right e-commerce niche to focus on. Before Tiket, he founded a digital lifestyle directory, an online reservation system for golf courses, and an entrepreneur community in quick succession.

By December 2012, Tiket had partnered with 1,000 hotels, six airlines, 30 events, and 300 travel agents.[27] It also made a strong case for a now-key Indonesian demographic: young, middle-income, digitally savvy consumers. Tiket remained flexible on the payment side, supporting online payment methods, credit cards, bank transfers, and even a cash option.

Between 2012 and 2013, Tiket's revenue skyrocketed by 1,300%, and the startup reached profitability in early 2013.[28] However, Tiket's decision to bootstrap rather than pitch for venture funding meant it turned out very different from its VC-backed challenger.

THE RETURNING DIASPORA

From 2009 to 2011, Ferry Unardi—one of the 9 million people who formed the global Indonesian diaspora—was finishing up his bachelor's degree at Purdue University and following it up with a Harvard Business School MBA.[29]

For eight years, this future Indonesian startup founder had been flying back regularly to his hometown of Padang from Indianapolis, Seattle, or Boston—a distance of more than 16,000 kilometers (almost 10,000 miles). Ferry was frequently frustrated by the complicated and time-consuming ticket booking process, the lack of direct flights, and the difficulties of finding connecting flights.

Previously a software engineer at Microsoft in Seattle, Ferry left his job to attend Harvard Business School but dropped out after a semester in 2011. Along with two fellow Indonesians in the United States, Albert Zhang and Derianto Kusuma, he decided to return to his home country to build a company. In 2012, the trio launched Traveloka, an online travel startup, in Jakarta.[30]

Almost immediately, Traveloka picked up seed funding from East Ventures in 2012, followed by a series A funding round in 2013 from one of the world's most aggressive e-commerce investors, Global Founders Capital (GFC).[31]

GFC is the VC arm of the Samwer brothers' (Marc, Alexander, and Oliver) Berlin-based technology incubator, Rocket Internet, the same name behind now-famous internet companies like Delivery Hero, Lazada Group, and Global Fashion Group.

Where Tokopedia's William had trouble finding early investors, the Traveloka trio's blue-chip resumes (Harvard and Microsoft) bridged the gap with foreign investors who were unfamiliar with the Indonesian landscape.

Similarly, while investors were skeptical about Tokopedia's ability to duplicate models from the United States or Europe in Indonesia, Rocket Internet had no such qualms about Traveloka. After all, the German internet brothers had made it their business model to clone proven US business models and adapt them for high-potential markets elsewhere.

THE DOOR IS OPEN, AND EVERYONE IS WELCOME

Indonesia's adjacent e-commerce verticals continued to grow and build on the foundation set by Remco and Arnold. Standing on the shoulders of Tokobagus, Bukalapak, and Tokopedia, the next cohort of companies took things further and faster.

But even though these players opened the door, it took the aggressive growth and hiring strategies of Rocket Internet to catalyze the next phase of the local digital landscape. As we will see in the next chapter, Rocket was not only responsible for the launch of well-known platforms like Lazada, Zalora, Foodpanda, and Lamudi, but it stepped up the local game by instilling a "whatever it takes" culture that can still be seen in local entrepreneurs today.

CHAPTER TWO

A GERMAN ROCKET SHIP ARRIVES

When it comes to hyperscalability in any market, all startups find two big issues challenging: funding and hiring. In emerging markets like Indonesia, however, these challenges are more pronounced.

In the previous chapter, we observed that William from Tokopedia spent years pitching to investors for funding and searching for local talent to hire. We noticed that both Bukalapak and Tokopedia had to rely on Japanese venture funding because the regional VC market in Southeast Asia had not yet developed and traditional investors could not understand the potential for internet businesses.

Additionally, we saw that a German investor quickly provided funding for Traveloka in 2013, despite weaker interest from other Western investors, which turned out to be a highly prescient decision. That

German investor was GFC, the venture arm of Berlin-based technology incubator Rocket Internet.

In this chapter, we look into the operations of the Samwer brothers. Their strategy of blitzscaling, applied in Indonesia and across Southeast Asia, led to the rise of notable unicorns. Their impact drew global VC attention to Indonesian startups and paved the way for a new wave of both local and expatriate entrepreneurial talent—a movement I found myself a part of.

NOT SUCH A CRAZY FROG AFTER ALL

Remco's idea of introducing e-commerce to Indonesians by bankrolling massive TV and billboard advertising campaigns may have seemed ahead of its time in Southeast Asia, but it was not at all new for internet companies back in Europe. Not everyone has been around long enough to remember "Crazy Frog." It was an animated frog character that danced to the distinctly catchy ringtones that played in TV adverts in the early 2000s. The reason many people can immediately call to mind the jingle and character is because German mobile phone content company Jamba! had bankrolled the creation of Crazy Frog and the blitz of TV ads that followed.[1]

Oliver, Marc, and Alexander Samwer were behind Jamba!. They were then known as the "Crazy Frog trio" in Europe. The siblings made £15 million (US$28 million) from Crazy Frog, which at one point was the most commercially successful ringtone.[2]

The Sanwer brothers went on to establish Rocket Internet in 2007.[3] It would become the parent company of more than 100 businesses across emerging markets such as China, India, Latin America, the Middle East, and Africa. To this day, it specializes in taking successful business models from developed markets like the United States, localizing said models, and quickly launching startups in other countries.

In 2010 the brothers' venture CityDeal was acquired by Groupon, and subsequently Oliver, or "Oli" for short, embarked on an international expansion program for Groupon.[4] Following the purchase, Marc Samwer started heading international operations for Groupon while also rolling out startups via Rocket.

In early 2011, Oli's team reached out to me with an offer to join as the managing director of Groupon China, an impressive organization of 3,000 people despite being only six months old. Although I passed on that particular opportunity, I later accepted the CEO position at Airizu, another venture incubated by the Samwers. It was an Airbnb-esque platform tailored for the China market, and I reported directly to Oli.

The incubator's previous "simple" business strategy was to avoid the world's two largest e-commerce markets in the United States and China, instead establishing dominant clones in other markets to make them attractive acquisition targets. That said, the sale of CityDeal earned the Samwers more than US$100 million and their understanding of Groupon's work around the world did make China seem like an appealing place for business. However, they quickly realized that the competition there was too strong and decided to focus Rocket on different emerging markets instead.

Today, in Southeast Asia, the Samwers are synonymous with their signature incubator-turned-venture builder, which introduced their uniquely aggressive "blitzkrieg" approach of venture building to Southeast Asia in 2011.[5]

ATTACK OF THE CLONES

In 2012, Indonesia's e-commerce scene was home to Tokobagus copycats (e-classifieds sites) and Tokopedia/Bukalapak clones (C2C marketplaces), but none had taken an unassailable lead yet, despite the e-commerce space receiving several early investment rounds and interest from foreign backers. This made the country a perfect target for Rocket, the kingmaker of internet clones.

The Samwer brothers made their name as "copycats" almost a decade before Rocket was incorporated, however. In 1998, while at the WHU-Otto Beisheim School of Management, Oli and his classmate Max Finger published their study of US innovation, distilling nearly 100 interviews with tech and venture figures into a document called "America's Most Successful Startups." Their findings formed the basis for Rocket's "blitzkrieg" (German for "lightning war") strategy: hyper-aggressive marketing and product development; centralized IT, design, marketing, and search engine optimization (SEO); hiring former investment bankers and management consultants as "founders" or CEOs to launch businesses on the ground; and data-driven execution.[6]

That same year when the brothers were living in San Francisco, Marc realized that many people in his office were using eBay and that it would be easily accepted in Germany. They emailed eBay with their idea to set up and run the business in Germany but didn't receive a reply. So the Samwers did it themselves by launching Alando in February 1999. Within 100 days, the Samwers sold Alando to eBay for US$43 million.

The next idea was Jamba! with its frog jingle leading to global notoriety and an eventual sale to Verisign for a staggering US$273 million in 2004. But the Samwers weren't done yet: the next few years saw them create German clones of YouTube, Twitter, Facebook, and Groupon.

In 2011, a year after the CityDeal sale, Groupon acquired Disdus, its Indonesian clone.[7] That same year, Rocket Internet entered Indonesia with boots on the ground.

SKEPTICAL GLOBAL INVESTORS VS GERMAN VISIONARIES

At the time, despite Tokobagus, Tokopedia, Bukalapak, Blibli, and Traveloka providing ample proof that e-commerce worked well in Indonesia, skepticism remained about the market's ability to grow even further.

An insider account from the book *Digital Indonesia: Connectivity and Divergence* on how Lazada started in Indonesia noted: "Even in 2012, no company had yet managed to secure an exit of meaningful proportions. The general sentiment among many foreign and domestic digital entrepreneurs was that Indonesia promised so much, but had actually delivered so little."[8]

The same barriers that held back significant cross-border trade before the introduction of e-commerce, such as poor infrastructure, lack of trust in e-commerce sites, and shifting government regulations, were still seen by Indonesian investors and entrepreneurs as largely insurmountable.

However, the Samwers' brute-force tactics proved it possible.

Ideas were never in short supply in Indonesia nor at Rocket. But the first barrier to hyper scaling that the Samwers had to cope with in Indonesia was a shortage of tech talent. While Tokopedia's William worked to cultivate talent organically via college kids, Rocket shortened this process to months, sometimes weeks.

The Rocket pipeline for creating companies was distilled down to a factory assembly line: the Samwers or their brain trust would conceive an idea. They would then appoint "founders" or "CEOs" and dispatch them with a modest equity stake to a market to get the company going. These founders were to adhere to the Rocket blueprint, which involved recruiting management from leading consulting firms or banks, or hiring local fresh graduates from top universities as "foot soldiers" at competitive salaries above the market rate. Clear KPIs (key performance indicators) were established, and the founders were expected to do whatever it took to meet those KPIs.

Unlike typical incubators, which may take a 10% stake in startups they fund and leave 90% to the founders, ownership percentages were inverted at Rocket.

So-called founders were typically MBA graduates from blue-chip schools (Ivy League universities, Stanford, Oxford, Cambridge, INSEAD, etc.).[9]

Individuals from prestigious consulting firms like McKinsey or Boston Consulting Group, as well as investment banks, were the primary targets for recruitment. To entice them away from their secure corporate positions, it was essential to provide attractive compensation packages, promising career advancement opportunities and equity stakes in the startups they were tasked to develop.

Although the equity stakes were inverted, Rocket typically applied pressure on founders and imposed tight deadlines for launching a new venture. It always aimed to get a company off the ground in 100 days—a callback to the Samwers' first success in 1999 with Alando.

An email leaked in 2011 sheds light on Oli's management ethos: meticulous German precision, swiftness, assertiveness, and a reliance on data.[10] His fondness for military jargon (like "blitzkrieg" and "sign it with your blood") combined with coarse language as motivational tools was often jarring in regions like Asia, where decorum is traditionally upheld in business. Yet, his relentless focus on data and metrics, which might have seemed extreme in 2011, fostered a robust culture of accountability that has significantly benefited Rocket Internet alumni.

In his email titled "When is it time for blitzkrieg," Oli pushes Rocket's teams in India, Turkey, Australia, South Africa, and Southeast Asia to achieve market dominance: "You must be in two seasons from now, have at least 50% market share of the total online market in all your categories.

A scenario where you have 35%, next 25%, next 20% will not give you the valuation that we need. We need an Amazon valuation: seen as the 80% leader in the market."

It was this same obsession with figures that impacted how quickly brands were launched, closed, and relaunched when Rocket finally set foot in Indonesia.

THE ROCKET INTERNET WAY

In my first encounter with Rocket, I was struck by the company's unwavering dedication to data and its penchant for micromanagement to ensure teams hit their performance targets.

I remember my initial meeting with Oli vividly. He was casually dressed in a white low-neck t-shirt and jeans, yet fervently grilling one of his leaders about the firm's growth metrics. If something didn't sit right with him, he wouldn't hesitate to drill down and check. On one occasion, he immediately rang up the head of customer service to cross-check the leader's figures.

Despite overseeing the vast expanse of the global business builder, Oli had a hand in everything. It amazed me how he found the time to respond to every email that mentioned him, always in a direct and no-nonsense manner. This wasn't a mere quirk; it reflected his belief in micromanagement. He orchestrated monthly global roll calls and marathon sessions where he would sit for nearly 24 hours nonstop. Teams from his various companies would have a mere 15 minutes to present their numbers, during which he'd readily offer critique or feedback. Oli wasn't just a micromanager; he actively encouraged his subordinates to do the same with their teams.

In a landscape dominated by copycat enterprises, speed and hitting targets became paramount. Oli's obsessive attention to detail, bordering on paranoia, cascaded down. It forced everyone to dive deep into the minutiae. We all learned to be prepared, knowing that Oli could quiz us on any aspect at any time.

In Rocket's early days, while founders like me didn't have a say in major equity decisions, we did possess autonomy over certain operational elements like tech stacks and hiring. But as Rocket expanded its reach into Southeast Asia, Oli began centralizing everything—from technology to marketing strategies. This shift eroded the individuality of the firms, replacing any emerging cultures with a singular, omnipresent Rocket ethos: succeed or be sidelined. Ultimately, it wasn't a culture conducive to loyalty or long-term commitment.

When things soured, people would exit. Even during successful phases, many would depart, overwhelmed by the relentless pressure. This might explain why a significant number of Rocket companies, despite their aggressive strategies and ample capital, weren't sustainable in the long run.

From my perspective, the most successful startups were those helmed by founders who, while analytical, weren't overly clinical. They were deeply invested in the culture and truly resonated with the mission and vision of their business.

ROCKETING INTO INDONESIA: A BRIEF TIMELINE

Tracking Rocket's footprint in Indonesia is a tough thing to do. Often, the incubator announces a company's launch months after the fact, while some companies are cut quickly even before news of their launch is made public.

Table 2.1 shows a timeline of how Rocket's arrival in Southeast Asia in 2011 quickly impacted Indonesia.

Table 2.1 Rocket's Arrival in Southeast Asia in 2011

Month/Year	Company Status
June 2011	Berlin-based Wimdu, a clone of Airbnb, announced it had rolled out in 50 countries within 100 days of its launch.[11] Wimdu was led by two Germans: global CEO and cofounder Arne Bleckwenn and cofounder Hinrich Dreiling (both serial entrepreneurs and graduates of Oli's alma mater, WHU-Otto Beisheim School of Management).
February 2012	Pinspire, a clone of Pinterest, launched in Indonesia, Malaysia, Singapore, the Philippines, and Vietnam. Austrian Karl Josef Seilern (serial entrepreneur), who was Rocket Korea's managing director, became interim co-CEO of Pinspire. Also in the Berlin founding team was Dane Jonas Chelbat (ex-Deloitte).[12]
March 2012	Zalora went live in six Southeast Asian countries, including Indonesia. Rocket appointed Indonesian Nadiem Makarim (ex-McKinsey, Harvard MBA) as Zalora Indonesia CEO. A clone of US online footwear and apparel retailer Zappos, Zalora offered free shipping and returns.[13] Lazada launched in four countries, including Indonesia. A clone of Amazon, Lazada focused on electronics as its beachhead strategy.[14] Foodpanda rolled out in 25 countries simultaneously, including Indonesia.[15] The Berlin-based food delivery company was led by two Swissmen, founder and global CEO Lukas Nagel (ex-Boston Consulting Group, Accenture) and global cofounder Rico Wyder (serial entrepreneur).
June 2012	B2B office supplies marketplace OfficeFab launched in Indonesia, the Philippines, Vietnam, and Malaysia. Based out of Jakarta, OfficeFab Southeast Asia was led by Korean cofounder and managing director Steven Kim (ex-AT Kearney, INSEAD). It was reported that payment app Payleven, a Square clone, bought domain names in Singapore, Malaysia, Indonesia, Vietnam, the Philippines, and Hong Kong. However, the site never appeared to have launched in Asia at all.[16]

(Continued)

Table 2.1 (Continued)

Month/Year	Company Status
September 2012	Pricepanda, a price comparison platform, launched in Singapore and Malaysia, with Indonesia and the Philippines following quickly after.[17] Based out of Berlin, the founding team was led by German Christian Schiller (ex-Credit Suisse, Rocket entrepreneur-in-residence).
November 2013	Rocket rolled out C2C marketplace Lamido in Indonesia. While Lazada targeted large sellers, small and medium-sized sellers fit better on Lamido. Italian Giacomo Ficari (ex-Barclays, Universita Bocconi) was named managing director of Lamido Indonesia and the Philippines, having previously been managing director of Lazada Malaysia.[18]
January 2014	Vehicle classifieds platform Carmudi expands in Indonesia, enabling customers to find or sell new and used cars, motorcycles, and commercial vehicles online.[19] Rocket's global CEO for its automotive classifieds and marketplaces, Stefan Haubold has previous experience cofounding a pet e-commerce startup in Munich and graduated from Leipzig University.
February 2014	Real estate marketplace Lamudi launches its Indonesia website.[20] Global cofounder and CEO Kian Moini is a graduate of the University of Amsterdam and was previously an associate at McKinsey.

DEEP POCKETS, LOYAL BACKERS

The Samwers' story is certainly not one of the rags-to-riches variety: their great-grandfather Karl Samwer created German insurance company Gothaer Versicherung.[21] Today, Gothaer Group is one of Germany's largest insurance companies, with €4.6 billion (US$4.85 billion) in premium income and approximately 4.1 million insured members.[22] The siblings' parents were both lawyers, with their father having represented Karl Carstens, who later became president of West Germany.

After their early 2000s success in selling startups, the brothers plowed their profits into obtaining a stake in Facebook in 2008.[23] They also maintained strong ties to the VCs and companies that they sold their startups to, such as German VC Holtzbrinck Ventures, to whom they sold German social network StudiVZ in 2007. Holtzbrinck Ventures would return time and again to back multiple Rocket startups' funding rounds.[24]

In August 2014, Holtzbrinck Ventures converted its stakes in seven Rocket startups in exchange for 2.5% of Rocket itself, before the incubator's listing on the Frankfurt Stock Exchange in October 2014.[25,26]

One of the earliest outside investors in Rocket after its launch in 2007 was Swedish family conglomerate Kinnevik AB, owned by the Stenbeck family. In 2009, Kinnevik invested €35 million (US$48 million) into Rocket.[27] In 2013, Rocket raised another US$500 million from Kinnevik and Len Blavatnik's Access Industries. This came a year after Access Industries invested US$200 million in Rocket directly.[28]

Access Industries was another regular backer of the Samwers' companies. It led a US$112 million round in Asia Pacific fashion site Zalora. It also led a US$130 million round in Russian fashion commerce site Lamoda, in addition to investing in Pinspire and home furnishings site Westwing.[29]

In August 2014, Rocket sold a 10.7% stake of itself to German internet service provider United Internet for €435 million (US$582 million) and a further 10% stake to telecom operator Philippine Long Distance Telephone Company (PLDT) for €333 million (about US$445 million).[30,31]

Such financial heft was necessary to get multiple businesses off the ground—often simultaneously across dozens of different markets and founding teams. In 2011, the Indonesian market began to show promise, as the strong initial backing of Rocket's startups in the region led to additional funding from newer and, in some cases, more traditional sources.

Founders still had to reach their KPIs and raise funding targets or face the Samwer axe. Over time, a few brands began growing and fundraising on their own merits, not just because they were under the Rocket umbrella. (See Table 2.2.)

Table 2.2 Summary of Key Fundraising Rounds of Rocket's Indonesian/Southeast Asian Startups (2011–2013)[32]

Month/Year	Company	Round Value	Investor(s)
September 2012	Lazada	More than US$50 million	JPMorgan
September 2012	Zalora	"Double-digit millions"	JPMorgan
November 2012	Lazada	US$40 million	Kinnevik
December 2012	Lazada	US$26 million	US private equity firm Summit Partners
January 2013	Lazada	Nearly US$20 million	German retail group Tengelmann
March 2013	Zalora	US$26 million	Tengelmann Group
May 2013	Foodpanda	More than US$20 million	Kinnevik and Russia's Phenomen Ventures
May 2013	Zalora	US$100 million	Rocket, Summit Partners, Kinnevik, Verlinvest, and Tengelmann Group
June 2013	Lazada	US$100 million	Holtzbrinck Ventures, Kinnevik, Summit Partners, and Tengelmann Group
December 2013	Lazada	"Tens of millions of pounds"	UK grocer Tesco Plc

THE BOLD AND THE BRUTE FORCE

By the end of 2013, Rocket had amassed more than 20,000 employees in over 100 countries and had aggregated revenues of more than €700 million (about US$936 million) for the year.

The ability to launch new products in new markets in a cohesive manner called for highly localized talent pipelines, which meant Rocket spent massively on aggressive hiring tactics. Not only were paychecks markedly higher than its peers (if it had any), but so were headhunters and recruiter bills. In Lazada Indonesia's earliest days, hundreds of young Indonesian graduates were pulled from elite universities in the United States and Australia to kick-start what would become lasting careers in the technology sector.[33]

Once the founding teams were set up, the aggressive hiring continued with executives, who were typically new graduates from local universities. These fresh graduates were pulled to Rocket companies with medium-range salaries and the attraction of learning while undertaking their own entrepreneurial journeys (in launching new products).[34]

Rocket's trademark style was most visible to the public through its assertive marketing tactics. A Google case study in 2015 found that Lazada employed a strategy known as "target outranking share," which allowed a brand to outrank its competitors in search engine results by aggressively bidding on keywords that its competitors were also paying for. In this way, Lazada would increase its cost per click price to help its ads "outrank" those of its competitors. In short, Rocket was willing to overspend to make competitors less visible.

"The team used this technique to position Lazada's keywords in new categories," Google explained. "The strategy also conveniently offered the team the opportunity to bid against strategic competitors, securing visibility and traffic among a new set of customers by targeting their competitors' keywords."

The strategy paid off: Lazada increased its market share within new categories; ad impression share rose by 50%; and traffic increased by more than 30%.[35]

Rocket executives across different startups also often teamed up for large marketing campaigns, such as 12.12.12, a jointly run day of discounts on December 12, 2012, modeled on the world's largest online shopping day: China's Singles Day. This is now the norm, so much so that every e-commerce site holds similar monthly sales. More than a decade ago, such a marketing spree was novel to Indonesia.

Zalora Indonesia also leveraged TV advertising campaigns in the lead-up to the year-end festivities in 2012. The campaign increased the site's traffic to 150,000 visits every day, while orders rose by up to 300%. Zalora also planned to roll out a mobile version of its website in January 2013, driving more mobile-first usage in tandem with rising mobile penetration rates across Indonesia.[36]

The influx of funding at both the incubator and startup levels upped the competition for Rocket's competitors in Indonesia while drawing deep-pocketed foreign brands to the archipelago. Existing e-commerce companies like Tokopedia and Bukalapak ramped up fundraising efforts to keep pace.

This resulted in two major global e-commerce brands setting foot on Indonesian shores in 2013: US-based eBay entered Indonesia under the brand name Blanja via a joint venture with local telco Telkom Indonesia;[37] South Korea's SK Planet formed a joint venture with another telco XL Axiata to launch an e-marketplace called Elevenia.[38]

ROCKET MAFIA

The Samwers call themselves "execution entrepreneurs," and their hiring strategies have led to the emergence of a so-called "Rocket Mafia," similar to the PayPal Mafia—the group of former PayPal employees and founders who went on to create LinkedIn, YouTube, Palantir, and Tesla, among others. Over the years, more than 400 founders have emerged from Rocket Internet.[39]

Arguably the most famous of the Rocket family in Indonesia is Zalora Indonesia's founding CEO Nadiem Makarim. When he joined Zalora in late 2011, Nadiem was already cofounder of his own motorcycle ride-hailing startup Gojek, which eventually became one of Indonesia's first unicorns. Gojek served to address the chokehold traffic that Jakarta is notorious for by leveraging the *ojek* (informal motorbike taxis) that pervade the capital city.

Nadiem left Zalora in 2012 to devote his time to Gojek, which eventually grew into a Southeast Asian super app comprising almost 20 service verticals. In 2019, Nadiem stepped down as Gojek CEO to become Indonesia's Minister of Education, Culture, Research, and Technology. He was succeeded by Gojek Group President Andre Soelistyo and Chief Financial Officer Kevin Aluwi (ex-head of business intelligence at Zalora Indonesia) as co-CEOs.[40]

Nadiem's early exit just one year into Zalora Indonesia's operation meant Hadi Wenas stepped in to lead the brand's expansion across the archipelago. But Wenas quickly moved on in 2013 to head up e-commerce solutions provider aCommerce Indonesia before jumping again in 2015 to lead Indonesian conglomerate Lippo Group's e-commerce play Matahari Mall.[41]

Hadi Kuncoro, who was operations director at Zalora Indonesia from 2012 to 2015, took over the reins of aCommerce when Wenas left. Kuncoro helped facilitate the growth of Indonesia's e-commerce regulatory space and planning within the public sector, serving as senior advisor on the e-commerce roadmap committee under Indonesia's Coordinating Ministry for Economic Affairs from 2017 to 2019.[42]

I am also a Rocket Internet alum. After earning my Stanford MBA in 2006, I moved to Beijing, China, to cofound Idapted. By 2010, it became one of the top providers of live, one-on-one language instruction in China. By 2011, our venture was acquired by Eleutian Technology, a US-based online English language training powerhouse.[43]

Later, I collaborated with Oli to build Airizu, a short-term lodging marketplace in China. By 2012, my journey brought me to Indonesia with Rocket, spearheading the launch of OfficeFab. The following year, in Jakarta, I teamed up with fellow Rocket Mafia members Sean Liao (formerly the managing director of Rocket China) and Steven Kim (ex-managing director of Zalora Singapore) to establish the food curation platform Qraved.[44]

By 2014, I branched out to set up Convergence Ventures, one of Indonesia's pioneering VC firms. In 2019, we merged with Agaeti Venture Capital, led by Pandu Sjahrir and Michael Soerijadji, ultimately culminating in the formation of AC Ventures.

Another foreign national who has made Indonesia his home thanks to Rocket is Nathanael Faibis from France, who worked in various capacities and across different Lazada Southeast Asia markets between 2012 and 2013. In 2014, Nathanael cofounded Alodokter, which subsequently became one of Indonesia's top healthcare apps with more than 24 million monthly active users connected to over 20,000 doctors.[45]

Another Rocket alum was Riky Tenggara (Stanford), who quickly rose through the Lazada and Rocket ranks between 2012 and 2014, overseeing regional products by the end of his stint there. Riky went on to become a serial entrepreneur, first founding printing startup Prinzio in 2015 (which was acquired by Gogoprint) and then cofounding Ula, an e-commerce enabler for MSMEs, in 2019.[46]

On LinkedIn, "ex-Rocket" became a powerful descriptor: a shorthand that meant someone was a mafia member with a valuable network and higher credibility with investors. In Southeast Asia, it became akin to how some folks in the United States claim "ex-Google," "ex-Facebook," or "ex-Tesla" on their profiles.[47]

ROCKET INDONESIA'S WIN–LOSS COLUMN

Not all the Samwer startups took off in Southeast Asia. Some, like Pinspire, Payleven, and online furniture retailer Home24, barely got a toe into the region before being axed. Others rumbled on for a while before being sold off or consolidated with competitors, such as Foodpanda and Zalora.

But what was clear to the Samwers was that Indonesia was a market that required sticking around. Gone were the days of flipping startups to buyers within 100 days of launching. Investors in Southeast Asia were slow to trust and needed time to drum up interest in any acquisition or consolidation moves.

Just over a decade after Rocket's entry into Indonesia in 2012, the incubator's scorecard in the region appears pretty balanced. In the loss column, OfficeFab's closure in July 2013—just over a year in, despite purportedly having good numbers—spoke to the Samwers' all-or-nothing aggressiveness.[48] Despite the company's high revenue and margins, OfficeFab was shut down after all the founders left, and Rocket higher-ups elected to make a change in strategy.

An even faster flop was Pinspire, which collapsed in just two months (February to April 2012). It quickly lost organic users due to an onslaught of spam. Would any other incubator spend money to address the fraud issue? Maybe, but that was not in Rocket's concern. You make your own fortune, and Pinspire had clearly misfired upon launch.

In August 2016, Foodpanda decided to sell its operations in Indonesia while evaluating its other Southeast Asian operations as it carved a path to profitability. Indonesia may be Southeast Asia's largest economy, but it has proven tough to conquer due to factors including competition and local market dynamics.[49]

Gojek's continuous fundraising and expansion into the food delivery space, coupled with its massive fleet of riders, was consistently outpacing Foodpanda's in Indonesia. Two months later, in October 2016, Foodpanda Indonesia announced its closure.[50] Another two months later, the overall Foodpanda brand was sold to rival firm DeliveryHero (in which Rocket had a minority stake).[51]

Wimdu, the Airbnb clone, took longer to close. In September 2018, it announced that it would be shutting down at the end of the year, citing "significant financial and business challenges." This was partly due to Wimdu's inability to raise funding beyond its initial US$90 million.[52]

The two brightest beacons were the two best fundraisers: Lazada and Zalora. Lazada's most formidable competitor was Tokopedia, which closely trailed in fundraising. By the end of 2014, both startups were the front runners in Indonesian e-commerce.

Key data collated by Forbes in October that year showed that while Lazada was "handily" beating Tokopedia in visitor traffic, Lazada Indonesia visitors spent less time and browsed fewer pages in a single visit than they did on Tokopedia.[53]

More firepower was needed, and bigger guns came to Lazada's aid, necessitating Rocket's exit. In 2016, Chinese e-commerce giant Alibaba acquired a 51% stake in Lazada for US$1 billion and then later increased its stake to 83% by injecting another US$1 billion. Despite the tough regional and local competition in 2023 (Gojek and Tokopedia having merged to form GoTo), Alibaba aims to increase Lazada's gross merchandise value to US$100 billion and double its number of customers to 300 million users by 2030.[54]

Zalora, meanwhile, remains part of the Rocket family. In 2014, Rocket decided to merge its five fashion commerce businesses into an e-commerce giant called Global Fashion Group (GFG). It is made up of Dafiti (Latin America), Jabong (India), Lamoda (Russia and the Commonwealth of Independent States), Namshi (Middle East), and Zalora (Southeast Asia and Australia). The group is headquartered in Singapore but trades publicly on the Frankfurt Stock Exchange. In recent years, GFG has divested from parts of its business, but Zalora Indonesia remains an active and integral component.[55]

See Table 2.3 for a summary of Indonesian startups from 2013.

Table 2.3 Summary of Key Indonesian Startups Backed by Global Founders Capital (2013–1H2023)

Startup	Sector	Round Value	Co-investors
Traveloka	Online travel agent	Series A: Undisclosed (Aug 2013)	None
Bridestory	Online wedding marketplace	Series A: Undisclosed (Mar 2015)	Rocket Internet, Venturra, Sovereign's Capital, East Ventures, Fenox VC, Skystar Capital, Lippo Digital Ventures, Pegasus Tech Ventures
Qlapa	Marketplace for handmade products	Seed: Undisclosed (Jan 2016)	Ideosource, Budi Setiadharma
Hipcar	Car-sharing service	Venture round: Undisclosed (Mar 2017)	Prasetia Dwidharma
Klikdaily	B2B supply chain	Seed: US$3 million (Aug 2019)	Pegasus Tech Ventures, FundedHere, Teja Ventures
Klikdaily	B2B supply chain	Series A: Undisclosed (May 2020)	Undisclosed
Crewdible	Micro warehousing	Seed: US$1.5m (Oct 2019)	None
Pintek	Education fintech	Seed: Undisclosed (Nov 2019)	Finch Capital, Amand Ventures
Pintek	Education fintech	Series A: US$7 million (Nov 2021)	STRIVE, Kube VC, Kaizenvest, Heritas Capital, Fox Ventures, Finch Capital, Earlsfield Capital, Blue7, Accion Venture Lab

(Continued)

Table 2.3 (Continued)

Startup	Sector	Round Value	Co-investors
Pinhome	Real estate fintech	Seed: Undisclosed (Dec 2019)	Insignia Ventures Partners
		Series A: US$25.5 million (Jul 2021)	Rocket Internet, Ribbit Capital, Goodwater Capital, Insignia Ventures Partners
		Series B: US$50 million (Apr 2022)	Ribbit Capital, Iterative Venture, Intudo Ventures, Goodwater Capital, Insignia Ventures Partners, Eurazeo Smart City, Alto Partners Multi-family Office
Finantier	Open finance API platform	Seed: Undisclosed (Jun 2021)	East Ventures, AC Ventures, Y Combinator, Genesia Ventures, Two Culture Capital, Taurus Ventures, Saison Capital, Partech, GMO VenturePartners, Future Shape
Finku	Budgeting and expense tracking	Pre-seed: Undisclosed (Aug 2021)	500 Global
		Seed: US$2.8 million (May 2022)	B Capital Group, Trihill Capital, Golden Gate Ventures, Goodwater Capital, Alto Partners, Hi2 Global Venture Fund, Y Combinator

Startup	Sector	Round Value	Co-investors
Astro	Quick commerce	Seed: US$4.5 million (Nov 2021)	AC Ventures, Lightspeed Venture Partners, Goodwater Capital
		Series A: US$27 million (Jan 2022)	Accel, Sequoia Capital India, AC Ventures, Lightspeed Venture Partners, Goodwater Capital
		Series B: US$60 million (May 2022)	Accel, Citius, Tiger Global Management, AC Ventures, Lightspeed Venture Partners, Sequoia Capital India, FJ Labs
Moladin	Used car platform	Series A: US$42 million (Jan 2022)	Sequoia Capital India, Northstar Group, East Ventures, K3 Ventures, Alto Partners Multi-Family Office
		Series B: US$95 million (May 2022)	DST Global, East Ventures, Northstar Group, Sequoia Capital India
NOBI	Crypto asset management platform	Seed: US$4 million (Feb 2022)	AC Ventures, Appworks, Skystar Capital, Cakra Ventures
Wagely	Financial wellness platform	Pre-series A: US$8.3 million (Mar 2022)	East Ventures, Integra Partners, Asian Development Bank, Trihill Capital, Blauwpark Partners, 1982 Ventures

(Continued)

Table 2.3 (Continued)

Startup	Sector	Round Value	Co-investors
Fithub	Affordable gym	Seed: US$3 million (Mar 2022)	Goodwater Capital, Trihill Capital, Bukuwarung co-founder Abhinay Peddisetty, Hangry co-founder Robin Tan, Koinworks co-founder Benedicto Haryono, Super co-founder Steven Wongsoredjo, Impack Ventures' Phillip Tjipto
Offmeat	Plant-based meat	Seed: US$1.7 million (Apr 2022)	Alpha JWC Ventures, Creative Gorilla Capital, United Family Capital, Lemonilo
Atma	Social job platform	Pre-seed: US$5 million (May 2022)	AC Ventures; founders and executives of GoTo Group, Advance Intelligence Group, Ula, Lummo, Kopi Kenangan, Sampoerna Strategic, MMS Group, and Xiaomi
Aman	Employee benefits platform	Pre-seed: US$1.2 million (May 2022)	Trihill Capital, 1982 Ventures, Alto Partners Multi-Family Office, Antonio Mazza, Atlas Global Kapital

Through GFC, the Samwers continue to support Rocket Mafia members such as Flash Coffee founder and CEO David Brunier, who was previously chief marketing officer at the consolidated Delivery-Hero operation. In April 2021, Flash Coffee raised a US$15 million series A round backed by DeliveryHero-linked DX Ventures, GFC, and

Conny & Co. Flash Coffee is based in Singapore, with operations in Thailand and Indonesia.[56]

Outside of GFC, the Rocket legacy remains strong in Indonesia. Former members have gone on to establish a new generation of homegrown Indonesian startups, advise entrepreneurs, become investors themselves, and even create public policy that may improve the digital economy in Indonesia for decades to come.

In hindsight, however, the Samwers' quick hire-and-fire strategies led to low employee retention rates, creating weaker continuity in company culture across the board. Personally, I believe a company with staying power needs time to build a strong culture driven by founders to get teams to pull together through ups and downs.

For all the execution prowess Rocket represented, it lacked in true founder-driven culture, which resulted in a revolving door of talent joining and subsequently leaving in a matter of months.

Rocket was a lightning rod that catalyzed the Southeast Asian digital "gold rush" bringing in talent, training, capital, and awareness. It was a training ground and delivered a very important cohort of tech leaders we now see today. The history of Indonesia's tech space cannot be retold without first unpacking how Rocket entered the sector, birthing a new generation of founders, and igniting a wave of funding never before seen—all in a span of two to three years.

As a result of Rocket's explosive impact, a new generation of e-commerce players arose in Indonesia from 2014 to 2018. The next chapter will take a look at the brisk pace and level of competition that would see a few major players dominating the market and the backers who helped push these commercial behemoths to the top.

CHAPTER THREE

THE EARLY ERA OF E-COMMERCE BATTLES

Rocket Internet's hyperscaling strategies, fueled by aggressive marketing and outsized financial backing for the region in the early 2010s, ignited a wildfire in the Indonesian e commerce sector. The impact of the Rocket mafia was far-reaching, spawning a host of new e-commerce ventures while also driving established homegrown brands like Tokopedia, Bukalapak, and Blibli to accumulate significant resources of their own. This transformative period saw the Indonesian e-commerce landscape evolve rapidly.

This chapter explores the explosive growth and intense competition within Indonesia's e-commerce sector during the early 2010s, catalyzed by Rocket

Internet's aggressive expansion tactics and substantial investment activity. It details the transformative impact these strategies had, not only spurring the rise of new ventures but also compelling established local brands such as Tokopedia, Bukalapak, and Blibli to escalate their resource accumulation, significantly altering the landscape and dynamics of the Indonesian digital market.

Indonesia's internet user population surged to 92 million by 2015, driven by a cumulative effect of various factors. Within three years of Rocket Internet's entry into the archipelago, a Google report revealed that Indonesia had become the world's fastest growing internet market, registering an impressive compound annual growth rate of 19%. In 2015, Indonesia's e-commerce market was valued at US$1.7 billion, representing a third of Southeast Asia's total online retail value.[1]

Compared to nearby countries, Indonesia experienced a huge increase in online shopping activity, new e-commerce users, and overall sales. This growth happened despite several challenges: slow internet speeds (Indonesia's average was 6.7 Mbps compared to the global average of 23.3 Mbps), many people not yet having internet access, limited online shopping infrastructure outside of major cities, and nearly 63.7% of the population not using banks.

The Google study also highlighted long-standing issues with fraudulent goods and high logistics costs. Orders originating in Indonesia were 12 times more likely to turn out fraudulent than the global average. Meanwhile, delivering goods outside of the central island of Java could take more than 10 days, and sea freight costs could even exceed US$1,000 per 20-foot container.

The report also made clear to the world what Indonesians and savvy foreign investors like Rocket had already realized years before. Any exponential growth that could already be seen would be dwarfed by further acceleration in the next few years.

The race was on, and in addition to established players like Tokopedia, Bukalapak, Lazada, and Blibli, new market entrants made their way into Indonesia from 2015 onward, such as Shopee (backed by Singapore-based tech company Garena, which later rebranded as Sea Limited and listed on the New York Stock Exchange [NYSE]) and Matahari Mall (backed by Lippo Group, one of Indonesia's large conglomerates).

Each player took a different route when seeking to corner Indonesia's burgeoning e-commerce market, while also carving out niches within the sector and addressing Indonesia-specific pain points for consumers.

TOKOPEDIA: EMBRACING FINTECH

If you recall, Tokopedia's unique selling proposition when it launched in 2009 was its debut escrow system to address the pain point of fraud. Simply put, users could withhold payment if they received counterfeit goods, nothing at all, or were otherwise scammed.

But the escrow feature soon became commoditized with other e-commerce players all incorporating it. Lazada and Zalora's entry into Indonesia in 2012 surely grew the sector, but also took a chunk of the C2C market from Tokopedia, which at the time was the nation's largest online marketplace. Founder William recognized that Tokopedia needed funds to enter the next phase of innovation and match the multimillion-dollar rounds the Rocket brands were refueling with.

In June 2013, Tokopedia quietly onboarded Japanese conglomerate SoftBank in a series D funding round, with the invested amount left undisclosed. A year later, Tokopedia made Southeast Asian history by becoming the first company in the region to raise a US$100 million series E funding round from SoftBank and Sequoia Capital.[2]

In a market where most funds were still focused on seed and early-stage deals and lacking a healthy mergers-and-acquisition paradigm, the mega round put Tokopedia's e-commerce competitors and their deep-pocketed backers on notice. By 2014, Tokopedia was selling 6 million items per month, with a 10% to 20% monthly growth rate.[3]

The funding enabled Tokopedia to expand its offerings by introducing new product categories. Recognizing that a significant portion of Indonesia's internet users were now using mobile devices to come online for the first time, Tokopedia launched an Android app in 2015.[4] That same year, it also teamed up with ride-hailing services like Gojek to introduce instant delivery, a concept that was previously hard to imagine due to Indonesia's struggles with last-mile delivery.[5]

Under the banner of democratizing commerce through technology, Tokopedia began developing its "Digital Products and Fintech" arm in 2016, bringing the app to the large number of unbanked, yet smartphone-savvy, Indonesians in the archipelago's satellite cities.[6]

Although credit cards to this day have minimal penetration in Indonesia, Tokopedia partnered with credit card issuers at the time in a bid to help people apply for credit cards via its platform. Its early fintech diversification set it apart from its e-commerce-focused competitors, with the app also acting as a payment channel for users to top-up mobile phone credit; pay utility bills, such as electricity; make social security contributions; and even buy train tickets—all on one app.

In April 2016, Tokopedia went back to the fundraising market for a follow-on US$147 million funding round from undisclosed investors. This additional funding led to the launch of its "Deals" arm in 2017, aimed at helping people find the best deals from eight main categories, including beauty, travel, and activities. Deals also helped Indonesia's offline businesses expand online. March 2017 marked the arrival of Tokopedia's e-wallet, TokoCash.[7]

In August 2017, Tokopedia's US$1.1 billion funding round set a new milestone in Southeast Asia's fast-growing digital ecosystem. The deal valued Tokopedia at US$7 billion and added a new name to its list of investors: Alibaba.[8]

Curiously, the e-commerce behemoth out of China was playing multiple sides of the Indonesian e-commerce market, having already acquired a controlling stake in Lazada regionally in 2016.[9]

The billion-dollar round was followed by yet another US$1.1 billion fundraise in 2018, this time with both Alibaba and SoftBank participating.[10] The year marked the rollout of more fintech services on Tokopedia, including the launch of a gold trading service.

Tokopedia then decided to bridge the gap between online and offline retail. In November 2018, Mitra Tokopedia launched as a separate app for micro-enterprises, such as mom-and-pop shops and outdoor food stalls (*warung*), to sell products on Tokopedia, including data packages, electricity tokens, and game vouchers.[11]

This innovation essentially turned *warung* sellers into online-to-offline (O2O) agents for villages in rural Indonesia where internet connectivity was less stable and users were doing business primarily offline. Mitra Tokopedia helped small businesses supplement their incomes while bringing millions of Indonesians online for the first time. In 2018, Tokopedia contributed Rp58 trillion (US$4 billion) to the nation's overall economy.[12]

BUKALAPAK: PIONEERING *WARUNG* TECH AND INVESTING IN LOCAL TALENT

Founded as an online marketplace for small to medium enterprises (SMEs) in 2010, Bukalapak facilitated more than US$80 million in transactions in 2014, passing the 160,000-merchant mark on its platform. In February 2015, the C2C marketplace secured its first big backer in the form of Indonesia's second-largest media company, Emtek Group, in a series B funding round.[13] Onboarding a media power like Emtek gave Bukalapak immediate help on the marketing end, especially against large, well-funded brands like Lazada and Shopee.

In fact, it was Bukalapak that invented the O2O *warung-tech* concept in 2016, a full two years before Tokopedia launched Mitra Tokopedia. Similarly dubbed Mitra Bukalapak, the initiative launched to give *mitra* (Indonesian for "partners") or *warung* owners the same resources and opportunities as a modern retailer. These included tools such as bookkeeping and customer relationship management software. As many of these mom-and-pop store operators were not very tech-savvy, Mitra Bukalapak also featured a community called *Juwara* that connected *warung* owners, where they could share tips and tricks, and discuss problems that the Bukalapak team could fix.[14]

The same year, Bukalapak launched BukaPengadaan, a B2B e-procurement platform that brought products by Indonesian SMEs listed on Bukalapak to the eyes of large corporate or government buyers.[15] Its comprehensive system made things easy for both buyers and vendors, including closed ecosystems for registered users, provision of goods and services, online approval systems, monitoring of goods orders, payments, and e-invoicing.

Just like Tokopedia, Bukalapak recognized that fintech was the next frontier. It introduced its first investment service called BukaReksa in 2016, in partnership with online mutual funds platform Bareksa.[16] This was followed up by a sharia-compliant mutual fund product, a gold transaction feature, and expanded virtual bank accounts in partnership with Bank Rakyat Indonesia (BRI) in 2017, as well as e-wallet BukaDana in 2018.[17-20]

These forays into different fintech spaces were partly financed by a series C funding round in November 2017, when Bukalapak raised an undisclosed round of funding, and then announced that it had attained unicorn status.[21] Bukalapak also expanded its product offerings in the C2C space when it acquired Indonesian secondhand goods marketplace Prelo in October 2018.[22]

To fuel its expansion across different product segments, Bukalapak invested heavily in hiring local engineers and software developers, building a center for R&D in Bandung in 2018 to support 200 in-house engineers.[23] By early 2019, Bukalapak had a roster of more than 1,100 top Indonesian tech talents.[24]

BLIBLI: CATERING TO THE AFFLUENT AND GUARANTEEING AUTHENTICITY

Unlike the bigger e-commerce names that chose to go the VC route in the arms race for expansion in Indonesia, Blibli chose a more traditional path to both brand building and fundraising. From the outset, Blibli had a strong financial foundation and business network, thanks to it being a subsidiary of Djarum Group, a diversified conglomerate owned by the Hartonos, one of Indonesia's wealthiest families. The Hartonos also own a majority share in Bank Central Asia (BCA), one of the largest banks in Indonesia.[25]

Launched in May 2011, Blibli is officially backed by Djarum Group's VC firm GDP Venture, led by Martin Hartono. GDP Venture also invested in Kaskus, which by April 2015 had amassed 8 million members.

Cognizant of the Indonesian e-commerce market's propensity for counterfeit goods, Blibli guaranteed that products sold on its platform were all original. In doing so, it was able to speak to a more focused audience of middle-class affluent consumers.[26]

To this day, a key difference between Blibli and other e-marketplaces is its sellers. Tokopedia and Shopee are primarily C2C platforms, while Blibli focuses on B2B, B2C, and B2B2C. Official stores are often placed prominently on Blibli's platform. This also leaves the door open to different forms of monetization.

By focusing on Indonesia's mass affluent segment and branded products, Blibli does not command a user or merchant base as large as Tokopedia's, but instead makes efforts to expand its part of the pie.

While Blibli has not repeatedly raised funding from outside Djarum Group, the e-commerce marketplace has been active as an investor and acquirer of other startups. In 2016, Blibli participated in online healthcare platform HaloDoc's US$13 million series A deal, together with ride-hailing firm Gojek, among others.[27] In 2017, Blibli outright acquired two online travel agents: Tiket.com and IndonesiaFlight.[28]

Additionally, Blibli's ties with fellow Djarum subsidiary BCA mean that the bank's credit cards, internet banking services, and other payment methods have been part of Blibli's ecosystem from the early days.[29] When BCA introduced its OneKlik deposit service for e-commerce portals, Blibli was its launch partner.[30]

In 2018, Blibli rolled out two new O2O initiatives: apartment rentals and expanding the Blibli InStore Kiosks to rural Indonesia.[31] The apartment rental service is a partnership with Jendela360, a property agent that provides 360-degree virtual images of apartments available for rent. Customers can browse for apartments on Blibli, contact agents for appointments, and make direct transactions using the Blibli InStore app, an O2O app that supports on-the-spot transactions.

Separately, Blibli expanded its reach to unbanked Indonesians in rural areas of the archipelago by partnering with Pos Indonesia (the national postal service) and placing Blibli InStore kiosks in post offices. Customers can place orders and pay with cash at the kiosks, with delivery fulfillment carried out by Pos Indonesia's quick service.

Even within its more affluent niche, Blibli still had to address the logistical hurdles of delivering across Indonesia by continuously investing in new warehouses to enable faster delivery, instead of just centralizing deliveries in the capital city of Jakarta. It also backed Gojek's US$250 million funding round in February 2018, leveraging Gojek's large fleet of *ojek* riders for delivery services. At the time, Blibli's website and mobile app totaled 40 million to 50 million unique visitors per month.[32]

LAZADA: FULL SUPPLY CHAIN CONTROL AND CROSS-BORDER TRADE

Two years after landing on Indonesian shores in 2012, Lazada announced that it had recorded more than US$105 million in local transactions in 2014. Indonesia was Lazada's top market, with local shoppers accounting for more than 30% of total regional expenditure on the platform.[33]

With the financial power of the Samwers and Rocket's European backers, Lazada looked to overcome Indonesian shoppers' trust deficit by introducing cash-on-delivery (COD) as a key payment method. It also navigated Indonesia's logistics roadblocks by spending massively on end-to-end logistics capabilities to give it full control over the supply chain. Lazada invested in warehouses and sorting centers while building out its partner network, as well as cross-border and last-mile arrangements.[34]

In August 2014, Rocket secured a significant investment of US$445 million from the Philippine telecommunications company PLDT, which directly benefited Lazada.[35] A key shareholder in PLDT is Anthony Salim, head of the local conglomerate Salim Group and another one of the wealthiest tycoons in Indonesia. Via PLDT's investment in Rocket, Anthony came to own a 10% stake in the German internet company builder.[36]

In November 2014, Lazada raised US$250 million from a group of investors, led by Singaporean sovereign wealth fund Temasek.[37] Nonetheless, heavy competition finally led to the largest capital injection in April

2016, when Alibaba spent US$1 billion to acquire a controlling stake in Lazada.[38] In June 2017, Alibaba doubled down, investing another US$1 billion to up its stake to 83%.[39]

Given Alibaba founder Jack Ma's involvement in encouraging regional trade and the "Digital Free Trade Zone," Lazada embraced regional trade in 2018, supporting sellers who wanted to market their products outside their own countries.[40] In August 2018, Lazada launched LazMall, a curated selection of more than 1,000 international and local brands from reputable retailers and resellers.[41] LazMall sold only authentic and original branded products and offered both a hassle-free return policy and next-day delivery.

Lazada continued its aggressive marketing campaigns with the monthly 9.9 (September 9) and 10.10 (October 10, and so on) one-day shopping festivals, which frequently rang up sales totals that were 30 times more than the typical daily gross merchandise value.

MATAHARI MALL: O2O BACKED BY BRICKS AND MORTAR

Another major Indonesian conglomerate decided to enter the e-commerce race in February 2015 with the launch of Matahari Mall. Claiming a US$500 million investment commitment from the Riady family-owned Lippo Group—which owns Lippo malls and Matahari Department Stores (MDS)—the marketplace raised a further US$200 million via bank financing in April the same year.[42]

Aiming to be the "Alibaba of Indonesia," Matahari Mall set itself apart from its e-commerce competitors with a unique O2O concept, which was designed to build consumer trust by allowing shoppers to redeem and return the items they purchase online at Matahari's 127 offline stores in 62 cities nationwide.

Matahari Mall users were able to access an array of products and services from the Lippo Group's diverse portfolio, including fresh products from Hypermart and movie tickets from Lippo's Cinemaxx theaters.

In 2016, Matahari Mall rolled out several programs in keeping with its trust-bridging and O2O themes, such as the "Super Sakti" program (via its partnership with LippoInsurance), which enables customers to claim insurance for damaged electronic products with the Super Sakti logo. The marketplace's "Super Cintaku" program, meanwhile, allowed customers to buy items through an installment payment scheme without needing to hold credit cards.[43]

On the delivery front, within a year of its launch, Matahari Mall boasted more than 650 pickup points across the archipelago, plus an additional 4,600 post-office pickup points via its own partnership with Pos Indonesia. This accessibility, coupled with the Lippo and MDS brand names, served to introduce e-commerce to Indonesians who were still unfamiliar with it, especially in satellite cities.

However, Matahari Mall was unable to match the sums of capital other e-commerce players were able to raise. It eventually merged with its shareholder and traditional retailer MDS in November 2018, with the site being folded into Matahari.com, the MDS online representation.[44]

SHOPEE: A BRAND-FIRST AND GAMIFIED APPROACH

Of this crop of e-commerce pioneers, Shopee was the last to enter Indonesia in mid-2015.[45] But it was by no means the least equipped. At the time, Shopee was a C2C marketplace backed by Garena Interactive Holding, a late 2000s game development and publishing company based out of Singapore.

Garena, which later rebranded as Sea Limited, already had massive backers, such as Chinese tech giant Tencent, before launching the Shopee brand in Southeast Asia. It also had institutional investors such as the US private equity firm General Atlantic, Canadian pension fund Ontario Teachers Pension Plan, Malaysian sovereign fund Khazanah Nasional Bhd, and Chinese VC firm Keytone Ventures.[46]

This meant Shopee hit the ground running in Indonesia. The marketplace launched as an app first, taking note of the archipelago's high mobile penetration rate and 65% of Indonesians already using social media to buy and sell items.

Shopee quickly attracted attention for its user-friendly features, including secure payment options, a logistics fee calculator integrated into the platform, and engaging social and gamified elements. A key factor in its early popularity was the Shopee Guarantee, which promised users a full refund if their purchases did not arrive as described or expected.

Arriving on the scene late also meant that Shopee benefited from the hundreds of millions of dollars other firms had spent on consumer education, which had by this point built much greater customer confidence in online commerce. This set off another phase of aggressive subsidies in logistics and merchant incentives bringing another front to the e-commerce war.

In 2017, Shopee introduced Shopee Mall—a separate portal from the regular Shopee marketplace—which provided access to thousands of products from more than 200 top sellers and brands such as 3M, L'Oreal, Philips, Adidas, and more.[47] This worked to scale up Shopee's B2C efforts.

In May 2018, this brand-first approach continued with the launch of Shopee's first "Super Brand Day" in Indonesia with its partner, fast-moving consumer goods giant P&G. That same year, Shopee introduced celebrity endorsers across the region, announcing K-pop band Blackpink as a regional ambassador.[48]

Like Lazada, Shopee also held monthly one-day shopping festivals that boosted sales figures. In Indonesia—by then Shopee's largest market—the platform recorded 83.8 million orders in the fourth quarter of 2018, or a daily average of 900,000. The marketplace set a new record for orders in a single day, with more than 12 million recorded over the 24 hours of December 12, 2018 (12.12). Close to half of the orders recorded (5.4 million) were from Indonesia alone.[49]

AN EVOLVING REGULATORY AND E-COMMERCE ECOSYSTEM

During the 2014 to 2018 period, the early e-commerce wars claimed many victims. It was not just the small brands that fell by the wayside; the "winners" or larger players also had to keep raising capital to continuously fight for a share of the user pie, while dealing with millions (sometimes hundreds of millions) of dollars in losses. Even Alibaba-owned Lazada required multiple billion-dollar capital injections to stay competitive.

Meanwhile, e-marketplaces backed by local conglomerates and Indonesia's wealthiest families still had to carve out niches rather than take a head-on attack strategy. Blibli immediately identified that it would target the affluent market with a focus on higher-end brands, while Matahari Mall was largely dependent on the strength of Lippo Group's umbrella of companies and its brick-and-mortar presence in shopping malls.

At the time, Indonesia also saw the rise and fall of several e-commerce firms that had high ambitions, such as JD.com's subsidiary JD.ID; Blanja, a joint venture between eBay and state-owned telecommunications firm Telkom Group; and Elevenia, a joint venture by South Korea-based SK Planet and XL Axiata.

It was a hypercompetitive time, when marketplaces needed to take key measures:

- Address trust deficits in a market where consumers had concerns about counterfeit goods and fraudulent transactions
- Cater to the large portion of the Indonesian populace who remain unbanked, or who are without constant access to the internet in satellite cities
- Offer O2O services that further bridged the trust gap and eased the lack of e-payment facilities for rural consumers through COD methods
- Ensure end-to-end logistics operations became more efficient and reliable for a better customer experience

On the regulatory front, this illuminated specific issues that Indonesia's policymakers had to address to further accelerate the growth of the country's e-commerce sector. In August 2017, the government issued Indonesia's E-Commerce Road Map covering eight areas: funding, taxation, customer protection, education and human resources, telecommunications infrastructure, logistics, cybersecurity, and the establishment of a steering and management committee.[50]

Of the 26 programs set to be carried out under the roadmap between 2017 and 2019, a notable one was the *Kredit Usaha Rakyat* program, which increased credit facilities for MSMEs. Other programs revolved around providing education for local e-commerce companies, creating incubators to support local startups, and beefing up telecommunications with regard to internet speeds, networks, and security.

Given the propensity of multiple local players (such as Tokopedia and Bukalapak) to undertake their own fintech projects, OJK—Indonesia's financial services authority—in September 2018 issued an umbrella regulation for fintech development and established a regulatory sandbox regime.[51]

The regulation required all existing and prospective digital financial innovation providers in Indonesia to be recorded with OJK (which encompassed all fintech services). After that, OJK would review over one year whether a provider was qualified to participate in the regulatory sandbox. Upon completing the sandbox process, OJK would then issue a recommendation for the provider to be (1) registered with the OJK; (2) improved upon, in which case the sandbox period would be extended for six months; or (3) denied registration, meaning the fintech provider would lose recordation and could not be sandboxed again.

Eventually, these policies and regulations were either superseded or augmented with expanded issuances from the Indonesian government. But the seeds of regulation would not be planted without the early era of e-commerce battles laying bare the key issues and roadblocks to digital economic growth.

All things considered, the sheer scale of the Indonesian market meant that even the big players were not able to take on the entire ecosystem, which enabled other startups to address not only different core industries like fintech but also sectors in e-commerce itself as the market continued to develop.

This created more specialization within the local ecosystem, further encouraging local innovation and entrepreneurship. The next chapter looks at how the hustle and bustle around payments, logistics, and policy were tackled and resolved, thus helping to transform Indonesian e-commerce into what it is today.

CHAPTER FOUR

PAYMENTS, LOGISTICS, AND POLICY SCRAMBLE TO KEEP PACE

With a baseline of e-commerce validation, a vast market, a growing middle class, and a multitude of greenfield tech opportunities, a winner-takes-all competitive mindset began to set in for Indonesia's largest e-marketplaces.

As outlined in the previous chapter, Indonesians' lack of trust in payment systems and the market's fragmented logistics and supply chain led many major players—including Lazada and Shopee—to seek full control over their entire value chains. In parallel, with no clear payments winners on the scene yet, companies like Tokopedia and Bukalapak sought to plant the seeds of early fintech.

These kinds of support pillars needed significant capital investment, in addition to technical expertise which, at the time, was not common in Indonesia. While the big platforms were able to foot massive R&D and operational bills (thanks either to fundraising from foreign VCs or the country's biggest conglomerates), they were stretched thin in trying to build up supporting e-commerce infrastructure related to payments and logistics.

This opened up new opportunities for specialized players to come in and fix specific problems. Specialists arose in the digital payment space that sought to quell worries about fraudulent transactions, while legacy logistics service providers ramped up their offerings to better serve e-commerce players.

This chapter addresses these important businesses and how they helped to enable the continued growth and rise of e-commerce. It shows how this all led to early efforts to regulate the payments space as policymakers scrambled to keep pace.

DOKU: A PAYMENTS PIONEER EMERGES FROM BALI'S DARK PAST

Before the nation's e-commerce boom in the mid-2010s, there were only a few payment gateways—and hardly any were as well known as Doku. While officially launched in 2007 by Singaporean national Nabilah Alsagoff, Doku was originally conceived back in 2002 as a unifier for the tourism community in Bali, which was hit hard that year by terrorist bombings in October.[1]

At first, Alsagoff and her partners planned to pull resources from the international community for rebuilding efforts so that accommodations in Bali (including hotels) could be perused and booked through a single website. Instead, years later, she established PT Nusa Satu Inti Artha, the first electronic payment and risk management company in the nation.

A year later, it became the first company to receive a global certificate for data security (Payment Card Industry Data Security Standard), a nod to growing privacy and fraud concerns in a very new e-commerce space.

The following years saw a rapid change: a rebrand to Doku in 2010, followed by receiving an electronic money license from the central bank (BI) in 2012. In 2014—a full seven years after it was founded—Doku had reached US$1.1 billion in total transactions and had launched its e-wallet. By that point, 80% of Doku's business came from large corporations such as Sinar Mas Land, AirAsia, and Oppo, all of which required a high volume of complex monthly transactions. Doku's payment gateway could process online payments via credit cards, major local banks (including Mandiri and BCA), and PayPal, among other methods.[2]

However, Doku also catered to SMEs via MyShortCart, a payment link launched in 2013 that helps small businesses that may only exist on social networks (like Instagram or Facebook) accept digital payments.[3] Sound familiar? Probably because PayPal launched a similar product two years later, whereas Stripe launched its payment links for businesses *eight years later*.[4,5] Doku also allied with PayPal directly in December 2012, enabling its merchants to accept payments in foreign currencies—a notable early development, considering Doku's origin story in the tourism sector.[6]

Global e-commerce players who wanted to follow Rocket and Shopee into Indonesia without the same massive investments in handling payments in-house were soon eyeing Doku as a payments partner that could accelerate their growth in the market. In February 2015, AliExpress, a marketplace under Alibaba that allowed Chinese suppliers to reach international buyers, partnered with Doku to immediately bring a diversity of payment options to its Indonesian customers.[7]

Via AliExpress's service agreement with Doku, customers could pay online through DOKU Wallet, Mandiri Clickpay, and BRI e-Pay, or offline either through 9,000 brick-and-mortar stores owned by Alfa Group or via ATM machines. Offline payments were of particular importance in 2015, as only 3.2% of Indonesia's 250-million-strong population at the time had credit cards, a percentage that, to this day and despite a recent credit boom, has not grown substantially.

IPAYMU: MARRYING A WIDE LOGISTICS FOOTPRINT WITH SECURE PAYMENTS

While the majority of Doku's clients were large corporations, SMEs were the focus for iPayMu. Founded by Riyeke Ustadiyanto, iPayMu launched in December 2012 with the idea of bringing Indonesia's SMEs online to take advantage of the early days of e-commerce growth.[8]

iPayMu hit the ground running on launch day, announcing partnerships with PayPal, national courier Pos Indonesia, and commercial bank CIMB Niaga. Pos Indonesia's then-4,000 branches across the nation gave iPayMu immediate access to one of the nation's largest distribution networks. Meanwhile, CIMB Niaga was instrumental in supporting the security of iPayMu's transactions, by offering its banking platform to support users.

iPayMu spread quickly through word of mouth among small business owners due to its transparent costing model for a variety of payment solutions. Within two years of its establishment, the payment gateway had racked up more than 26 million users.

Despite the relative ease of selling on the internet in the early 2010s, payments remained a minefield. To allay trust concerns, iPayMu was built as Indonesia's first debit-based payment system with embedded escrow for transactions. In 2014, the archipelago's SMEs faced difficulties in accessing banking services—a gap iPayMu was only too happy to fill, thanks to its integrations with more than 137 foreign and local banks.

In 2016, iPayMu simplified payments further for peer-to-peer transactions with the launch of its BayarDisini (Indonesian for "pay here") product. BayarDisini payment links could be shared quickly on social media channels and messengers—platforms that typically have a high risk of fraud.[9]

In 2020, iPayMu updated its payment link universe by introducing several enhancements. First, it automatically secured transactions with an escrow facility. Additionally, it integrated GoSend for local-area delivery of goods. For inter-regional delivery, it partnered with JNE, TIKI, or Pos Indonesia. This update allowed SME owners to have a clear view of all the service partners and the costs involved in the fulfillment process.

VERITRANS (MIDTRANS): QUICK INTEGRATION AND A SIMPLE USER INTERFACE

The local payments space proved too alluring for foreign investors to ignore; unsurprisingly, Japanese e-commerce players were soon keen to tap into Indonesia's potential.

In 2012, the same year iPayMu launched, Veritrans Indonesia (since rebranded as Midtrans) was launched as a "payments user experience" company. The company was a joint venture between Veritrans Japan; Netprice, a Japanese consumer internet incubation-turned-investment firm that backed Tokopedia; and MidPlaza, a pioneering Indonesian IT services company.[10]

Among the company's earliest customers was Japanese tech conglomerate Rakuten's Indonesian e-commerce site, which switched over from Doku due to Veritrans's fraud detection system.[11] In 2015, Veritrans began positioning itself as more than a payment gateway, transitioning into an e-commerce enablement company during a period that coincided with its rebrand into Midtrans.

Over the next year, it rolled out several tools, including pattern detection platform Aegis and chat commerce channel Prism.

Aegis incorporates algorithmic fraud scoring, transaction relationship visualization, and advanced fraud pattern analytics reporting. These proved instrumental in reducing fraud rates, while at the same time increasing the overall acceptance rate of transactions for businesses.

Prism, meanwhile, is a single chat window to explore products, talk with customer service representatives, check out products or services, and complete payments. Buyers that open the Prism window with customer service professionals have a transaction conversion rate of 12% to 15% versus 1% to 3% for customers that explore an e-commerce website themselves.

By October 2016, Midtrans was serving more than 1,700 merchants in Indonesia, including major e-commerce players Blibli, Bukalapak, Gojek, MAPeMall, Matahari Mall, Tokopedia, and Traveloka.[12]

XENDIT: FROM MONEY TRANSFERS TO A B2B PAYMENTS FACILITATOR

When Xendit launched as a simple money-transfer service in August 2015, it was attempting to bring a seamless C2C payments app to the market.[13] Observing that Indonesians frequently dined out together, Xendit cofounder

Moses Lo believed that a purpose-built bill-splitting application could get some early adoption.

Unlike all the other players which were B2B focused, Xendit would address consumers directly. In addition, Doku, iPayMu, and Midtrans, Indonesia's conglomerate-owned payments gateways, like Finpay and Faspay, were already entrenched, with a slew of services catering to businesses in almost all sectors, suggesting that B2B was already saturated.

The idea was that Xendit's easy user experience would set it apart, where users only needed phone numbers to send or request money (like Venmo in the United States). Within just a few months of its beta launch, Xendit racked up 13,000 users. The company's official launch was also notable in the headlines: Xendit was the first Indonesian startup to be accepted into Silicon Valley's prestigious Y Combinator incubator program (YC S15).[14]

Several local and regional investors also participated in Xendit's seed round, including Convergence Ventures (our former fund before it merged with Agaeti Venture Capital and became AC Ventures in 2019).

At the time, Xendit was a consumer play—not focused on SMEs or large corporations that had been the target of other major payment players. People selling through WhatsApp would already have buyers' numbers, for which instant payments via Xendit proved a logical next step. At the time, both Venmo and PayPal had no direct presence in Indonesia. But even early on, there were concerns that the money transfer service could be replicated by bigger entities such as WeChat.

In 2016, the team faced a setback when they realized that their product was ahead of its time for the Indonesian market. Recognizing this, Xendit shifted its focus in 2017 to support B2B transactions.[15] This new direction allowed banks and businesses to handle several payments at once, instead of processing them individually. To support this change, Xendit needed fresh capital. Its fundraising efforts were boosted by the team's participation in Y Combinator. Additionally, the backgrounds of

Moses and cofounders Tessa Wijaya, Juan Gonzalez, and Bo Chen, who had studied and worked in the United States, made them more appealing to US-based investors.

In June 2018, Xendit raised a series A funding round of US$20 million that was led by one of the biggest names in VC investing, Kleiner Perkins.[16] Over the next few years, Xendit began launching more products. It was the first platform to offer automated disbursements to more than 130 banks in Indonesia. It was also the first company to build fully developed custodian accounts for clients to segregate investments from operations.

To prevent fraud and ensure secure connections to customer bank accounts, Xendit introduced a method to verify bank accounts using an application programming interface (API) prior to completing a payment. By confirming the bank account name, this approach enhanced transfer security and minimized the risk of fraud.

At the same time, Indonesians were trying to take advantage of digital disruption by looking for more attractive investment assets. This resulted in the surge of P2P digital lending, which allowed individual lenders to give loans to people and businesses. This would soon be followed by the crypto craze, which gave birth to local crypto exchanges.

Both business models have a common denominator: the need for a complete, easy, and reliable payment gateway. This was a perfect opportunity for Xendit.

Currently approaching a US$2 billion valuation, Xendit processed more than US$25 billion in 2023.[17] Today, the company is recognized as one of Indonesia's top fintech pioneers, as it now aspires to become the "Stripe of Southeast Asia." Businesses can use Xendit to accept and send payments, get business financing, and manage taxes, among other services.

In the early and mid-2010s, payment players were plentiful, with many focusing on bringing SMEs online. However, bringing merchants to meet with customers in a secure situation online was only one part of the trust equation. The other was delivering products as and when promised. With Indonesia being an archipelago, the nation's logistics sector was a tough nut to crack, and in some ways still is.

17,000 ISLANDS MEANS DISTRIBUTION MAKES EVERYTHING WORK

Forward-thinking payment gateways quickly forged partnerships with legacy couriers and logistics companies that offered wide networks as part of their unique selling propositions to business owners who did not want to devote too many hours and resources to managing e-commerce deliveries.

Indonesia's end-to-end logistics costs for e-commerce deliveries will always dwarf those of its Southeast Asian peers, purely because its archipelagic makeup calls for multimodal transportation (land, rail, sea, and air) to move goods from port to doorstep. Compounding this problem is the lack of developed infrastructure in roads and ports, which makes it hard to route efficiently. At the same time, customer demand and the early e-commerce battles among the various platforms resulted in delivery services for express and small parcels in Indonesia growing by 17% compound annual growth rate (CAGR) from 2013 to 2017.[18]

By this time, despite progress and skyrocketing e-commerce sales, logistics costs in Indonesia still outpaced those of its Southeast Asian neighbors by a significant margin.

Moreover, despite being largely dependent on truckers, Indonesia's truck utilization was incredibly low compared to regional peers. Our team attributed this to a lack of infrastructure development, leading to inefficiencies and low utilization as the majority of trucks experienced empty backhaul rates, as did almost every ship returning from remote areas.

In 2019, each Indonesian truck only covered an average of 50,000 kilometers annually, compared to trucks in Thailand (150,000 kilometers) and across Europe (200,000 kilometers) that were three to four times more efficient.

This led to a new wave of startups that aimed to address inefficiencies in logistics by employing smart warehousing tech, utilizing sensors, and implementing IT dashboards.

But back in the early 2010s, it was still vital for e-commerce players to tap into the widest distribution networks at the onset of their online selling journeys. These massive networks were often serviced by legacy logistics companies that have operated in the archipelago for decades, such as TIKI, JNE, and, of course, Pos Indonesia.

A 300-YEAR-OLD NATIONAL COURIER EVOLVES

Having been around the longest, established in 1746, the state-owned postal service Pos Indonesia had the widest reach for e-commerce deliveries. Its 24,000 service points cover all cities, districts, and subdistricts in Indonesia, including 940 locations in some of the country's most isolated places. Pos Indonesia's network also includes more than 3,800 offline post offices.[19]

In November 2016, Pos Indonesia was named as a key player in the government's 14th Economic Policy Package on the E-commerce Road Map 2017–2019.[20] The roadmap was Indonesia's first piece of major policy concerning the country's growing e-commerce sector, and the logistics aspect involved the following:

- Improving the e-commerce logistics ecosystem through the National Logistics Blueprint to further accelerate shipments and cut shipping costs
- Revitalizing, restructuring, and modernizing Pos Indonesia as the provider of national post services
- Outsourcing e-commerce logistics facilities
- Developing logistics systems from villages to cities

The repositioning strategy aimed to transform Pos Indonesia from focusing on mail delivery to becoming the logistical backbone of Indonesia's e-commerce sector. The ICT Minister at the time, Rudiantara, framed it this way:

> With more than 3,000 outlets across the nation, Pos Indonesia could offer reliable services at relatively low prices to help e-commerce companies reduce expenses. E-commerce players don't need to establish their own logistical units, as they can share a single logistical platform provided by Pos Indonesia.[21]

In a step toward modernization, Pos Logistik Indonesia (Poslog), the logistics subsidiary of Pos Indonesia, entered into a partnership with Anchanto, a Singapore-based e-commerce fulfillment company, in February 2016.[22] This collaboration aimed to digitize Poslog's delivery systems, warehouses, sorting centers, and trucking networks.

Anchanto and Poslog set up a dedicated team to offer real-time order visibility, efficient picking and packing, channel sales management, persistent inventory listing across local and regional marketplaces, and customer support.

Although these served to address a pain point faced by the Indonesian e-commerce sector, logistics providers continued to use processes built especially for B2B logistics, which resulted in a lack of end-to-end visibility of orders. This led to errors and delivery delays as well as higher costs.

In the previous chapter, we explored how homegrown e-commerce platforms like Matahari Mall partnered with the national logistics brand for its O2O services (enabling payment and goods pick-up in post offices across the country), one avenue to circumvent problems related to payments on the last mile of delivery.[23] In 2018, Pos Indonesia inked a similar agreement with O2O e-commerce startup Kioson, which would expand Pos Indonesia's network by turning Kioson partner kiosks into postal service agents (in addition to receiving e-commerce deliveries).[24]

Since then, Pos Indonesia has continued to digitize its ever-growing network and offer its warehousing and distributing expertise to e-commerce players. In December 2021, e-commerce contender Bhinneka collaborated with Pos Indonesia to build an optimal warehousing and distribution system, including express delivery, a BNPL (buy-now-pay-later) service, APIs for application developers, and shipment tracking services.[25]

PRIVATE LOGISTICS PLAYERS PAIR UP WITH MARKETPLACES

In Indonesia, last-mile delivery is particularly complex. Outside of Pos Indonesia, legacy firms have the largest networks. Among private-sector players, two of the local names that have been around for decades are TIKI and JNE, both founded by Soeprapto Suparno in 1970 and 1990, respectively.[26]

PT Citra Van Titipan Kilat (TIKI) was initially made to cater to the high traffic for domestic shipments, largely packages and documents, outside of Central Jakarta. Over time, TIKI expanded across the archipelago, and Soeprapto started exploring the possibility of servicing overseas shipments. Two decades after establishing TIKI, Soeprapto and Johari Zein cofounded PT TIKI JNE (Tiki Jalur Nugraha Ekakurir) in 1990. The rapid pace of industrialization in the 1990s across Southeast Asia meant that JNE not only competed with foreign shippers but, eventually, its own parent company TIKI. In 1994, JNE and TIKI split, and JNE opened its domestic services arm.

The rising tide of e-commerce growth boosted all logistics players in the mid-2010s.[27] In 2015, JNE was Indonesia's market leader with 13,000 employees, 3,500 brick-and-mortar storefronts, 7,000 motorcycles, and 2,000 vans, in addition to a fleet of hired trucks and boats.[28] With the ability to spend Rp760 billion (US$55 million) annually, JNE was delivering an average of 4 million e-commerce packages per month. The company boasted annual revenue increases of 30% to 40% thanks to Indonesia's e-commerce boom. By 2017, Tokopedia, Shopee, Lazada, and Blibli were all using JNE for their deliveries.[29]

Meanwhile, TIKI saw 50% of its deliveries come from the capital city. In December 2017, TIKI sought to increase efficiency by launching the free online pickup service Jempol, which was expected to result in a 30% increase in deliveries in Jakarta, where the service was integrated with TIKI's mobile app. In 2016, TIKI delivered 25 million packages across Indonesia, and e-commerce accounted for 25% to 30% of its revenue.[30]

In contrast, FedEx subsidiary RPX was shipping 100,000 e-commerce packages monthly in 2015, a far cry from the numbers that both JNE and TIKI were pulling in. However, RPX handled deliveries for major e-commerce marketplaces, including Lazada, Zalora, and Blibli. Working around Indonesians' distrust of e-payments led to initiatives like O2O and COD. However, marketplaces that offered COD had to work in tandem with their logistics partners to mitigate risks for delivery riders and drivers who were left holding cash. As such, RPX used its in-house couriers for COD, and could only offer the service in 28 cities across Indonesia.

EXPRESS COURIER SERVICES INTRODUCE THE TECH EDGE

Despite the availability of existing logistics firms, both e-commerce buyers and sellers were still hungry for an improved experience. They needed solutions that could cater to specific needs, including cheaper delivery costs, same-day delivery options, package pick-up, and COD.

For these reasons, The Kim Hai and Rudy Darwin Swigo, local founders with experience in the cargo business, decided to launch SiCepat Express in 2014.[31] The company rolled out a variety of tailored services, such as affordable e-commerce delivery to all Indonesian cities, bulk delivery, international delivery, and COD.

From the beginning, SiCepat had partnered with almost all major e-commerce firms in the country and participated in giving discounts during promotional times, such as National Online Buying Day.

In 2020, the company delivered more than 1 million packages per day, from 5 million seller partners, and the total transaction value had tripled compared to the previous year.[32]

A year after SiCepat was established, the former CEO of OPPO Indonesia, Jet Lee, founded another e-commerce-focused logistics firm called J&T Express.[33] The name came from the combination of his name with OPPO's founder Tony Chen, who was also involved in the new company.

Having been in Indonesia since 2013, Jet recognized the growing potential of e-commerce. Drawing upon his deep experience in selling popular smartphone brands, he decided to resign from his position and founded J&T. He aimed to tap into both his expertise and the emerging logistics market in Indonesia.

In a short time, the company expanded not only in Southeast Asia but also to Jet's home country of China by acquiring Shanghai-based Longbang Express. By then, the firm also operated in Saudi Arabia, the United Arab Emirates, Brazil, and Egypt.

Similar to SiCepat, J&T gained momentum by collaborating with local e-commerce firms. By creating a logistics network that was more efficient than the existing one, thanks to the use of technology, it was able to provide better services at a more affordable cost.

In 2022, J&T raised US$2 billion in fresh funding from Temasek, Boyu Capital, and Sequoia Capital China.[34] In late 2023, it went public on the Hong Kong Stock Exchange, successfully raising a further US$500 million.[35]

Less than a decade after the emergence of early e-commerce players, Indonesia had various logistic options, from conventional ones to firms that focused on e-commerce. However, local serial entrepreneur Budi Handoko and ex-McKinsey consultant Phil Opamuratawongse believed that there was still a missing piece in the landscape: an aggregator that could merge all networks into a single platform. It is similar to the concept of Cainiao, a China-based third-party logistics aggregator.

That is the birth story of Shipper, a logistics and warehouse aggregator that was founded in 2017.[36] It offers practical, safe, and convenient service solutions for customers' business needs within the country and abroad. The firm could mitigate inefficiencies and save costs for merchants, which is a strong value proposition for both logistics providers and merchants.

Shipper allowed customers to ship packages from anywhere with no minimum order or additional costs. MSMEs and micro-sellers also did not have to bother leaving the house because Shipper would pick up packages directly from the sender's address.

"The rapid growth of e-commerce transactions in Indonesia has prompted new needs for integrated logistics services from upstream to downstream, including warehousing services. Shipper's mission is to provide broader and more equitable access to high-class logistics services throughout Indonesia, especially for MSMEs," explained Budi Handoko, cofounder and chief operations officer at Shipper.

AC Ventures joined Shipper's US$20 million series A round led by Naspers in May 2020.[37] In 2021, amidst the COVID-19 pandemic, Shipper raised US$63 million in series B funding from AC Ventures, DST Global, Sequoia Capital India, Prosus Ventures, Floodgate, Lightspeed, Y Combinator, and Insignia Ventures Partners.[38] It had 300 warehouses throughout the country and thousands of corporate clients.

While startups and their logistics and payment providers were busy experimenting and innovating, policymakers reacted quickly to the new risks that emerged in the payments and fraud space.

PAYMENTS POLICY EVOLVES AT BREAKNECK SPEED

Before 2010 and the emergence of early e-wallets from Doku and iPayMu, Indonesian retailers, banks, and telcos used e-money tools to reach 200 million unbanked Indonesians.[39] Services like m-payment, mobile money transfers, and m-wallets (linked to mobile numbers) were prevalent and aided by the large number of Indonesian migrant workers remitting money home regularly.

In 2008, Indonesia's 4.3 million documented migrant workers were the second largest contributor to its foreign exchange incomes, amounting to US$8.24 billion in remittances.[40]

As early as 2008, the number of e-money instruments in Indonesia, from prepaid cards to telco e-wallets, had proliferated. This led Bank Indonesia (the nation's central bank) to roll out its first e-money licensing regulation in 2009, which indirectly stimulated early payments innovation in the country and has shaped the landscape we see today.[41]

By the mid-2010s, it had become clear that credit cards would never take hold in Indonesia the way they did in other markets, which opened the gates for e-wallets to thrive in e-commerce.

A 2017 KPMG report attributed Indonesia's low credit card growth to consumer protection regulations issued by Bank Indonesia in January 2015, which specified age- and income-based restrictions around credit card ownership, as well as a government decree effective in 2016 requiring credit card providers to submit transaction details (including customer identity) to the Indonesian tax office, which discouraged the use of credit cards due to privacy concerns.[42]

As the payments space and e-commerce evolved further, Bank Indonesia and OJK had to keep pace with new policy updates.

The rise of regulation in fintech only served to draw more interest in Indonesia's digital economy, fueling a new breed of entrepreneurs (see: the Rocket Mafia) as well as giving the green light to brick-and-mortar conglomerates to enter the digital space with renewed investment interest.

With some e-commerce players choosing to build payments and logistics systems in-house, and others choosing to partner with third-party providers with better reach and specialist expertise, it was only a matter of time before super apps emerged in Indonesia. VC investments fueled the race for the most users. When blue oceans became red, startups in verticals with large user bases (such as ride-hailing apps) looked to expand into e-commerce, payments, and logistics to offer a more complete package to Indonesians.

The next chapter explores the journeys of Southeast Asia's two largest super apps from their shared origin in ride-hailing.

CHAPTER FIVE

GOJEK, GRAB, AND THE WAR FOR TWO-WHEELED DOMINANCE

The previous chapters touched on Indonesia's massive population, large unbanked and underbanked communities, and its archipelago makeup causing region-high logistics costs as key recurring issues for e-commerce, payments, and logistics players.

The nation's current capital city of Jakarta, however, is a different story entirely. In the booming metropolitan area of Jakarta, home to approximately 30 million residents, the main concern is not about how to deliver goods by boat, truck, or plane. Instead, one of the single biggest pain points revolves around debilitating traffic conditions that persist today.

For many, it's a given in Jakarta that if you commute to work, you spend a significant amount of time in traffic: in extreme cases up to three or four hours in the morning rush, repeating the same drill in the evening. In 2010, the gridlock was so bad that Jakarta's daily traffic jams cost the nation around Rp12.8 trillion (US$1.4 billion) annually in wasted petrol, health problems, and lower overall productivity.[1]

Statistics Indonesia reported that in 2022 there were a staggering 3.8 million cars and 17.3 million motorbikes in the Special Capital Region of Jakarta alone, not counting the surrounding metro area.[2] Juxtapose that against London, a city over twice the size of Jakarta, which has a mere 2.6 million registered cars.[3]

With millions of cars sitting idle for hours on end, it became the norm to see passengers, even business travelers and expats, make it quickly from one end of the city to the other riding on a motorbike taxi (*ojek* in Indonesian).

Indonesia's growth in the mid-2010s, similar to other developing megacities like Beijing and Delhi, fueled massive demand for personal mobility that quickly outgrew the existing infrastructure. While the taxis were regulated by licensed companies and came with a controlled fare structure, *ojek* drivers were essentially just individuals earning a living on their motorbikes, with rates negotiated on the spot in a highly informal way.

It was common to see groups of *ojek* drivers whiling away the hours in the shade outside office buildings, waiting for passengers.[4] Often, their only advertisement was a small hand-drawn sign tied to a post with a bit of wire.[5]

It appears obvious now, but innovating in this transportation subsector led to yet another inflection point in the growth of Indonesia's digital economy. Disrupting the informal *ojek* practice the way Uber revolutionized the taxi sector in the West led to the birth of Southeast Asia's (and Indonesia's) two dominant super apps today: Gojek and Grab.

This chapter looks at how both Gojek and Grab fended off the global fight from Uber with innovative solutions for a local problem. We also explore how this massive untapped user base (*ojek* drivers) served as the cornerstone for a revolution in Indonesia's nascent payment space at the perfect time, just as the e-commerce boom had primed the market.

FORMALIZING THE *OJEK*

Ojek drivers were far from efficient, spending at least a third of their time idle while waiting for fares. Passengers, meanwhile, had no means to book or call drivers to their location. Fares were erratic and only settled in cash, and *ojek* were considered so unsafe that some foreign companies would not let their expatriate employees ride them.

The complication pushed many Jakartans to opt for owning their own motorbikes, braving the notorious traffic daily, rather than dealing with the vagaries and inconsistencies of an *ojek*.

In 2006, Nadiem Makarim returned to Jakarta after graduating from Brown University to work as a consultant with McKinsey. Though the firm provided a company car and driver, Nadiem was partial to the *ojek* due to its ability to bypass Jakarta's traffic. However, at the same time, he also realized that those riders are usually wasting their time waiting for passengers.

The idea for a more efficient *ojek* service in the form of a call center began to germinate in Nadiem's mind.

By 2010, while pursuing his MBA at Harvard Business School (HBS), he had established Gojek as a call center with 20 or so driver partners. With Nadiem working remotely from the United States and his Jakarta-based cofounders running Gojek part-time, it was a start-and-stop venture for a few years. While at HBS, Nadiem shared his idea with Malaysian classmates Anthony Tan and Tan Hooi Ling.

Plans were laid, per Nadiem: "We were always consulting each other on our businesses. I was going to take over bikes, and Anthony was going to take over cabs."[6]

After they graduated from Harvard in 2011, Anthony and Hooi Ling returned to Malaysia to set up MyTeksi in 2012 and started what would eventually become Grab, quickly upending Malaysia's friction-filled taxi sector and building a regional footprint.

Nadiem took a more indirect route. While his cofounders oversaw Gojek in the background, Nadiem's McKinsey experience and Harvard credentials had drawn the attention of the Samwer brothers. In 2011 and 2012, he was recruited to start the fashion e-commerce site Zalora in Jakarta as the first managing director of Zalora Indonesia, while also helping launch Lazada Indonesia. Gojek benefited too, as *ojek* drivers were roped in for Zalora and Lazada deliveries.

Pricing was transparent, and drivers' incomes doubled. The strength of the two Rocket brands also added a veneer of trust to Gojek. Drivers received road safety training and insurance. For passengers, they began offering raincoats and surgical masks to protect against pollution. Given the large number of unbanked Indonesians, Gojek's ability to accept cash on the spot (compared to Uber's obstinacy in sticking to a card-only cashless offering when it entered Indonesia in 2013) was a big advantage in the market.

By mid-2012, when Nadiem left Zalora, Gojek was already exploring ways to bring additional income to drivers, the start of its path toward pivoting to other sectors. Gojek had 15 employees and 450 drivers who, besides ferrying passengers, were also becoming dedicated COD agents for e-commerce ventures.[7]

But with little tech and funding, scaling up Gojek was a daunting endeavor. Nadiem took his time, moving on to a chief innovation role at Kartuku (bookmark this name for later), a local payments startup, in 2013 and 2014.

In mid-2014, Nadiem and Gojek began seeing renewed interest from investors, in response to Uber's entry into Indonesia in 2013 and Anthony and Hooi Ling's GrabTaxi in July 2014.[8,9] However, both of those foreign apps were only focused on car transportation.

Patrick Walujo, founding partner of Northstar Group, took an early and bold step by becoming the first angel investor in Gojek. Being a close confidant of Nadiem, he also urged the budding startup to transform its ride-hailing call center into a digital app.

In January 2015, Gojek released its mobile app without much fanfare.[10] Besides introducing the unique two-wheeler ride-hailing service, a feature neither Uber nor Grab had at the time, the company also seamlessly integrated food delivery and courier services within the same app.

TAKING THE (PRICE) FIGHT TO THE STREETS

Given Indonesia's economic dominance in Southeast Asia, it is challenging for any company to assert regional conquest without a firm grip on the Indonesian market. This realization struck Uber and Grab in 2015. Despite their strong positions in other Southeast Asian markets, establishing supremacy in the Indonesian market remained a crucial objective they couldn't afford to overlook.

In May 2015, Anthony's GrabTaxi took on the *ojek* space, with the launch of GrabBike, which it had previously pioneered in Vietnam.[11] Uber also began wising up, accepting cash payments in November 2015 and launching UberMotor in April 2016.[12] The war for two-wheeled dominance was officially on.

The script had already been written in the West: Uber would come into a new market with a huge influx of cash, slash ride prices aggressively, and dominate local competition, eventually obliterating competitors who could not stomach massive losses.

In 2015, Uber and Grab's deep pockets (Grab had raised US$340 million by then) were facing off against Gojek's first-mover advantage, multiservice offerings (personal transport, food delivery, and instant courier), and support from the Indonesian government for a local champion. Soon enough, drivers used multiple apps, so the battle came down to who could command the largest *ojek* user base.

The intense competition between ride-hailing apps in Jakarta in 2015 led to dramatically low prices. Travelers could ride with GrabBike for as little as Rp5,000 (approximately US$0.35) or choose Gojek at a fixed rate of Rp15,000.[13] Gojek kept its courier and delivery services at Rp10,000. Though Uber was a year late to the two-wheeled arena, its fare structure upon launching UberMotor in 2016 was hypercompetitive, starting with a base fare of Rp1,000, and proceeding with an additional Rp1,000 per kilometer and Rp100 per minute of travel.[14]

Both Gojek and Grab were up to the task of fighting Uber on the pricing stage, thanks to fundraising and acquisition sprees, which led to the rollout of more services. Gojek, operating from a base of three services, beta tested or soft-launched as many as 20 services, from event ticketing to grocery delivery, massages, and even a virtual mall, shutting down or replacing those that didn't work.

Diversifying the riders' roles was essential, in line with Nadiem's mission to maximize the efficiency of *ojek* by ensuring they stay consistently busy and earning.

Nonetheless, these rollouts demanded rapid expansion maneuvers and specialized expertise—capabilities that exceeded the level of Indonesia's technology talent pool at the time. Gojek decided to buy its engineering talent by amassing developers from a slew of Indian startups it acquired, all in 2016. After acquiring software companies C42 and CodeIgnition to gain access to tech talent, Gojek set up an R&D center in Bangalore.[15] It followed up by buying healthcare startup Pianta and mobile app developer Leftshift.[16,17]

By then, Gojek's funding had taken off, drawing foreign investors from Japan, India, and the United States. The firm raised an undisclosed amount of series B funding from the Southeast Asia and India unit of Sequoia Capital (now called Peak XV Partners) and DST Global in 2015.[18] The following year, Gojek announced US$550 million in new funding from KKR, Warburg Pincus, Farallon Capital, and Capital Group Private Markets, which pushed its valuation to the unicorn territory, around US$1.3 billion.[19]

Armed with new ammunition and a bench of top tech talent who were dedicated to building tools for the Indonesian market out of India, Gojek was able to weather the storm of discounts it took to fight Grab and Uber for market share.

Grab, which had already racked up large institutional backers such as renowned US VC firm Tiger Global and Japan's SoftBank before entering Indonesia, ramped up efforts by adding Chinese ride-hailing giant Didi Kuaidi and sovereign wealth fund China Investment Corporation to its cap table.[20,21]

The Malaysian ride-hailing startup did not neglect its tech R&D, opening centers in Seattle, Singapore, Beijing, Ho Chi Minh City, and Bangalore via acquisitions of its own.

TWO DIFFERENT ROUTES TO SUPER APP-HOOD

In March 2018, Uber bowed out of Southeast Asia, selling its assets to Grab, resulting in a regional launch of GrabFood (previously Uber Eats) later that year.[22] This allowed both Grab and Gojek to bring massive financial resources to support their respective super-app ambitions.

Although Gojek did enter Vietnam and Thailand following the announcement of a US$500 million plan to expand outside Indonesia in May 2018, the majority of its new services were still focused and tailored to the Indonesian market.[23] Meanwhile, Grab continued its mission to become Southeast Asia's everyday super app, juggling the hyperlocal needs of Indonesian users while maintaining its dominance in the other seven Southeast Asian markets that it was active in.

The startups, by now both unicorns and with more investor expectations on their shoulders, took different routes to realize their super-app visions. Gojek chose to take the fintech path, acquiring three Indonesian fintech companies (one of which was Kartuku, which Nadiem previously worked at) in 2017 to beef up its GoPay e-wallet services.[24] Gojek leveraged the large unbanked segment of Indonesia's population, given its reach across the country. A microloan product for SME merchants was rolled out in 2018, followed by virtual credit card PayLater, an investment into Indonesian insurtech startup PasarPolis (which led to the launch of online insurance offering GoSure in 2020) and Indonesian fintech startup Pluang, resulting in the online investment product GoInvestasi in 2020.[25,26] It all culminated with Gojek acquiring 22% of publicly listed Bank Jago to offer full-fledged digital banking services.[27]

But that didn't stop Nadiem from continuing in the strong Rocket Internet tradition of blitzscaling new verticals, trying them out, and dropping them if they did not work. Via both corporate partnerships and acquisitions, the myriad of services trialed and beta tested between 2018 and 2020 were mind-boggling: in-car entertainment products GoIce and GoVend; e-commerce feature GoMall (replacing GoShop, which had itself replaced GoMart); online donation service GoGive; news aggregator GoNews; comic reader GoKomik; GoTravel; and GoScreen, a digital outdoor advertising service with signage mounted on motorbikes.

Meanwhile, Anthony and Hooi Ling made similar investments but instead positioned themselves for the enterprise customer via their Grab for Business Suite, understanding that their regional presence and massive fleets were boons to companies that wanted to bring their brands and solutions to the 600-million-strong Southeast Asian community. These include the fraud detection and prevention system GrabDefence; e-voucher service GrabGifts (offered as part of Grab Platform); and O2O advertising platform GrabAds.[28–30]

In addition to the Grab Platform API suite for third-party developers, Grab's acquisitions and partnerships with investors or other startups birthed new offerings: GrabFresh with e-grocery player HappyFresh; Trip Planner and hotel booking features with Booking.com, OYO, and Agoda; GrabCycle with oBike; and Grab Rentals with Tokyo Century.

Finance was also a major foundation to Grab's super-app dream, with the Grab Financial Group encompassing e-wallet GrabPay; merchant financing solutions via GrabFinance; insurance products under Grab-Insure; investment solutions under GrabInvest; and loyalty program GrabRewards.

Grab Financial Group was bolstered by acquisitions of Indian mobile payments startup iKaaz, Singaporean robo-advisor Bento, and Indonesian O2O payments startup Kudo, as well as investments into Indonesian e-wallet LinkAja.[31–34] Grab also tapped the financial expertise of institutional brand names in its cap table, such as Japanese banking group Mitsubishi UFJ, Thailand's Kasikornbank and Bank of Ayudhya, Chinese insurer Ping An, and global credit reporting brand Experian, to build out the Grab Financial Group suite of solutions.[35–38]

Today, Grab and Gojek continue to dominate the Southeast Asian super-app arena, with Gojek making inroads in countries outside its home base of Indonesia. It is currently also present in Vietnam and Singapore. Meanwhile, Grab is pursuing digital banking licenses across different Southeast Asian markets to expand its financial reach.

Both have publicly listed, Grab on the NYSE via a SPAC merger, and Gojek on the Indonesian Stock Exchange (IDX) as part of GoTo, the merger between Gojek and fellow Indonesian tech unicorn Tokopedia.[39,40] Cognizant of their massive footprints across the region, both Grab and Gojek have begun focusing on environmental, social, and governance (ESG) issues in their future growth plans.

These startups have evolved far beyond their initial missions to alleviate traffic woes in Indonesia's major cities. They have become indispensable to Indonesian daily life, seamlessly integrating a broad spectrum of services that address the diverse needs of its people. Their journey from simple solutions to massive organizations, rivaling the gross domestic product (GDP) of small countries, exemplifies not just a blend of luck, good timing, and strategic investments but also their commitment to serving the community.

Their integration into the fabric of society shows that, irrespective of valuations, stock prices, or market fluctuations, Gojek and Grab maintain their indispensability. They have positioned themselves as critical pillars, facilitating mobility, convenience, and economic opportunities for millions, thereby positively impacting the daily lives of a vast portion of the population.

Gojek's ecosystem contributed Rp249 trillion (US$17.6 billion) to the Indonesian economy in recent years and accounted for 1.6% of the archipelago's GDP.[41] The latest figures for Grab date back to 2019, when it contributed Rp77.4 trillion (US$5.45 billion) to the Indonesian economy, largely thanks to its food delivery service, while providing gig work for the country's informal workers.[42]

The growth of Gojek and Grab, as well as their ability to fend off Uber's advances, were thanks in no small part to overseas capital that began flowing into Indonesia in search of local champions. It's inarguable that without these institutional backers, there would be no engineering and R&D teams in Seattle or Bangalore to make up for the arrears in Indonesia's local talent pipeline.

The next chapter explores this flurry of funding through the eyes of local players who were present when record-breaking deals were inked, such as JD.com's entry into Indonesia, Alibaba's acquisition of Lazada, and its subsequent US$1.1 billion injection into Tokopedia.

IRON SHARPENS IRON

Table 5.1 provides a detailed timeline comparing the developmental milestones of Gojek and Grab, highlighting key events from their founding moments as MBA ideas to becoming dominant players in Southeast Asia's online transportation and services sectors.

Table 5.1 Gojek and Grab: A Decade of Hyper Growth[43]

Gojek	Year	Grab
Nadiem Makarim starts his MBA studies at HBS. Nadiem was previously an Associate at McKinsey in Jakarta, Indonesia.	2009	Anthony Tan and Tan Hooi Ling also pursue their MBAs at HBS. Anthony is a scion of Tan Chong Group, a manufacturer and distributor of Nissan vehicles in Malaysia. Hooi Ling was previously an Associate at McKinsey in Kuala Lumpur, Malaysia.
While still at Harvard, Nadiem founded Gojek as an *ojek* phone-booking service in Indonesia. Gojek operates in Jakarta under the part-time leadership of cofounders Jurist Tan and Brian Cu.	2010	
Nadiem graduates from HBS with his MBA. November: Joins Rocket Internet fashion e-commerce startup Zalora as managing director of Zalora Indonesia. Helps out with Lazada Indonesia.	2011	Anthony and Hooi Ling graduate from HBS with their MBAs.
Gojek wins the Global Entrepreneurship Program Indonesia, gaining recognition as a call center for *ojek*. It is positioned as a social enterprise focused on increasing driver income. August: Nadiem leaves Zalora Indonesia.	2012	MyTeksi launches in Kuala Lumpur as a taxi-hailing app with GPS enhancements in June 2012. By December, it reaches 700 drivers, a 350% jump since launch.
April: Nadiem joins Indonesian payments startup Kartuku as chief innovation officer.	2013	Rebrands to GrabTaxi for regional expansion into Singapore, Thailand, and the Philippines. Acquires Chinese ride-sharing startup Youche to form Grab's Beijing office. January: Seed funding from Germany's Rheingau Founders. September: Series A funding from Singaporean government-linked Vertex Ventures and US VC 500 Global.

(Continued)

Table 5.1 (Continued)

Gojek	Year	Grab
	2014	Expands to Indonesia and Vietnam. May: US$15 million series B funding from Vertex and US VC GGV Capital. July: Launches GrabCar for private cars. October: US$65 million series C funding from US VC Tiger Global and China's Hillhouse Capital. November: Launches GrabBike for motorcycles in Vietnam. December: US$250 million series D funding from Tiger Global and Japan's SoftBank Capital.
May: Nadiem leaves Kartuku to concentrate full-time on Gojek. December: US$2 million series A funding from NSI Ventures (now known as Openspace). Following the round, Nadiem buys out his cofounders.		
Gojek's mobile app goes live. September: Launches on-demand services, including package (GoBox), meal (GoFood), and grocery (GoMart) delivery services, massages, and event ticketing (GoTix). October: US$26 million series B funding from Sequoia Capital India, Openspace, and DST Global.	2015	April: Opens Singapore R&D center. May: Opens Beijing R&D center. Launches GrabBike for *ojek* in Indonesia. July: Launches GrabExpress courier service. August: US$350 million series E funding from Tiger Global, SoftBank, Chinese ride-sharing startup Didi Kuaidi, and Chinese sovereign wealth fund China Investment Corporation. November: Launches GrabHitch carpooling service. December: Joins global pact with ride-sharing startups Didi Kuaidi (China), Lyft (United States), and Ola (India).

Gojek	Year	Grab
February: Acquires Indian software companies C42 and CodeIgnition to gain access to tech talents and set up an R&D center in Bangalore. April: Launches GoCar private car-hailing service. US$170 million series C funding from Japan's Rakuten Capital and Openspace. May: Invests in Indonesian health-tech startup Halodoc's series A round. August: US$550 million series D funding led by US PE firm Warburg Pincus and US asset manager KKR. September: Acquires Indian healthcare startup Pianta. October: Acquires Indonesian fintech startup MVCommerce so that Gojek's wallet GoPay has regulatory clearance via an active e-money license. November: Acquires Indian mobile app developer Leftshift to boost Gojek's engineering team in India.	2016	January: GrabTaxi rebrands as Grab, bringing all its services under an umbrella brand. It also launches the GrabPay e-wallet and opens its Seattle R&D center. May: Launches beta test of GrabFood delivery service in Jakarta. June: Launches GrabWork for working professionals to expense business rides. September: US$750 million series F funding from SoftBank and Honda. October: Launches a two-wheel version of the GrabHitch ride-sharing service as *Nebeng* in Jakarta. November: Launches GrabPay Credits, a cashless stored value option allowing top-ups, in Indonesia. December: Launches GrabShare, an on-demand commercial carpooling service. Raises private equity funding from Tokyo Century, a Japanese leasing company, to help Grab drivers buy their cars.

(Continued)

Table 5.1 (Continued)

Gojek	Year	Grab
March: Launches GoBlueBird, in partnership with Blue Bird, the largest taxi operator in Indonesia. August: Acquires Indonesian event management and ticketing platform Loket to boost GoTix. Undisclosed series E funding from Singaporean VC K3 Ventures. November: Invests US$2 million in Bangladeshi ride-hailing startup Pathao. December: Acquires Indonesian fintech startups Kartuku, Midtrans, and Mapan to expand GoPay services.	2017	February: Launches GrabCoach for group travelers and corporate customers. March: Launches GrabShuttle shuttle bus service. Grab also opens its Bangalore and Ho Chi Minh City R&D centers. April: Acquires Indonesian O2O payments startup Kudo to boost GrabPay. Kudo later rebrands into GrabKios. June: Private equity funding from Indonesian media conglomerate Emtek Group. July: US$2 billion series G funding from SoftBank, Third Point Ventures, Macquaries, GGV, Emtek, and Didi. August: Launches GrabRewards, an expanded loyalty program with merchant partners. It also invests in Singaporean dockless bike startup oBike. October: US$700 million debt financing from HSBC to create the largest car rental program in Southeast Asia.

Gojek	Year	Grab
February: US$1.5 billion series E funding led by Tencent, with participation from Singaporean sovereign wealth fund Temasek, Chinese e-commerce giants Meituan and JD.com, Google, Blibli, and others. March: Launches microloans for SME merchants, in partnership with Bank Negara Indonesia and other financial services. May: Announces US$500 million plan to expand beyond Indonesia. August: Invests in Indonesian insurtech startup PasarPolis. September: Discontinues GoMart, and replaces it with a stripped-down shopping feature named GoShop. Acquires Indonesian adtech startup Promogo to enable GoCar drivers to place ads on their vehicles for extra income. Also launches in-car entertainment products Golce and GoVend. Invests in the news app Kumparan through GoVentures. Launches localized brand GoViet for Vietnam. Launches PayLater, a virtual credit card for in-app payments. October: Invests in US IT company Escapex's venture round. US$920 million series F funding from Tencent, Google, and JD.com. December: Launches localized brand "Get" for Thailand with motorbike hailing and on-demand delivery services.	2018	Launches microloans and other financial services. January: Acquires Indian mobile payments startup iKaaz. Undisclosed series G funding led by Hyundai. March: Launches GrabCycle, a bike-sharing marketplace app combining different mobility partner brands including oBike. May: Acquires Uber's Southeast Asia business and officially launches GrabFood (formerly UberEats) across the region. July: Launches GrabPlatform API suite for third-party developers. It also invests in grocery delivery startup HappyFresh and launches GrabFresh, an on-demand grocery delivery service. August: Launches innovation arm GrabVentures in Indonesia with plans to invest US$250 million in Indonesian startups. US$2 billion series H funding led by Toyota, with China's Ping An Capital and others. October: Undisclosed series H funding from Microsoft and another US$200 million from travel giant Booking.com. November: US$250 million series H funding from Hyundai and another US$50 million from Beacon VC, owned by Thailand's Kasikornbank, to expand GrabPay services in Thailand. December: Invests US$100 million into Indian budget hotel network OYO. US$150 million series H funding from Yamaha to expand GrabBike services in Indonesia.

(Continued)

Table 5.1 (Continued)

Gojek	Year	Grab
January: Acquires Filipino fintech startup Coins.ph for US$72 million ahead of expansion into the Philippines. Invests in JDID, the Indonesian arm of China's JD.com. Undisclosed series F funding from Swiss investment club French Partners. March: US$100 million series F funding from Indonesian conglomerate PT Astra International Tbk, forms transportation joint venture. April: Launches e-commerce feature GoMall in partnership with the Indonesian arm of Chinese e-commerce giant JD and Blibli. Also launches a news aggregator (GoNews) with Kumparan and comic reader GoKomik in collaboration with local comic artists. May: Launches online donation service GoGive in partnership with fundraising platform Kitabisa and GoTravel with Tiket.com (owned by Blibli). Invests in Ugandan urban transportation network Safeboda. June: Acquires Indian AI-powered recruitment platform AirCTO to expand development team in India. July: Invests in Indian food delivery platform Rebel Foods via GoVentures. September: Invests in Indonesian fintech startup Pluang via GoVentures.	2019	January: US$350 million series H funding from Tokyo Century to expand car rental service Grab Rentals. Gets another US$200 million from Thai retail conglomerate Central Group into Grab Thailand. March: US$1.5 billion series H funding from SoftBank and the VC arm of French energy giant TotalEnergies. April: Invests in regional logistics provider Ninja Van. May: Launches hotel-booking feature in Indonesia in partnership with online reservation platforms Agoda and Booking.com. June: Invested in UK global mobility marketplace Splyt Technologies. US$300 million series H funding from US investment management firm Invesco. July: Launches GrabWheels, a green e-scooter solution with Universitas Indonesia. Undisclosed funding from multinational credit reporting firm Experian to boost mobility and financial services to the underbanked across Southeast Asia. October: Invests in Indonesian O2O advertising technology company StickEarn. Undisclosed funding from Japan's MUFG Innovation Partners.

Gojek	Year	Grab
January: Invests in Indonesian tech wearables startup Zulu. February: Invests in Indonesian taxi company Bluebird Group. Launches online insurance offering GoSure, in partnership with PasarPolis. March: US$1.2 billion series F funding from Visa, Mitsubishi Motors, Mitsubishi UFJ Financial Group, and Mitsubishi Corporation. April: Acquires Indonesian mobile point-of-sales startup Moka for US$130 million. May: Launches online investment product GoInvestasi, in partnership with Pluang. June: US$375 million series F funding led by PayPal and Meta. November: Launches GoScreen, a digital outdoor advertising service with driver-partners. US$150 million in corporate funding from Indonesian telecommunications giant Telkomsel. September: Acquires Vietnamese payments provider WePay to secure a license to operate e-wallets in Vietnam. December: Purchases 22% stake in publicly listed Indonesian bank Bank Jago.	2020	February: Acquires Singaporean robo-advisor Bento (rebranded as GrabInvest) to offer retail wealth management services. US$856 million series I funding from Japanese banking group Mitsubishi UFJ, Japanese IT company TIS, and Krungsri Finnovate, the VC arm of Thailand's Bank of Ayudhya to boost financial services push. August: US$200 million PE funding from Korean firm STIC Investment. November: Invests in Indonesian state-backed e-wallet LinkAja. December: Undisclosed venture round from Hong Kong asset manager Jeneration Capital.

CHAPTER SIX

INDONESIA'S VENTURE OPPORTUNITY, HIDDEN IN PLAIN SIGHT

In the present day, Indonesian startups have emerged as prime targets for investors hailing from the United States, China, Europe, the Middle East, and even Australia. However, this scenario was quite different in the past.

A decade ago, foreign investors viewed Indonesia through a mostly regional lens, often favoring Singapore as the primary investment destination. Indonesia's lagging internet infrastructure, low credit card usage, and its classification as a low-income nation often dissuaded global investors from allocating funds here.

Yet, local VC firms like AC Ventures, as well as names like East Ventures and Alpha JWC Ventures, held a distinct viewpoint. Established by in-market investors, they recognized the immense potential in the country's vast consumer-driven economy, supported by a large, young, and growing middle-class demographic, envisioning it as an attractive and investable market ready to flourish.

While digital infrastructure may have been still nascent at the time, a concerted push from the government to expand mobile data coverage, coupled with the eagerness of the local populace to join the online economy, led to a surge in internet adoption. Moreover, Indonesia boasted a vibrant community of passionate entrepreneurs and a resourceful diaspora, poised to forge innovative digital enterprises.

Indonesia's pioneering venture capitalists, mainly seasoned entrepreneurs themselves, held a deep belief in the market's potential and were keen to demonstrate it. Most sourced their early funding from family offices and local conglomerates. During this period, the atmosphere was more cooperative than competitive, with many of us looking to co-invest and share the risk.

Meanwhile, the Singaporean government had a program running since 2009 aimed at supporting nascent startup incubators and VC firms in the city-state.[1] The National Research Foundation (NRF) implemented the Technology Incubation Scheme to offer government funding. This scheme matched up to 85% of investments made by VCs operating incubators, with a maximum cap of S$500,000 (approximately US$360,000).

These incubators gave support to the companies they backed, including providing physical space and strategic guidance. A key benefit for the VCs managing these incubators was the option to buy out the NRF's stake in the startups within three years by repaying the initial investment plus nominal interest. This arrangement proved beneficial for private investors and their limited partners (LPs), enabling them to realize significant financial gains from subsequent funding rounds secured by the startups.

This program catalyzed the establishment of various regional VC firms, including names like Jungle Ventures, Wavemaker, and Golden Gate Ventures. As time progressed, these firms began investing in Indonesian startups.

However, the early Indonesian VC pioneers encountered hurdles in convincing LPs who believed that the key to market dominance lay in operating across every Southeast Asian country. Local VCs persisted in underlining the significance of Indonesia and a key beachhead approach. As time unfolded, it became evident that they were correct.

As shown in the previous chapter, after the meteoric rise of local champions like Tokopedia and Gojek, the Indonesian market experienced an influx of global capital, starting in 2014. This phenomenon triggered a wave of investment from renowned global VC and private equity players from the United States and India, as well as from tech giants and the Fortune 500, propelling Indonesia's startup ecosystem to new heights.

THE SEQUOIA EFFECT

Grab's entry into Indonesia in 2014 drew investor attention to up-and-coming local ride-hailing startup Gojek, but the timing was also fortuitous for the booming e-commerce industry. By then, it had been nearly two years since Indonesia's introduction to the Samwers' "blitzkrieg" strategy of funding, marketing, launching, and killing brands when necessary in the e-commerce space.

Not only was Indonesia primed for growth capital by that time, but the proliferation of the "Rocket Mafia," mainly ex-Zalora and ex-Lazada Indonesia employees, meant that over time, deep-pocketed investors became more amenable to backing local founders.

Before 2014, it was common to see local startups racking up seed-stage to series B funding rounds. Publicly announced series B funding rounds were lucky to reach the US$10 million mark, and most of the action was coming from local VCs, family-owned conglomerates, or foreign VCs testing out the Indonesian market.[2] The big funding rounds were going to the Samwers and, if you look at disclosed deal amounts, *only* the Samwers.

Tokopedia, which was by then five years old and a well-entrenched name in the e-commerce space, had announced funding rounds in its battle against Lazada, Blibli, and Matahari Mall. But until then, it had not disclosed exact funding amounts.

In October 2014, the dam holding back growth funding to local founders broke with Tokopedia's US$100 million round, led by Japan's SoftBank and Sequoia Capital. A landmark deal, the round was also Sequoia's very first investment into Indonesia.

GOJEK PROVES INDONESIANS' HUNGER FOR MORE DIGITAL SERVICES, AND INVESTORS ANSWER THE CALL

While Grab focused on expanding in the transport vertical, Gojek leveraged its *ojek* base (ramping up to 200,000 riders by February 2016) by pushing out as many as 20 new services in 2015 and 2016.[3] These ranged from expected services (transport, courier, shopping, etc.) to uniquely Indonesian ones (on-demand makeup, spa, massage, air conditioner repair, at-home car wash services, etc.).[4]

This strategy showed investors that the massive market potential in Indonesia, which at the time possessed a 20-million-strong middle class, extended far beyond e-commerce and ride-hailing. Indonesians who had already gotten used to digital purchases were now ready to try new products online, and they could get it all from a single super app, run by a local champion that had the support of Indonesian policymakers.[5]

After Tokopedia's historic round, it was no surprise that already-surging Gojek was the next to make headlines. On the surface, its October 2015 series A funding round was relatively small: just US$26 million. However, two very big names, Sequoia and late-stage investor DST Global, were added to Gojek's cap table. This also marked DST's first startup investment in Indonesia.

Two other growth investors and renowned US private equity firms, Warburg Pincus and KKR, made Gojek their first deal in the archipelago in a blockbuster US$550 million round in August 2016.[6] This was then one-upped by Tokopedia's record-breaking US$1.1 billion funding round from China's e-commerce giant Alibaba in August 2017, which was followed by Gojek's US$1.5 billion round from Chinese digital household names Tencent, Meituan, and JD.com, alongside Google and German insurance giant Allianz in February 2018.[7-9]

A SERIES OF FIRSTS ENSUE, AS US AND CHINESE INVESTORS PILE INTO INDONESIA

Earlier chapters covered the role of Japanese internet companies like Rakuten and Netprice, banks like Mitsui and MUFG, and VCs like SoftBank, Rebright Partners, and CyberAgent in helping fund early-stage rounds for Indonesian e-commerce companies in the late 2000s and early 2010s.[10]

Chinese tech conglomerates took different routes, preferring to explore joint ventures with Indonesian conglomerates that already had market leadership in the space. But eventually, they too began investing directly and partnering with local startups, as shown in Table 6.1.

Table 6.1   Chinese Tech Giants' Investments in Indonesia (2010s)*

Tech company	Indonesia entry	First startup investment
Alibaba	AliExpress launches a localized site in October 2014 and acquires Lazada (including Lazada Indonesia) for US$1 billion in April 2016.[11]	Leads a US$1.1 billion round into Tokopedia in August 2017.
Tencent	Joint venture with Indonesia's biggest media group PT Global Mediacom in February 2013 to boost WeChat.[12]	Invests up to US$150 million in Gojek in July 2017.[13]
JD.com	Launches localized site JD.ID in October 2015.[14]	Invests in travel startup Traveloka's US$500 million round in July 2017.[15]
Meituan	N/A	Invests in Gojek's US$1.5 billion round in February 2018.

*List not exhaustive

While working with local conglomerates or setting up Indonesian teams to build localized sites and run marketing plays, eventually Alibaba, Tencent, Meituan, and JD.com began investing directly in local startups. In August 2017, Alibaba put more than US$1.1 billion into Tokopedia, betting on its first-mover upper hand and mulling parallels and synergy with Lazada's regional operations. Meanwhile, Tencent, Meituan, and JD.com saw super-app potential in Gojek, with all three participating in its US$1.5 billion mega-round in April 2018.

US investors also took seats at the funding table. Renowned tech investors with decades-long track records such as KKR, Tiger Global, and Accel followed Sequoia's lead to make their initial bets in Indonesia's venture space. Starting in 2018, it was the turn of blue-chip internet and finance brands, including Facebook, Google, PayPal, Amazon, and Visa, to make direct investments in Indonesia's startups. (See Table 6.2 for details.)

Whatever trust issues US investors may have had with Indonesia's nascent startup ecosystem were effectively put to bed by 2020.

Table 6.2 US Investors Enter Indonesia (2010s)*

Company	Indonesia entry	First startup investment
KKR	Acquires stake in food company PT Tiga Pilar Sejahtera Food in July 2013.[16]	Invests in Gojek's US$550 million round in August 2016.
Sequoia	N/A	Invests in Tokopedia's US$100 million round in October 2014.
500 Startups	N/A	Invests in restaurant-booking site Qraved's seed round in September 2013.[17]
Warburg Pincus	Invests US$125 million in a joint venture with local real estate company Nirvana to develop retail malls in Indonesia in February 2015.[18]	Invests in Gojek's US$550 million round in August 2016.
Tiger Global	N/A	Invests in fintech firm Payfazz's US$21 million round in November 2018.[19]
PayPal	Enters partnership with payments firm Doku to reach Indonesian SMEs in December 2012.	Invests in Gojek's US$375 million round in June 2020.[20]
Google	Opens Google Indonesia office in January 2012.[21]	Invests in Gojek's US$1.5 billion round in February 2018.
Amazon	Plans US$1 billion investment into Indonesia in September 2018.[22]	Amazon founder Jeff Bezos, through Bezos Expeditions, participates in a US$87 million funding round for B2B e-commerce startup Ula in October 2021.[23]
Visa	N/A	Invests in Gojek in July 2019, part of its US$1.2 billion round that closed in March 2020.[24]
Accel	N/A	Invests in insurtech firm Qoala's pre-seed round in March 2018 via Singaporean VC SeedPlus.[25]
Facebook	Opens Indonesia office in August 2017.[26]	Invests in Gojek's US$375 million round in June 2020.

*List not exhaustive

LOCAL INVESTORS STEP UP TO STRENGTHEN THE EARLY-STAGE PIPELINE

The influx of growth and late-stage capital was a boon for Indonesia's unicorns, fueling Gojek, Tokopedia, Bukalapak, Traveloka, and others with war chests to acquire tech talent and expand their logistics footprints across the archipelago. At the same time, newer startups still needed early-stage and seed investment support, which largely came from the venture arms of local conglomerates, founders-turned-VCs, or in some unique circumstances, scions of family offices who became active tech investors.

One of these was Pandu Sjahrir, whose family history is deeply interwoven into the fabric of Indonesia's modern political, business, and military landscape. Raised and educated in the United States, Pandu returned to Indonesia in 2010. He then steered his family's local energy company PT Toba Bara Sejahtra (TBS) toward its initial public offering (IPO) on the IDX just two years later.[27]

Pandu's timing could not have been better. The particular period of growth-stage investing, defined by Tokopedia's US$100 million round in 2014 and Gojek's US$550 million round in 2016, was pivotal for Indonesia's tech ecosystem. Before that, local angel investors, VCs, and conglomerates were predominantly active in series A or B funding rounds. This began to change. Gojek and Tokopedia's funding sprees were, in part, a response to Rocket's bevy of big international backers.

Pandu, who had pursued his Stanford MBA from 2005 to 2007, joined Sea Limited in 2016 to help Shopee gain a foothold in Indonesia.[28]

FOUNDERS-TURNED-VCS LEND EXPERTISE TO THE NEXT GENERATION

Pandu and I overlapped at Stanford. I graduated in 2006 while he was in the class of 2007. Later on, back in Indonesia, while he was getting things underway with Shopee, I was setting up a new early-stage VC firm in Jakarta called Convergence Ventures. I had initially teamed up with Donald Wihardja, then-head of the Indonesia E-commerce Association, who would go on to become CEO of MDI Ventures under the state-owned Telkom Group.

Banking on my background building and scaling companies as an entrepreneur and with Rocket Internet, I leveraged my network and know-how in two different Asian markets in a bid to find and invest in the most promising Indonesian tech startups.

Convergence Ventures also brought on board several successful entrepreneurs from China as early LPs, such as Xu Xiao Ping, founder of New Oriental Group and Zhen Fund, as well as Zhang Tao, founder of Dian Ping.[29]

Having previously cofounded and exited a language learning startup in China called Idapted, my foodtech venture Qraved was, in September 2013, the first investment in Indonesia for early-stage VC firm 500 Startups (now known as 500 Global). Next, Convergence Ventures was my bet on investing in Indonesian startups and propelling the ecosystem toward maturity.

Over the next four years, this bet paid off via successful early-stage and first-check investments in startups that have since achieved unicorn status. These include Xendit, which has become one of Indonesia's top private fintech companies, and Carsome, recognized as Southeast Asia's largest marketplace for secondhand cars. Convergence Ventures also made marquee investments in other high-value companies. Among these, Moka was acquired by Gojek, while Payfazz, and Julo have each achieved valuations ranging from US$300 million to US$500 million.

By 2018, more Indonesian startups began raising mega-rounds, and deep-pocketed foreign investors started seeking Indonesian VCs with local know-how. Pandu, whose name fortuitously means "guide" in Bahasa Indonesia, became the go-to person for connecting investors with startups.

By then, Pandu was already holding multiple key roles in the ecosystem. He was the managing partner of leading alternative asset management firm Indies Capital Partners; chairman of Sea Indonesia (overseeing Shopee Indonesia); and a board member of Gojek. Add to that his Stanford education, his corporate and VC expertise, and his family links within Indonesian business and government circles, and it was clear: if you wanted to invest quickly and wisely in Indonesia, Pandu could guide the way.

After a few years of active angel investing in Indonesian startups, Pandu took the leap himself in 2018, setting up his own VC firm Agaeti Venture Capital with long-time TBS colleague and family friend Michael Soerijadji.

In 2019, Michael, Pandu, and I met up to discuss how we could build something greater than the sum of its parts. With my shared history alongside Pandu at Stanford and with a clear compatibility in investment philosophies between the three of us, we decided to boldly combine Convergence and Agaeti into a single outfit.

The firms merged to form AC Ventures, with a combined portfolio of 80 companies.[30] By then, both Agaeti and Convergence's debut funds had been fully deployed. So we went to market together to raise our inaugural fund as a combined team. AC Ventures' objective was, and still is, to consolidate resources to create a platform of exponential value that offers significant support to portfolio founders as they build and scale successful businesses across Indonesia.

THE LONG-TERM EFFECTS OF BREAKING THE FUNDING DAM

The AT Kearney-Google 2017 report on Indonesia's VC landscape revealed that in 2012, only 18 deals were finalized in the country, each averaging a size of US$2.5 million.[31] By 2014, a significant increase in both the number of transactions and the size of each deal was evident. Tokopedia's funding round that year, which secured US$100 million, stood out as an exception in a year when most disclosed funding amounts fell below US$1 million. During the same year, Indonesian startups tripled their number of funding rounds to 54, and the average deal size grew to US$4.3 million.[32]

Once the funding floodgates were open, the size and quantity of deals escalated so rapidly that in the first eight months of 2017, the average deal size skyrocketed to an astounding US$56 million, resulting in a cumulative total of US$3 billion. This surge was propelled by three enormous funding rounds, all driven by Chinese tech powerhouses: Tencent's US$1.2 billion investment in Gojek, Alibaba's US$1.1 billion injection into Tokopedia, and approximately US$500 million invested by JD.com in Traveloka.

Advancing to 2021, Indonesian startups managed to raise a megasized US$9.4 billion through 213 deals, with the average deal size standing at about US$44 million.[33] The presence of foreign venture firms, private equity firms, tech giants, and large conglomerates incited similar enthusiasm from local investors.

Notably, AC Ventures, under the combined leadership of Michael, Pandu, and I, successfully raised US$205 million for the firm's Fund III, doubling the initial target.[34] Our counterparts at Alpha JWC and East Ventures also achieved success, raising new funds of similar amounts during this cycle.

In the next chapter, we will explore how Tokopedia, Gojek, Grab, and Bukalapak's entrance into fintech spurred a strong response from incumbent banks and fostered the emergence of a new generation of fintech startups focusing on specific subsectors, such as digital payments, lending, and insurance.

Indonesia's large unbanked population meant the pie was large enough for all players to compete, bringing financial inclusion to the most remote parts of the archipelago. Key ingredients included simple mobile apps, a healthy open banking system powered by APIs, and strong O2O integration across the board.

CHAPTER SEVEN

THE EVOLUTION OF FINTECH IN INDONESIA

Despite its substantial population, Indonesia's financial services space has remained relatively small compared to its regional peers, with its banking sector accounting for around 80% of the sector's assets.

Back in 2013, the ratio of financial sector assets to GDP stood at 103%. This paled in comparison to the Philippines' 194% and more than 300% in Malaysia, Singapore, and Thailand.[1]

From 2010 to 2015, Indonesia's financial sector assets as a percentage of GDP showed little change, indicating limited expansion since the global financial crisis of 2008. This stagnation could be attributed to a fragmented regulatory framework, nonalignment with international best practices, and an environment less conducive to growth.

Turning to the equities market, while the number of publicly listed companies increased from 440 in 2011 to 506 in 2014, market capitalization lingered around US$422 billion. This amounted to less than 50% of the country's GDP, a stark contrast to the higher ratios seen in the stock exchanges of Malaysia, Singapore, and Thailand, all surpassing 90%.

In the debt securities market, a significant challenge was illiquidity. Government bond market representation stood at a mere 13% of GDP, sharply contrasting with the Southeast Asian average of 58%. Similarly, corporate bond markets faced comparable hurdles, constituting just 2% of GDP, compared to a Southeast Asian average of 21%.

Indonesia's financial landscape is primarily dominated by banks, accounting for roughly 80% of the nation's total financial assets. Consequently, entities like insurance firms, pension funds, multifinance companies, securities firms, and pawnshops hold smaller stakes in the market.

Nonetheless, Indonesia's substantial population and consistent economic growth have provided fertile ground for expansion in the financial sector. By 2018, three local banks, BCA, BRI, and Bank Mandiri, had secured positions among the top 10 largest banks in Southeast Asia by market capitalization. The pivotal moment arrived three years later, when BCA surpassed Singapore-based DBS, claiming the title of the largest bank in the region, a distinction it still holds today. This is despite the number of underbanked consumers in Indonesia still ranging between 140 million and 180 million people.

In the late 2010s, investors recognized that the Indonesian e-commerce market had become highly competitive, with dominant players already solidified. Consequently, in the search for the next group of "centaurs" (startups valued at more than US$100 million), the financial technology sector, referred to as "fintech," emerged as an area of significant interest that could not be overlooked.

In the last chapter, we talked about how Indonesia's early fintech players mostly zeroed in on digital payments. They wanted to help small and medium-sized businesses quickly get online and start processing transactions via bank transfers, prepaid cards, e-wallets, and sometimes even mobile top-ups. This made it easier for customers to pay in all sorts of ways, depending on their internet access, how comfortable they were with online shopping, and whether they even had a bank account.

As covered, the early 2010s saw low trust in digital payments systems. In response, the concept of escrow and O2O payments was introduced by e-commerce players.

By the time Grab and Gojek launched in 2014 and 2015, people's trust in digital systems had started to grow. However, Indonesians still heavily relied on cash and used it as a go-to payment method. Before long, startups began marketing their e-wallets and cashless payment options as a more convenient alternative for both motorbike taxi drivers and passengers. As Gojek's services expanded and brand recognition increased, trust in digital wallets like GoPay also grew. The logic was simple: if you trust your e-wallet for daily commute expenses, why not use it for food and package deliveries as well?

In more rural locations, renowned e-commerce companies like Bukalapak and Tokopedia took significant steps by leveraging small, family-owned shops as local agents ("*mitra*") to cater to a multitude of unbanked Indonesians. These agents provided an accessible way to conduct a wide range of transactions—activities like topping up mobile phone credit, processing e-commerce orders, settling utility bills, investing in gold, transferring money, buying insurance, and more.

This chapter explores how the vast number of underbanked and unbanked Indonesians drew the attention of specialized fintech companies, with niches ranging from lending, insurance, and wealth technology to full-fledged neobanking. Local entrepreneurs began approaching the financial inclusion issue in Indonesia with unique solutions.

Fintech innovators quickly collaborated with conventional banks, insurance companies, and large corporations to start creating a more inclusive banking ecosystem.

THE FINANCIAL INCLUSION STORY

In 2010, around 200 million Indonesians of the country's then 250-million population were without bank accounts.² Fast forward to October 2019, just before the COVID-19 pandemic, and that number had more than halved to 92 million—serious progress but still with work to do.³

Around the world, financial exclusion is synonymous with an underdeveloped financial sector overall. Even today in Indonesia, 48% of the adult population remains unbanked. Forty percent of the population simply does not borrow. Only 13.1% has ever taken out a loan from a formal financial institution. This means that a sizable share of the population is unable to access fair credit to enable further investment in education or business. With limited opportunities to increase wealth via savings and mitigate financial risks to their livelihoods, they remain in poverty.

The main challenges in this area are low access to financial services; impediments to the delivery and usage of financial products and services; a low level of financial literacy; and weak consumer protection. Promoting financial inclusion presents an opportunity to address this developmental problem as increasing basic savings, especially among the poorest groups in society, can raise income levels and reduce the gap in income distribution.

While Tokopedia, Bukalapak, Gojek, and Grab helped bring financial inclusion to MSMEs and those in the gig economy in terms of deposits (income in their e-wallets), the super apps refused to rest on their laurels. With plenty of *mitra* and *ojek* riders in need of working capital to keep their shops supplied or their vehicles in good working condition, the next step was providing merchant and rider financing, with monthly payments to be automatically deducted from their e-wallets.

For decades, Indonesia's traditional banks were hesitant to lend to MSMEs, citing reasons like their lack of credit history. This was because most MSMEs operated on cash transactions or customer credit, leaving little documented evidence of their dealings. Additionally, many lacked assets that could be used as collateral. E-commerce platforms and ride-hailing services soon filled this void. They had a unique advantage: access to a vast pool of regularly updated and verified transaction data from their merchants. This data made lending decisions more informed and feasible.

The quantifiable elements like sales volume and transaction frequency, as well as qualitative factors such as customer reviews and ratings, collectively reflected a small business's capacity to repay loans. This comprehensive insight, coupled with personal and business data points—including national IDs, business licenses, and other pertinent documents—which are collected during the onboarding process for digital lending apps, quickly provided a robust framework to evaluate the creditworthiness of MSMEs.

Suddenly, know-your-customer (KYC), the one thing legacy banks held over fintech contenders, was not just sorted out but was almost fully automated, drastically reducing processing costs for digital lenders. This enabled tech companies to offer more competitive financing, as well as wealth and insurance products down the road, all from one app. But they were limited in the amounts they could disburse, and as invoice financing took a digital turn, digitally enabled consumer and SME lending finally arrived in Indonesia in 2016.

A SNAPSHOT ACROSS TIME

Between 2011 and 2022, the number of fintech startups in Indonesia skyrocketed, multiplying more than six times from a mere 51 in 2011 to 334 in 2022, as shown in Figure 7.1.[4] A little over a decade ago, the Indonesian fintech landscape was dominated (55%) by players in the payments sector. But by 2022, the spread across different services became more balanced, with lending (35%) and payments (33%) at the forefront, followed by wealthtech, which accounted for 17% of all fintech startups.

Figure 7.1 Indonesia's Fintech Space Has Seen Rapid Growth Over the Last Decade.

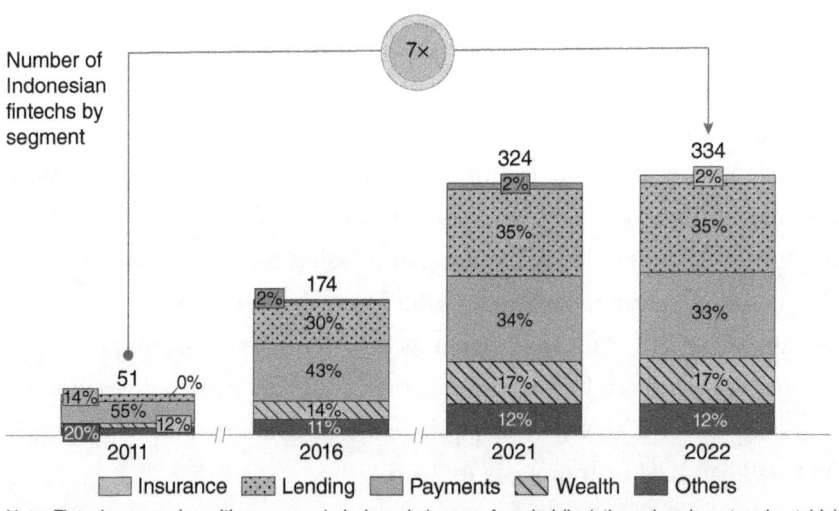

Note: Fintech companies with presence in Indonesia by year founded (incl. those headquartered outside)

Looking back, one can see how the fintech landscape evolved and built upon each successive innovation. Digital payments built the rails on which transactions and money flow could be more clearly identified. Next, digital lending came to address large credit gaps for both consumers and MSMEs. Consumers then became more comfortable with transacting and borrowing online. Next, wealth services were launched. Eventually, full-stack digital banks launched to aggregate all these verticals together.

Since 2011, there has also been a considerable rise in customer interaction with fintech services nationwide. The payments sector, which already had an impressive 60 million active users in 2020, is predicted to maintain a CAGR exceeding 20% through 2025. Leading the payments sector are gateways. These companies originally made their mark by linking businesses to various payment systems in the 2010s and have since broadened their services.

OVO first joined the e-money boom in 2017.[5] It later expanded to other financial services, including digital lending, investment, insurance, credit scoring, and multifinance. Today, it is a holistic digital payments platform that offers a wide range of services, including a mobile e-wallet, bill payments, merchant payments, and more.[6] In 2021, Grab acquired OVO to boost its fintech capabilities, buying out Lippo and Tokopedia (the other major shareholders).[7]

Xendit, often referred to as "the Stripe of Southeast Asia," focused on building payment systems for B2B. It accomplished this through simplifying and streamlining online and offline payments, money transfers, and other transactions. Native to Indonesia, the payments infrastructure platform now helps bridge the region's fragmented payments landscape and makes cross-border transactions easy for SMEs and larger enterprises alike.[8]

Digital lending has slowly grown to outpace payments, with super apps using their respective e-wallets to springboard into merchant cash advances, fixed deposits, and working capital financing, while specific lendtech names in BNPL and virtual credit cards have thrived.

With larger digital lenders helping banks channel MSME loans and even distributing *sukuk* (a *sharia*-compliant bond-like instrument used in Islamic finance), it was only a matter of time before fintech gave way to wealthtech in Indonesia.[9]

Take Stockbit, for instance. Launched in 2012 as a "social media platform for traders," the company gradually evolved into a full-on stock trading app.[10] It also introduced an investment app called Bibit, which empowers users to invest in mutual funds and government bonds. Research conducted in 2023 by Boston Consulting Group and AC Ventures reveals that wealthtech platforms in the archipelago are now catering to more than 9 million retail investors.

Insurance continues to lag behind other fintech verticals, at less than 2% penetration in Indonesia, thus representing the bluest of oceans.[11] Founded in 2016, insurtech startup PasarPolis offers affordable insurance products through digital channels, partnering with e-commerce players like Shopee to deliver product protection on packages (think insurance for high-value electronics).[12]

Despite massive growth in the uptake of digital financial services over the last decade, there is still room for growth, particularly in the lending, wealth, and insurance verticals. All this growth will continue to be driven by cross-industry efforts to complete Indonesia's massive financial inclusion puzzle.

DIGITAL LENDING LANDS IN INDONESIA

In Indonesia, the potential of digital lending (linking individual or corporate creditors with potential debtors on a platform) became evident in 2015. It was marked by the emergence of several early movers and the establishment of the Indonesian Fintech Association a year later. The enthusiasm for this novel lending approach was compelling, given that the country grapples with an annual loan gap exceeding US$63 billion, a challenge beyond the capacity of banks for various reasons.

Not long after, in January 2016, Modalku ("My Capital" in Bahasa Indonesia) launched as the localized offshoot of Singaporean lending platform Funding Societies.[13] Modalku started by providing noncollateral loans with interest rates between 15% and 20% and with loans ranging from Rp50 million (~US$3,300) to Rp500 million (~US$33,600), to be repaid over 3 to 12 months.

Suddenly, bigger ticket loans were a possibility for Indonesia's SMEs—though, of course, at higher interest rates, and depending on the type of loan. Because lending platforms had the capital to offer larger loans for longer durations compared to microloans offered by e-commerce marketplaces, it was a natural progression for the two to work together to give merchants and gig workers a wider variety of financing options.

Also launched in 2016 was KoinWorks, the brainchild of two Indonesian diaspora who met while attending the University of Michigan in the early 2000s.[14] KoinWorks was originally a digital lender meant to unlock funding for underbanked SMEs. Investors could start lending with as little as Rp100,000 (~US$6.50), while borrowers could apply for up to Rp2 billion (~US$134,000). The aspect that made KoinWorks different from other digital lenders was its target market (primarily e-commerce merchants).

While KoinWorks now offers a variety of features beyond digital lending, to date, it has facilitated more than Rp14 trillion (~US$922 million) in loans to MSMEs.

In 2016, a digital financial services platform named Julo emerged on the scene. Founded by Adrianus Hitijahubessy, an Indonesian with prior experience at Capital One in the United States, the startup centered its efforts on providing loans for productive needs like working capital, health expenses, home renovations, and tuition fees.

Julo secured US$80 million in series B funding, spearheaded by Credit Saison, in 2022.[15] Simultaneously, the company witnessed a threefold increase in transactions and doubled its revenue compared to the previous year. Since its inception, Julo has dispensed more than US$1 billion to borrowers.

In 2020, the number of registered and licensed digital lending firms under OJK reached a peak of approximately 150 companies.[16] Following this, the financial services watchdog initiated actions to improve sector governance by removing nonactive companies, shutting down illegal lending operations, and imposing a moratorium on new digital lending licenses. These measures signaled a mature approach to the budding digital lending sector.

There were more than 19 million active digital borrower accounts in August 2023, proving that while digital credit has taken a backseat in the rest of the world, it remains an integral part of Indonesia's microlending landscape.

BNPL AND ONLINE CREDIT CARDS

The BNPL sector in Indonesia was expected to grow by 94.7% on an annual basis to reach US$2.67 billion in 2022, with its gross merchandise value (GMV) estimated to reach US$25.3 billion by 2028.[17] Although BNPL has drawn headlines since the pandemic hit Indonesia, two pioneers in the country launched as early as 2016. Founded by expats from India and China, respectively, Kredivo and Akulaku introduced online credit facilities and BNPL installment financing via Indonesia's burgeoning e-commerce scene.

Kredivo targets buyers on e-commerce platforms and provides them with a straightforward BNPL service.[18] It allows users to pay their online transactions at a later date, or in monthly installments. The firm does not rely solely on traditional credit bureaus. Instead, it gauges the creditworthiness of potential borrowers through alternative data sources like telcos, e-commerce accounts, bank account history, and more.

Similarly, Akulaku also operates a BNPL service but through a virtual credit card, offering partnerships with e-commerce platforms.[19] Aside from that, it runs a lending platform called Asetku, and entered the digital banking space by acquiring a stake in Bank Yudha Bhakti in 2019.[20]

AGENT BANKING

Other fintech startups carved out niches in O2O, such as agent-banking pioneer Payfazz (now Fazz), which became the first Indonesian startup to be accepted into the Y Combinator accelerator program in 2017.[21] Payfazz began as an almost purely rural, unbanked play for Indonesians looking to make online bill payments without a bank account. Users topped up a mobile wallet through an agent and then used the balance for easy online payments. While GoPay and other super-app e-wallets could also facilitate bill payments, users still needed to top up their e-wallets by transferring from a bank.

With Payfazz, its network of 250,000 agents (often *warung* operators or individuals trusted within their neighborhoods) did most of the transacting, and in the process, helped familiarize locals with digital payments.[22] Brick-and-mortar banks that had stayed away from rural areas—due to the perceived lack of scalability, a shortage of revenue-generating transactions, and high overheads to open new branches—began copying the agent banking model; in some cases, pairing up with Payfazz directly to help rural Indonesians open bank accounts remotely.

BRI, the country's largest MSME lender, revived a 1970s project, the *Unit Desa* village banking network, as an independent profit center running savings and lending services in the mid-2010s and later named it BRILink.[23] Indonesians who previously kept cash stashed under their mattresses were now able to set up bank accounts and apply for loans, with loan officers being rated on the quality of loans approved. BRI also heavily invested in branchless banking, providing agents with electronic draft capture devices to offer simple banking services to the unbanked.

WORKING WITH, NOT AGAINST, BANKS

These collaborations extended throughout the ecosystem, taking different forms that ranged from fintech startups buying stakes in legacy banks to forging partnerships to working through APIs and initiating the banking-as-a-service model in Indonesia. (See Table 7.1.)

APIs empowered traditional banks, including BRI and Mandiri, to swiftly integrate with the systems of startups. Before long, both banks and fintech firms (alongside super apps) resolved to traverse the complex licensing landscape by establishing swift partnerships. Such tie-ups incorporated pipeline agreements, with digital lending platforms assisting in funding MSMEs, or O2O fintech firms like Payfazz operating as an integral part of BRI's branchless banking initiative, as illustrated in Figure 7.2.

The swift uptake and approval of e-wallet and QRIS payments by merchants in Indonesia has helped close the gap between the volume of payments processed by banks and fintech startups. Today, fintech startups handle a number of monthly payments that is practically neck-and-neck with banks, hitting 90% of what banks process. Meanwhile, the actual volume of processed payments by fintech companies has climbed to 80% of the banks' volumes for customers who utilize both service types.

Table 7.1 Fintech Tie-ups Across Indonesia*

Vertical	Startup	Year	Details
Payments	OVO	2018	Strategically partnered with four different brands: Bank Mandiri (traditional bank), Grab (super app), Moka (point-of-sale software), and Alfamart (convenience store chain).[24]
Lending	Bukalapak	2019	Bukalapak partnered with three digital lending platforms (Amartha, Modalku, and PohonDana) to provide loans to *Mitra Bukalapak* offline merchants.[25]
Insurance	PasarPolis	2020	Worked with Allianz Indonesia to provide hospitalization insurance on Gojek's GoSure service.[26]
Wealth	Tokopedia	2021	Tokopedia Keuangan offered two *sharia*-based mutual funds in collaboration with wealthtech startup Bareksa.[27]
Lending	Traveloka	2021	Developed Traveloka PayLater "Virtual Card Number" in partnership with Bank Negara Indonesia (BNI); allowed users to pay later on supported e-commerce platforms outside Traveloka using the card number.[28]
Lending	Payfazz	2021	Partnered with BRI Agro to bring BRI digital lending app Pinang, savings accounts, and lending solutions to 250,000 Payfazz agents and subsequently 10 million Indonesian customers.[29]
Lending	Alami	2021	Acquired majority stakes in regional bank Cempaka Al Amin, and turned it into Hijra Bank.[30]
Lending	Akulaku	2021	Acquired majority stakes in Bank Yudha Bhakti and turned it into Bank Neo Commerce. Partnered with Alipay+, allowing Indonesian consumers to use the Akulaku PayLater feature at Alipay+ global merchants.[31]
Payments	Xendit	2022	Acquired a minority stake in SME-focused Bank Sahabat Sampoerna. The bank is currently owned by two local conglomerates: Sampoerna Group and offline retail champion Alfa Group.[32]
Lending	Kredivo	2022	Acquired majority stakes in Bank Bisnis Internasional, and turned it into Krom Bank Indonesia.[33]
Investment	Ajaib	2022	Acquired controlling stakes in Bank Bumi Arta.[34]

*List not exhaustive

Figure 7.2 Rapid Rise of Digital Banks, Backed by Existing Banks, Business Groups, and Tech Players.

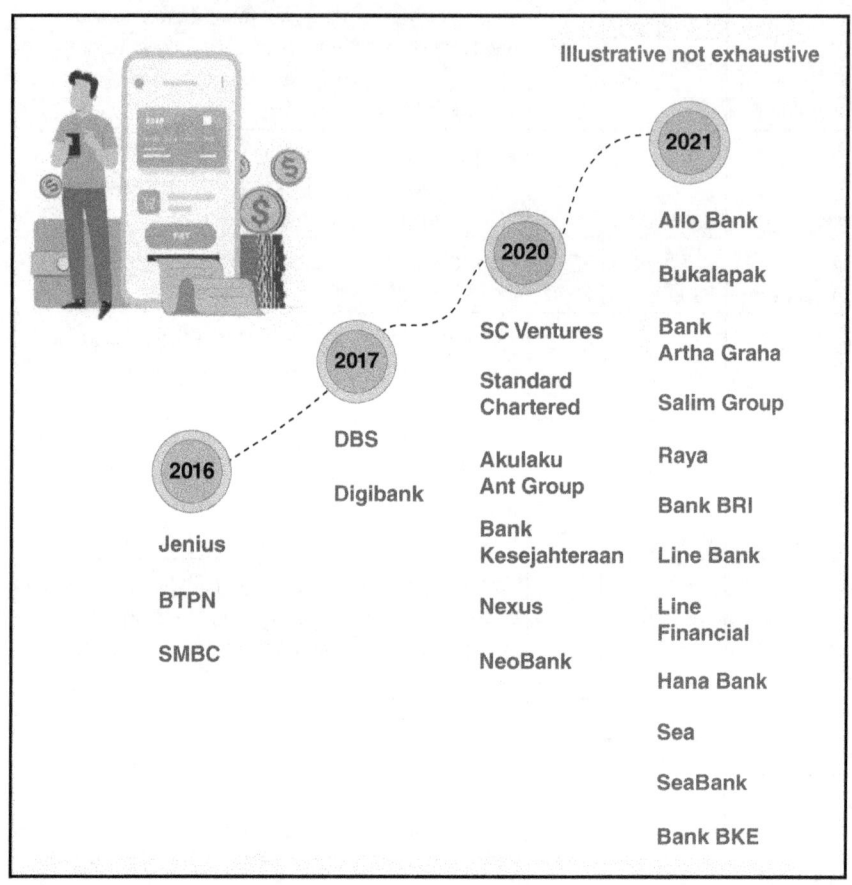

The Indonesian Payment System Blueprint 2025 and the SNAP national standard laid the groundwork for innovation to flourish in the open banking scene. One of the fascinating things about the SNAP standard is how it could democratize the space for payment innovation, giving startups a better shot at competing with the established players in the market.

Additionally, the fast payment system BI-FAST has also played a key role in creating a conducive environment for cashless payment, due to a more affordable transaction fee and real-time transactions time.

In the context of regulation, fintech business leaders have seen that more rules can actually make it easier for them to innovate. Essentially, supportive government actions and policies have helped the fintech industry in Indonesia grow.

THE FUTURE SITS WITH SMES

In the past decade, Indonesia has seen the number of fintech companies shoot up by 600%. At first, this boom was primarily fueled by the payments sector. But now, the fintech scene in Indonesia has blossomed into a diverse mix, with lending, payments, and wealthtech paving the way forward.

Today's fintech field is vibrant, featuring a blend of new and seasoned players. From 2020 to 2022, fintech investment in Indonesia hit US$3.2 billion.[35] Remarkably, that's 4.6 times the funding compared to 2017 to 2019, which goes to show strong investor confidence during and after the pandemic. Even though a good portion of this funding has gone to more developed companies, about 60% of the deals involved early-stage companies, demonstrating a keen interest from investors in future opportunities in this sector.

But when it comes to the local SME market, fintech companies still have some ground to cover. This is clear from the fact that, outside of payments, adoption rates are still under 10%. Even within the realm of payments, fintech companies only account for about a third of the total market. On top of that, around 70% to 80% of lending disbursements are still concentrated in Java Island. So, the opportunity for growth is still there.

The story of financial inclusion in Indonesia is still unfolding. MSMEs, which are major players in Indonesia's economic narrative, are just starting to dip their toes into fintech. With less than a 15% reach across all loan products, there's a big window for startups to step up and push financial inclusion further.

The game plan for most of these startups? Tap into the growing pool of data from digital transactions and payments. These data are crucial for finding new ways to determine whether local businesses are creditworthy. It is particularly helpful for MSMEs that struggle to get loans. This struggle is often due to the fact that they don't have the formal financial records that banks usually require for loan approval.

By pulling in extra data, whether that's teaming up with others in the industry or working with government bodies like the Strategic Industry Management Agency, startups can get a fuller picture and further propel financial inclusion. This is all about teamwork. Lending platforms and regulators have to come together to share vital data.

The next chapter will shine a light on how the COVID-19 pandemic shook up MSMEs and the digital economy in Indonesia. Regulators, already juggling with new sectors and innovations, suddenly had a bigger canvas with skyrocketing demand for digital services during the pandemic. Startups felt the tremors with some seeing a boom, particularly in e-commerce, while others, like travel and ride-hailing, hit a slump. Big business names, even while already revamping digitally, had to move faster to keep up with the swift shift in customer needs.

Interestingly, areas like healthtech, edtech, and online grocery shopping, which usually come into the digital spotlight later in a country's economic journey, got a strong push during the pandemic. This set the stage for nimble tech startups and adventurous investors ready to jump in where others might hesitate.

CHAPTER EIGHT

COVID-19 BRINGS DIGITAL ADOPTION FORWARD BY 10 YEARS

As the 2010s drew to a close, Indonesia's digital economy was on an impressive upward trajectory. High-performing local companies such as Gojek, Traveloka, Tokopedia, and Bukalapak had firmly established themselves. There was also an active investment scene, with investors eager to fund new and promising startups, many of which were launched by former employees of companies like Rocket and Gojek. Additionally, the talent pool was expanding, thanks to a growing number of

Indonesians returning home to contribute their skills and an ever-growing pool of expatriates willing to relocate to Indonesia.

With 68 million young people making up 28% of the population, the future was indeed promising, at least for the upcoming decade.[1] There was ample opportunity for further growth in the consumer market, particularly with a burgeoning middle class growing at a faster pace than other segments. Notably, at least 52 million Indonesians were considered economically stable, translating to one in every five locals enjoying a baseline of financial security.[2]

But things didn't turn out as anticipated. By April 2020, the once bustling streets of Jakarta, notorious for their three-hour-long traffic jams that led to the inception of Gojek, stood deserted. The sweeping impact of the COVID-19 pandemic was felt universally, leading to the closure of schools, places of worship, and shopping malls.

Even more adversely, the government's nonbinding "stay-at-home" request for everyone across this nation had already begun to take an economic toll: state data showed that 1.4 million workers in both the formal and informal sectors had either been told to stay home or would soon be laid off.

A wave of pessimism swept through the country with uncertainty bearing on everyone's minds, from the severity of the pandemic to the global and local economy and even people's very livelihoods. Yet, the reality revealed a more nuanced picture, far from the gloom that initially seemed to shroud it.

As people were restricted from shopping and socializing together, the realms of e-commerce and online food delivery witnessed an unprecedented surge, a boom that even pre-pandemic projections couldn't have foreseen. As homes transformed into havens of safety, gaming emerged as a favored pastime, captivating minds and screens alike.

On top of that, the domains of healthtech saw a major hike in interest, as individuals tended to put more focus on their well-being. Meanwhile, education technology (edtech) quickly gained traction in a world where schools were shuttered.

While some industries thrived, others suffered. The online travel sector took a big hit, and Traveloka, one of the country's leading tech companies, was significantly affected. This was the case even when some countries started to reopen their borders, introducing new virus testing rules and lots of paperwork.

In Q2 of 2020, investors faced a significant stock market downturn due to uncertainties surrounding COVID-19, leading to a widespread aversion to risk. For the majority of 2020, notably its first three quarters, there was a global slowdown in deal-making. However, as the effects of the US government's zero interest rate policy effectively reduced the cost of capital to zero, investor risk appetite rebounded. In 2021, this led to a marked increase in asset prices, especially for digital businesses. Investors were keen to invest in sectors reshaped by the implications of COVID-19.

The situation was like a double-edged sword. On one side, it drew investors to Indonesia, highlighting it as a lucrative market for higher returns. This visibility not only reaffirmed Indonesia's significance on the global digital stage but also attracted new direct investors and introduced new LPs to local venture capitalists. On the flip side, however, it escalated expectations and valuations for tech companies to levels beyond their achievable performance.

This chapter explores how the pandemic rapidly advanced Indonesia's digital adoption, significantly boosting sectors like e-commerce, healthtech, and edtech, while severely hindering others such as travel and fashion.

A TALE OF TWO FUNDING HALVES

According to the Google e-Conomy SEA report released in November 2020, the first half of the year saw investment in Indonesia's internet sector reach US$2.8 billion, close to the full-year figures for 2019 (US$3.2 billion).

However, more than half of this was due to Gojek wrapping up its series F fundraising: US$1.2 billion from multiple Mitsubishi affiliates and Visa in March 2020, followed by a much smaller US$375 million round from PayPal and Facebook in June.[3]

Aside from the two major funding rounds that Gojek received, the US$2.8 billion remainder was largely dispersed among smaller startups through about 200 different deals. Investors didn't entirely retreat from the game; instead, they adopted a more cautious approach with smaller rounds. This trend continued into the latter half of 2020. As the reality of COVID-19's enduring presence set in, both investors and startup founders had to adjust their strategies accordingly.

According to Google data, the total funding in the second half of 2020 dropped to half of the investments seen in the first half of the year, with US$1.6 billion spread across 235 deals. The economic downturn had started to affect all levels of business, and even the major players were beginning to feel the pinch.

Reports suggested that Traveloka was looking for new funding at a reduced valuation in July 2020.[4] Ultimately, it secured a funding round of US$250 million led by the Qatar Investment Authority, with a pre-money valuation of US$2.5 billion.[5] This was a noticeable drop from its reported valuation of US$4 billion before the pandemic hit.[6]

In November, Bukalapak and Tokopedia wrapped up their US$100 million and US$350 million rounds, respectively, with returning backers like Singaporean government-linked investment arms GIC and Temasek, as well as Indonesian media giant Emtek.[7,8] Notably, these deals attracted first-time investors with deep pockets as well, such as Microsoft and Google. However, lower valuations and smaller rounds were considered wins in 2020, compared to what smaller startups went through.

LOSSES IN TRAVEL, HOSPITALITY, OFFLINE RETAIL

Mid-sized startups, previously engaged in aggressive growth strategies, found the tougher fundraising landscape particularly challenging. Practices like heavy spending on marketing, promotions, and engaging in price competition to increase their user bases, which were once commonplace, turned out to be detrimental for several of these growth-oriented firms.

Every startup faced challenges similar to their traditional business counterparts: from a decrease in consumer spending to supply chain disruptions, along with the inability to have in-person interactions with employees, clients, and business partners. Startups in the travel, hospitality, and physical retail sectors were especially hard hit, experiencing considerable setbacks and in some cases, even shutting down. (See Table 8.1.)

Indonesia's online travel industry experienced a severe setback, with GMV plummeting 68%, from US$10 billion in 2019 to just US$3 billion in 2020. While Traveloka managed to weather the worst of the pandemic, some of the smaller companies in the travel industry, such as budget hotel aggregator Airy, weren't as fortunate.

By 2022, the travel sector was in a gradual recovery mode, with the ease of travel restrictions and quarantine requirements spurring a surge in demand. However, the full recovery to pre-pandemic level was only expected in the next one or two years.

Despite struggles in international travel that took longer to rebound, domestic travel saw a relatively quick revival, with hotels in Southeast Asia returning to around 80% of their pre-pandemic occupancies. Domestic air travel in Indonesia rebounded to 70% of its pre-pandemic passenger loads.

Table 8.1 Select Startups That Shut Down Due to COVID-19*

Startup	Service	Issues
CoHive	Coworking and coliving spaces	• Short-term demand at first as companies moved away from long-term leases due to economic uncertainty and no work-from-home setups, but eventually revenue dropped due to social distancing and screening protocols.[9] • Last funding round: US$13.5 million (June 2019).[10] • Eventually downsized from 30 coworking spaces to just six in January 2023, when it was declared bankrupt.[11]
Fabelio	Furniture e-commerce	• A D2C brand that manufactured its own products while working with local designers.[12] • Last funding round: US$9 million (May 2020).[13] • Announced plans to open three new centers, increase storage capacity, and expand same-day delivery (August 2020).[14] • Employees had been unpaid for multiple months in 2021.[15] Finally declared bankrupt in October 2022 due to the impact of COVID-19 and a delay in funding from investors.[16]
Sorabel	Fashion e-commerce	• Was on the path to profitability with gross margins of 58%, and aimed to raise US$30 million from Chinese investors by April 2020. • Travel restrictions in China and Indonesia forced investors to drop off, while customers cut down on discretionary spending.[17] • Last funding round: debt financing (August 2019).[18] • COVID-19 wiped out company cash, leaving Sorabel unable to pivot or pay salaries. Shut down in July 2020.[19]
Airy	Budget hotel aggregator	• Indonesia's largest aggregator of budget hotels (2,000 properties and 30,000 rooms) and a strategic partner of Traveloka. • Announced pivot to profitability, expressed optimism that COVID-19 will be resolved soon (March 2020). • Laid off 70% of staff in April 2020. • Permanently ceased operations at the end of May 2020 due to COVID-19 threatening tourism.[20]

Startup	Service	Issues
Stoqo	Food logistics	• Sold ingredients and other supplies to food and beverage SMEs through its platform. • Its costly labor-intensive operations and mispriced products led to minimal profit margins, which hindered its ability to scale.[21] • Last funding round: undisclosed series A (December 2018).[22] • Needed to close a series B round by the end of 2019, but failed to do so. The pandemic quickly ate into the cash runway. • Shut down in April 2020, becoming Indonesia's first tech casualty of the pandemic.[23]

* List not exhaustive

SURVIVING ON SHORT-TERM PIVOTS

Despite the difficult circumstances, not all startups in heavily impacted sectors faltered. Some had enough financial reserves to support changes to their business models, while others strategically conserved cash for long-term survival. Many adapted their models to the new market dynamics. For instance, some started offering COVID-19-related products or services or ventured into new markets entirely.

The swift spread of the outbreak in densely populated Indonesia underscored the urgent need for efficient screening and testing methods. The country's already strained healthcare system required quick digital solutions that Indonesians could access from their homes.

Two startups, Achiko, a mobile payments firm, and Nusantics, a genomics tech company, quickly shifted their focus to offer COVID-19 screening and testing services. Traveloka diversified its offerings by introducing services like on-demand food delivery and online grocery services. Social Bella, a beauty retailer, transitioned to hosting online events and shifted its focus from makeup to home-based self-care products. Akulaku adjusted its approach to target underserved markets and offer consumer loans via partnerships with e-commerce platforms, while also reducing loan sizes. (See Table 8.2.)

By and large, the distinguishing factors between startups that managed to successfully navigate the pandemic and those that did not were their pre-pandemic financial preparation and ability to conserve cash. For entrepreneurs who were in the middle of securing deals in early 2020 or those who only started engaging with investors as COVID-19 began to hit, their efforts proved to be mostly ill-fated.

Table 8.2 A Few Startups That Pivoted Strategies or Services During the Pandemic*

Startup	Service	Pivot points
Traveloka	Online travel → food delivery, online groceries, and more	• Launched Traveloka Eats (food delivery), Traveloka Send (on-demand courier), and Traveloka Mart (online grocery service) as part of its COVID-19 diversification strategy.[24] • Traveloka Eats was initially created to review and list restaurants in 2018. • 2020 or earlier funding: US$250 million (July 2020). • Shut down pandemic-response business units and refocused on travel in October 2022.
Nusantics	Genomics tech → COVID-19 testing	• Before COVID-19, the genomics tech company focused solely on microbiome analysis. • Within weeks of COVID-19 hitting Indonesia in March 2020, Nusantics produced a testing kit and offered assistance to the government. • 2020 or earlier funding: US$700,000 (March 2020).[25] • Now runs the testing kit arm of the business as a social enterprise.[26]

Startup	Service	Pivot points
Achiko	Mobile payments → COVID-19 testing	• Used technology developed for a payments aggregator to launch the Teman Sehat app that incentivizes people to get tested, make payments, and keep records of test results for entry into public places.[27] • 2020 or earlier funding: seed round (August 2018).[28] • Worked with a biotech company to develop an affordable screener that costs less than US$0.25 per kit.
Social Bella (Sociolla)	Beauty and personal care retailer (changed strategies)	• Had six physical stores across Indonesia and served 30 million annual users before the pandemic. • Added a live chat feature so users could directly interact with beauty consultants, resulting in a 50% increase in basket size on Sociolla. • 2020 or earlier funding: US$58 million (July 2020).[29] • Now boasts 48 stores in Indonesia, as well as 13 stores in Vietnam.[30]
Akulaku	Fintech (changed strategies)	• During the early days of the pandemic, Akulaku restructured thousands of loans as people lost their jobs or saw wages slashed. • Switched focus to consumer loans by working with e-commerce platforms. Also focused on underpenetrated markets, addressing incomplete credit history and lack of data, resulting in smaller loan sizes and revenue per customer.[31] • 2020 or earlier funding: US$100 million (January 2019).[32]

* List not exhaustive

WINNING SECTORS GET THEIR TURN IN THE LIMELIGHT

As history would show, the pandemic also accelerated digital adoption across the board and presented new opportunities for an entire cross-section of local digital businesses. Startups in sectors like e-commerce, healthtech, edtech, and remote-working tools saw a surge in demand as people turned to online solutions during lockdowns and social distancing measures. (See Table 8.3.)

Table 8.3 A Few Startups That Thrived During the Pandemic

Startup	Service	Winning strategy
Halodoc	Telemedicine	• Founded in 2016. Before the pandemic, it had 22,000 doctors on duty and 1,200 pharmacies on standby to send out prescriptions. • Funding: undisclosed series B (July 2019) from Allianz, Bill & Melinda Gates Foundation, Prudential.[33] • Launched "Check COVID-19" telemedicine service in partnership with the Ministry of Health, rolled out on Gojek and Blibli apps in March 2020.[34] • Users could check symptoms, get accurate COVID-19 information, consult with doctors, and order prescribed medication. • Extended its telemedicine service in the PeduliLindung COVID-19 tracking app by the ICT Ministry in June 2020.[35] • Partnered with Gojek and the Ministry of Health to offer drive-through vaccination services for at-risk groups in 2021.

Startup	Service	Winning strategy
CoLearn	Edtech for tuition centers and tutors	• Founded in 2018. It started with an offline model, offering supplementary English, mathematics, and coding classes to students. • Funding: undisclosed seed round (January and December 2020).[36] • Went fully digital in 2020, offering live online classes, AI-powered homework help, and exam assistance. • By mid-2021, it had 250,000 prerecorded videos available. The startup's AI answered 5 million questions monthly, matching users with video tutorials recorded by more than 400 tutors.[37]
Astro	Quick commerce	• Launched in September 2021 by Tokopedia alumni. An on-demand platform that could deliver groceries in 15 minutes or less. • Funding: undisclosed series B (January 2021).[38] • Collaborated with local businesses to launch private labels for food products including coffee, bread, and seasonal treats.[39] • Strong post-pandemic retention rate: after their first month of use, 30% to 35% of customers remained loyal to Astro due to the convenience of delivery and familiarity with the service.[40] • By mid-2022, Astro operated in 50 locations across the Jakarta Metro Area.[41]
ESB	Fully integrated restaurant operating platform	• Founded in 2014. Initially offered a customized enterprise resource planning (ERP) cloud solution to replace expensive traditional hardware-based systems. • During the pandemic, ESB started working on an all-in-one restaurant operating system covering point-of-sale and mobile self-ordering tech, effectively reducing the need for waitstaff. • Funding: seed round from AC Ventures (May 2020).[42]

(Continued)

Table 8.3 (Continued)

Startup	Service	Winning strategy
Shipper	One-stop logistics solution	• Founded in 2017, it offered a multi-courier shipping platform and a distributed warehousing and fulfillment network. • In 2020, worked with more than 100 express couriers and had over 30 fulfillment centers.[43] • Funding: US$20 million (May 2020).[44] • By November 2020, Shipper was operating in 70 cities across Indonesia, with around 2,500 logistics providers and 50 fulfillment centers.[45]

Online shopping continued to be the main factor boosting growth, increasing to a total sales value of US$32 billion in 2020. This was a substantial jump of 54% from US$21 billion in 2019. However, not all e-commerce startups did well. Those in the discretionary spending verticals (think Fabelio in furniture and Sorabel in fashion) were hit hard, as they relied on customers having extra cash to spend on nonessentials.

Similar to other countries in Southeast Asia, Indonesia's startups previously concentrated on expanding B2C e-commerce in rapidly growing areas such as clothing, travel, food delivery, and transportation. Sectors that were expanding at a slower pace, like healthtech and edtech, also attracted investment but these verticals, which often required cooperation with federal and local governments, traditional banks, and various communities, received funding at a slower rate and in smaller amounts. In 2020, this dynamic changed rapidly.

In response to the urgent need for digital solutions that could quickly and effectively monitor the spread of COVID-19 in Indonesia, the health technology sector garnered a lot of attention in the pandemic's early days. This came not just from investors, but also from founders.

Healthcare accessibility remains a significant challenge in Southeast Asia, with Indonesia exemplifying this issue. The country has a healthcare provision ratio of 0.4 doctors and 1.2 hospital beds per 1,000 residents.[46] As a benchmark, Singapore, which is better served in terms of healthcare, has ratios of 2.8 doctors and 2.5 hospital beds per 1,000 residents.

Given this situation, it's not surprising that the pandemic fast-tracked the development of digital healthcare solutions, including providing accurate health information, online pharmacy services, online medical consultations, and appointment scheduling. They also included health and disease management services for people with chronic conditions who needed to renew their prescriptions or had medical procedures postponed due to social distancing rules.

Telemedicine apps drew massive interest from banks, healthcare providers, insurers, and super apps, who rushed to partner with Halodoc and Alodokter. While Halodoc had already partnered with Gojek's on-demand medicine delivery service GoMed in 2017, in 2020 it worked with the Indonesian Ministry of Health to launch the "Check COVID-19" telemedicine service, which was subsequently rolled out on Gojek and Blibli.[47,48] This feature enabled users to check for COVID-19 risks via the Halodoc platform, consult with more than 22,000 licensed doctors, and buy medications without leaving home.

The pandemic taught us the importance of affordable and accessible healthcare. We can expect to see much higher adoption of digital medical services in the coming years, especially among Indonesia's rural population.

As time progressed, an emphasis on ensuring the continuity in children's education arose. The government launched "Belajar dari Rumah," a television educational program translated as "Learn from Home," to complement online classes. Additionally, universities without an existing platform were offered a complimentary learning management system.

Interestingly, while many Indonesian families lacked laptops to enable remote learning, smartphones and tablets were already ubiquitous. This led to an increase in edtech apps, like K12 live learning and homework assistance platform CoLearn. Launched in August 2020, the app could answer users' academic questions with an AI-powered homework assistant.

From August 2020 to April 2021, CoLearn was downloaded more than 3.5 million times and reached 1 million active users, mostly students in grades 7 to 12. As of mid-2021, CoLearn offered more than 250,000 prerecorded videos with homework help. Today, users ask about 5 million questions through the app each month, and the AI matches them with video tutorials, recorded by more than 400 tutors who break down key concepts.

Meanwhile, edtech contender Ruangguru launched a free online school service in March 2020 when schools across the nation were closed.[49] Users could enroll for free weekday virtual classes, which included live teaching, chats, and discussions.

With the return to in-person schooling, demand for online learning has cooled off compared to the peak levels of the pandemic. However, the experience has opened a possibility for new hybrid learning models going forward.

WINNERS IN B2B AND MSME TECH

Another key concern of policymakers was to ensure food security for hundreds of millions of Indonesians. The most logical point of entry for addressing the issue was via the nation's ubiquitous *warung* and informal neighborhood convenience shops.

As people began schooling, working, and even playing remotely, mom-and-pop shops became more important for communities than ever before. With movements restricted by districts or regions and borders tightened, rising supply chain costs and delays hit small retailers the hardest.

Financial and digital inclusion for MSMEs was not a novel idea by the time the pandemic hit. Neither were O2O solutions, COD, or pickup points for online purchases. But no Indonesian tech startup had yet tied it all together in a truly elegant way.

Some companies, such as Ula, Super, Sinbad, and GudangAda, stepped in to provide solutions that combined those services. However, at the time of writing it still remains to be seen if they will be able to build sustainable businesses.

Meanwhile, restaurants found themselves needing to swiftly transition to digital operations to stay in business.

Established in 2014, ESB, a company cofounded by entrepreneurs with decades of experience in the food and beverage industry, initially offered a solution to this challenge. They provided restaurants with an ERP cloud solution, offering a cost-effective alternative to traditional, more expensive hardware-based systems.

In response to the 2020 pandemic, ESB expanded to an "all-in-one" restaurant operating system including a point-of-sale (POS) system and a customer-facing, self-serve mobile ordering feature called ESB Order.[50] The startup grew 3× year-on-year during the pandemic, mainly due to robust demand for contactless ordering.

By 2021, ESB had worked with more than 500 food and beverage brands and annually processed more than 40 million API orders. ESB's fully integrated approach made it easier for restaurants to quickly transition to digital operations, a necessity during the pandemic. This was particularly beneficial for restaurants with multiple outlets across different cities and those utilizing a variety of consumer-facing channels such as websites, food delivery apps, social media, and super apps.

Looking at the broader picture, a wide range of businesses had to fast-track the digitization of their logistics systems during the pandemic, due to a multitude of supply chain challenges and the already significant transportation costs within Indonesia. Comprehensive logistics solutions like Shipper offered a valuable alternative for MSMEs. It allowed businesses to compare and select the best rates among various major carriers, instead of being restricted to a single shipping app such as Gojek or Lalamove.[51]

Shipper's platform provides sellers with the ability to create, track, and manage their orders. Its pick-up service involves couriers who gather packages and distribute them to various logistics providers across the country.

Its API equips MSMEs with the capacity to swiftly incorporate shipping and tracking services into their websites. By November 2020, this logistics aggregator was operating in 70 cities across Indonesia, utilizing approximately 2,500 logistics providers and 50 fulfillment centers.

During the pandemic, the Indonesian government implemented measures to aid the tech startup ecosystem. These steps included financial stimulus packages, regulatory reforms, and partnerships with industry leaders to encourage digital innovation. Evidence of this was seen in its telemedicine collaborations with Halodoc and Gojek, as well as the introduction of remote learning solutions for the millions of Indonesian students studying from home. These initiatives sought to boost digital transformation, stimulate innovation, and cultivate a favorable environment for startups to flourish amidst the "new normal."

Despite the challenges, startups needed to identify and leverage their unique strengths in successful sectors. While super apps and unicorns had ample funding and resources to explore fresh directions, many smaller startups chose to prioritize cash preservation. As a result, forging partnerships, whether with other digital entities, government agencies, or major corporations and banks, became a central strategy for many.

SECOND-ORDER EFFECTS

The focus on high-burn, win-at-all-cost expansion that marked the early years of Indonesia's startup boom (introduced by Rocket Internet and propagated by subsequent founders and VCs) was not sustainable once funding dried up after the US Fed started aggressively raising interest rates in early 2022.

Instead, the focus turned to existing startups with sustainable scalability and clear paths to profit, as well as viable avenues for investors to exit. Newer founders suffered due to a lower appetite from investors, but big players like Tokopedia and Traveloka continued to bring in massive funding rounds, albeit at lowered valuations.

Looking beyond the pandemic, even established names like Grab and Gojek took measures to cut spending, shifting toward sectors they believed would generate profits faster, such as fintech for Grab. They even outlined profitability pathways for individual products.

For VCs, however, the pandemic came with something of a silver lining, as it opened up previously untapped pools of foreign capital. The requirement for venture capitalists to traverse the planet for pitch meetings with global LPs was replaced by highly efficient online meetings.

While remote and hybrid working initially slowed down traditional businesses during the early days of the pandemic, VCs and their LPs adapted to remote deal-making necessitated by lockdowns.

AC Ventures successfully onboarded new LPs remotely, even as travel restrictions persisted into 2021. Western investors had to get comfortable putting money into companies and founders they could not meet in person. This is where our firm played a vital role in bridging the trust gap.

The arrival of cross-over funds and late-stage capital allocators increased, bypassing the need for excessive travel with a more direct approach. This hybrid strategy was highly effective, allowing us to secure a US$205 million fund mostly during the pandemic via Zoom calls. By 2022, we were meeting some of our existing LPs in person for the first time.

The capability to connect with key players from the other side of the world was immensely beneficial for startup backers in Southeast Asia—a region from which one would previously have had to endure a 23-hour journey to finalize a deal.[52]

INDONESIA'S MSMES ARE THE NEXT BLUE OCEAN

While the so-called slower-growth, harder-to-tap verticals like edtech, healthtech, and MSME enablement came to the foreground during the pandemic, there is still a lot of room to grow. Indonesia's more than 64 million MSMEs represent 98% of total business activities, account for 97% of employment, and contribute more than 60% of the nation's GDP.[53]

Even with the strong inroads B2B startups like Majoo, KoinWorks, ESB, and Shipper have made into Indonesia's *warung*, restaurants, and small retailers, millions of unbanked and underbanked MSMEs still continue to rely on outdated analog systems and processes. The accelerated pace of digitalization, fueled by the pandemic, has arguably advanced digital progress by a decade within just two years. This fast-forward may have opened the door wider for new B2B startups, but challenges remain. There is still a lot of work to be done, inefficiencies to iron out, and market gaps to bridge.

In the next chapter, we will go into the outsized role that MSMEs play in Indonesia's economic growth story while supporting societal progress and resilience at the grassroots level. MSMEs and the language of inclusion also align with the latest requirements of VCs and their LPs in this modern investment climate, which increasingly prioritized impact and sustainability.

CHAPTER NINE
IMPACT IN THE TIME OF DIGITIZED MICRO-BUSINESS

It is important to recognize that within the context of developing countries, Indonesia stands out as a prime example of an economy bolstered by its MSMEs. However, akin to many economic underdogs, these businesses face challenges in expansion. Their size, combined with constrained purchasing power and a limited footprint in the formal financial system, often curtails their growth potential.

Despite these challenges, the relevance of MSMEs to Indonesia's socioeconomic narrative cannot be overstated. Collectively, they are the pillar supporting inclusive and sustainable economic evolution, fortifying social progress from the ground up.

Local unicorn Bukalapak emerged as a trailblazer in tech empowerment for MSMEs through its Mitra Bukalapak initiative. Subsequently, numerous startups have also undertaken similar efforts.

Another significant effect of VC investing is its transformative influence on the investment landscape for climate solutions. More VC firms are being guided by their LPs and industry stakeholders. They are adapting their portfolios for a surge in ESG best practices that will redefine Southeast Asia.

In countries like Indonesia, compliance with ESG standards was, until recently, more of a peripheral consideration rather than a central one for investors. The scene is changing rapidly today. As an increasing amount of foreign institutional capital seeks to penetrate the market, local venture firms and startups are realizing the importance of staying ahead. Large multinational corporations, bound by strict ESG regulations in their home countries, are paving the way. Their overseas investments are not immune to their home-country rules, heralding a significant shift in international investment norms.

BRIDGING A US$63 BILLION FINANCING GAP

The outsized role MSMEs have in Indonesia's growing economy has made them the focus of policymakers, particularly in filling the digitization and financing gaps between MSMEs and multinationals in the archipelago.

While the idea is commendable, its execution proves challenging. Most of the country's MSMEs, particularly those in the microsegment, are situated in second- and third-tier cities. These areas often grapple with inconsistent internet connectivity, limited bandwidth, and underdeveloped infrastructure. Consequently, both established companies and startups face the substantial task of scaling in markets that aren't fully ripe for expansion.

Most of Indonesia's MSMEs are small-scale businesses with limited profit margins, and a significant number of them are in rural areas where internet access is still spotty. Consequently, many of these microentrepreneurs are not very familiar with digital tools. It's important for tech startups to understand these challenges. They should create applications that are simple to use and require minimal bandwidth and battery power.

With this in mind, the massive leapfrogging of digital acceleration forced by the pandemic and partial lockdowns led to an increase in both Indonesian consumers and MSME merchants adopting digital tools and services. Google found that 37% of all digital consumers in Indonesia were new to a particular service due to COVID-19. Drilling down further, of these new digital users, a majority were from outside the Jakarta Metro Area. On the merchant side, many MSMEs shifted online out of necessity: some directly, and some with the support of traditional banks introducing e-wallets and digital payments to their MSME clients.

This "new digital normal" post-pandemic has made it easier for e-commerce enablers and fintech startups to bring digital inclusion to MSMEs across Indonesia. But another big part of the scalability puzzle was giving MSMEs access to funding to grow their businesses. In 2021, the International Monetary Fund estimated that Indonesia's MSME financing gap was around US$165 billion. Notwithstanding several government initiatives, more than 70% of Indonesia's MSMEs still lack access to formal credit, where bank loans only make up 6% of MSME funding sources, driven largely by directives from Bank Indonesia.[1]

In August 2021, Bank Indonesia expanded its regulation to encourage banks to issue more loans to MSMEs. The new regulation required banks to disburse at least 20% of their loans to either MSMEs themselves, related supply chains, or low-income earners. At the time of writing, Bank Indonesia is expected to gradually raise the mandatory MSME credit ratio to 30% in 2024.[2] The high cost of setting up branches in remote towns, however, means many brick-and-mortar banks focus squarely on medium-sized businesses in first-tier cities—leaving microbusinesses like neighborhood *warung* to fintech players such as KoinWorks and others.

Unlike the blitzscaling of Indonesia's initial tech boom, new-age fintech startups need to find cost-efficient ways to onboard MSMEs across different cities while providing smaller ticket loans. As a result, they are only barely bridging the MSME financing gap, with data from OJK showing that fintech platforms only disbursed a total of US$5 billion in 2020—a mere droplet in what is otherwise an ocean of microfinance opportunity.[3]

On one of our recent podcasts, Angelique Timmer, senior vice president of Impact and ESG at KoinWorks, said that her company has provided access to capital for more than 500,000 businesses, with a total loan disbursement of around US$936 million, while still keeping nonperforming loans low at just 2%.[4] The speed of disbursement is instrumental for MSMEs' working capital needs in Indonesia, especially for rural microentrepreneurs who depend on daily and weekly income to survive.

MSMES AND OUTSIZED SOCIETAL IMPACT

In the bustling world of Indonesian e-commerce, it's easy to assume that every business has joined the digital movement, especially given the widespread influence of local giants like Tokopedia and Bukalapak. Despite this, a considerable portion of MSMEs are still not engaged with online platforms. A key barrier preventing these hold-outs from fully integrating into the digital economy is the challenge of managing first- and last-mile deliveries across Indonesia's sprawling archipelago. This requires a sophisticated mix of land, sea, and air transportation to ensure goods reach customers' doorsteps efficiently.

As discussed in the previous chapter, the role of *warung* in ensuring food security for rural Indonesian villages has been monumental. But despite the ease of downloading e-commerce apps, another real challenge presents itself in replenishing inventory for MSMEs that have become the lifeline for their communities.

Consider the example of a *warung* owner in Madura, a relatively remote island off the coast of East Java. Procuring inventory requires the owner to close her shop for one or two days to undertake a road trip. During this period, locals who rely on the *warung* are left without essential supplies.

A few local startups, like Super and Sinbad, have risen to the occasion by leveraging technology to streamline the supply chain. In some cases, they connect *warung* owners directly with suppliers, thereby eliminating the middlemen, ensuring quicker delivery, and expanding the range of products available at competitive prices.[5]

Beyond the supply chain, there's also an evident need for modernizing the physical infrastructure of many *warung* and integrating digital systems into their operations. WarungPintar was an early pioneer in this regard. In its early days, the company offered a novel approach of providing prefabricated kiosk-style shops equipped with a range of digital tools—from inventory management systems to digital payment options.[6]

The potential of these startups to revolutionize the traditional *warung* landscape in Indonesia is undeniable. Their integrated solutions address multiple pain points, bringing an era of digitization and modernization to an age-old sector.

However, it's crucial to note that this is an industry characterized by razor-thin distribution margins. As these tech-enabled businesses continue their pursuit of disruption, the question remains: will the blend of technology and tradition yield a sustainable and profitable future? Time will tell in the next couple of years.

REVENUE GENERATION VS POVERTY ALLEVIATION

In 2022, the Asian Development Bank reported a disheartening statistic: nearly 1 in 10 Indonesians lived below the international poverty line.[7] Faced with limited employment opportunities, many turn to entrepreneurship, creating micro-businesses out of sheer necessity. For these individuals, making sales is not simply about growing a business, but securing their daily bread.

Against this backdrop, lending products from firms like KoinWorks have played a transformative role. Supporting thousands of MSMEs, they've helped these businesses transition from mere survival to upward economic mobility.

As Angelique from KoinWorks explained, "About 70% of our borrowers receive their first-ever productivity loan from us. This loan helps them expand their businesses, leading to more stores, more branches, and eventually more jobs."

By improving productivity, reducing downtime, and enhancing scalability, MSMEs have started to tap into additional income streams. As we've already covered, Bukalapak launched its Mitra Bukalapak initiative, enabling *warung* to generate extra revenue by serving as e-commerce agents and pickup points. However, an initial plan to introduce a mobile POS and inventory management feature faced resistance from store owners, who preferred their own hands-on approach.

In response, Teddy Oetomo, president of Bukalapak, turned this inventory management feature into a clever digital marketing tool for MSMEs.

"MSMEs can itemize their inventory, along with volume and pricing, and with a single click, they can share it in their community via WhatsApp groups," he said on an episode of the Indonesia Digital Deconstructed podcast by AC Ventures. This direct marketing approach yielded immediate results, driving customers to stores, Teddy explained.[8]

But the pressure for offline MSMEs to embrace digital marketing across various channels and e-commerce marketplaces has sometimes cut into their margins and, in some cases, proven to be a time drain. To address this pain point, local startup Majoo has built an all-in-one platform that offers a variety of digital tools for Indonesian MSMEs, ranging from POS and backend management to payroll and even social media integration.

Adi Wahyu Rahadi is the founder and CEO of Majoo, a SaaS company that helps offline merchants sell through multiple online channels without friction, integrating them with e-marketplaces such as Tokopedia, Shopee, and Bukalapak. "We enable them to centralize and manage inventory easily and efficiently," Adi said on our podcast.[9]

Payment capabilities have also been simplified with Majoo. The platform cooperates with e-wallet providers to streamline the transition from cash to digital payments for MSMEs. Adi added, "Our users don't actually have to get onboarded with all of these e-wallets; instead, with Majoo, all e-payments can now be collected by arming merchants with a single QR code to show their customers."

By empowering these small businesses with advanced digital tools, they are stimulating an economic uplift for communities previously bound by the poverty line. This has had a profound and transformative impact, turning the tide of economic prosperity in favor of those who need it most.

INDONESIA'S MSMES AND THE GLOBAL FOOD SUPPLY

In rural Indonesia, small-scale farmers and fishermen perform the critical task of ensuring food security for the nation. But the fruits of their labor often don't reach them, as middlemen take the lion's share of profits or perishable produce goes to waste due to supply chain inefficiencies. The country's annual food waste is also responsible for more than 7% of the country's greenhouse gas emissions and is estimated to cost the economy up to US$37.1 billion per year.

Addressing this critical problem, two startups are delivering outsized impact, connecting agricultural entrepreneurs directly to high-value buyers and offering them price certainty. The role of these startups transcends mere business; they are minimizing food waste and reducing the effects of climate change and uncertain yields.

Consider Aruna, Indonesia's largest integrated fisheries platform. It focuses on optimizing the supply chain for the country's 12 million fishermen. Interestingly, while Indonesia ranks second only to China globally in terms of seafood production, it doesn't even appear in the top 10 for export value. This gap can be attributed to an inefficient, fragmented supply chain. Aruna addresses this by directly connecting local small-scale fishermen to international buyers.

With an integrated approach, Aruna also employs GPS trackers and other technologies to monitor and manage overfishing, contributing significantly to the sustainability of coastal communities. Aruna's intervention has already led to an increase of 200% to 300% in the income of local fishermen.[10]

On the agriculture side, a company called Koltiva helps Indonesia's farmers meet global sustainability and traceability standards, comply with international regulations, and thereby gain access to the global market.

In the context of agri-based product traceability, Koltiva is breaking new ground. By developing software that provides seed-to-table visibility, the company ensures that the journey from input materials, through farm operations and distribution, to the final consumer is fully transparent. This innovation helps large multinationals and enterprises trace the origin of their food supply, much of which comes from smallholder farms (MSMEs) in Indonesia and other countries where Koltiva operates.

The company's cofounder and CEO, Manfred Borer, explained, "Koltiva empowers corporations to wisely navigate the global landscape of evolving regulations and sustainability compliance while enhancing smallholder farmers' livelihoods. We aim to foster an ecosystem benefiting global brands while also uplifting the grassroots, MSME-driven level of the supply chain."

Koltiva already serves more than 1 million MSME farmers and 6,800 large enterprises, indicating a significant need for its innovative food supply chain tracing, climate tech offerings, and more.[11]

Ventures like Aruna and Koltiva are setting a transformative precedent. They're not only revolutionizing the agriculture and fisheries sectors but are also paving the way for a new kind of venture capitalism in Indonesia: investing driven by sustainability and impact considerations.

SOCIAL INCLUSION AND SKILL DEVELOPMENT

Venture investing has increasingly focused on social issues, especially after the pandemic underscored economic inequities in marginalized communities. Indonesia, a developing country, reflects this trend. Research by the

International Labour Organization shows that greater gender diversity in the workplace enhances profitability, productivity, talent retention, and creativity.

However, in Indonesia, gender diversity in the workplace trails behind its neighboring countries. Presently, only 55.9% of women participate in the Indonesian workforce, with the majority employed in the informal sector, despite two-thirds of the female population being of working age. This is an improvement from past years, but it still falls short of the 67.7% regional average for Asia Pacific. The World Bank points to inadequate childcare as the main hindrance for working Indonesian women, leading to an economic loss in terms of potential earnings.

Microentrepreneurship and MSMEs present a viable solution, enabling women to balance childcare with work. The International Finance Corporation (IFC) suggests that women-owned SMEs in Indonesia offer a "golden opportunity" for financial institutions seeking to invest or lend. This rapidly growing sector, despite being underserved historically, shows promise and is approaching a potential market size of US$10 billion. As Indonesia transitions from an economy reliant on labor and consumption to one that is more focused on capital investment, there is significant potential for growth and development.

Angelique of KoinWorks said the company will begin incorporating the United Nations Sustainable Development Goal of Gender Equality into its annual impact reports. Currently, women lead 43% of its MSME borrowers, a significant rise from 19% in 2017.

The advent of agent banking and other agent networks, which serve as the backbone of Indonesia's O2O sector, has also benefited female microentrepreneurs and stay-at-home moms. Startups like RAENA and Segari predominantly employ female agents, empowering women and enhancing supply chain efficiency across the archipelago.

Segari takes a novel approach to local food delivery by utilizing agents to distribute goods, acquire customers, and provide last-mile delivery, fostering a robust connection with end-users. RAENA, on the other hand, serves home-based beauty product resellers, offering them business training, online support, and competitively priced products via a dropship and resell system that requires no initial capital.

CEO of RAENA, Sreejita Deb, noted that 20% of the platform's resellers have progressed from being microinfluencers to opening their own stores over the past year, recognizing the potential for offline transactions in second- and third-tier cities.[12]

In promoting gender equality, these agent networks also provide tech tools and soft skills training that help microentrepreneurs learn how to run their businesses better. These experiences teach them about time and inventory management and cost-efficiency. This knowledge provides them with a foundation for entrepreneurship and, in the long term, further job creation.

WHAT STORIES WILL INDONESIA'S STARTUPS TELL OVER THE NEXT DECADE?

While investor interest in revamping Indonesia's MSMEs is largely driven by ESG and climate change considerations, the entrepreneurs themselves are equally concerned with enhancing efficiency, boosting margins, and generating returns.

Successfully engaging this diverse and distributed MSME population hinges on balancing ESG values with profitability from the outset. Aruna champions ESG because of its commitment to curbing overfishing and encouraging sustainable fishing practices. However, it also obtains higher prices for its fish, leading to a doubling of fishermen's revenue.

The potential economic boon from digitizing MSMEs in Indonesia is merely one aspect of the nation's prospective growth. As mentioned in the previous chapter, the swift digital transformation brought about by the pandemic not only impacted MSMEs but also previously underinvested sectors such as healthtech, agritech, and edtech.

Let's take a closer look in the next chapter at what the future holds for these sectors, along with a few others gaining momentum, as inclusivity and sustainability increasingly become key priorities for investors, policymakers, and startups alike.

CHAPTER TEN

THE NEXT 10 YEARS: INDONESIA'S DIGITAL DECADE

When early internet entrepreneurs laid the foundation for digital commerce in Indonesia, they were drawn by the nation's youthful, swelling population and rising disposable income levels. Intriguingly, the same qualities were used by the Samwer brothers to convince their European backers to venture into the archipelago.

We've witnessed the infancy and progression of Indonesia's e-commerce sector, the sudden surge of foreign capital, and the consequential development of infrastructure to support the economy's digitization. We've observed that it all led to the rise of Gojek, the nation's first homegrown unicorn and a brand around which the startup ecosystem quickly coalesced. The wave renewed investor interest in logistics and fintech startups, given their supportive roles in further propelling e-commerce growth.

As more investors, founders, and corporations became active players in Indonesia's digital growth story, massive funding rounds followed. By 2019, heavyweight US-listed tech companies and blue-chip multinationals began placing their bets on contenders in the Indonesian e-commerce race.[1]

The 2020 pandemic created a push for startups to adapt quickly to crisis. COVID-19 propelled the widespread adoption of digital services in Indonesia, far surpassing the most optimistic projections of 2019. This unexpected acceleration paved the way for investments in startups that cater to more than 64 million underserved MSMEs.

Fast forward four years, we can see clearly the impact that digital disruption has had on Indonesia with technology platforms such as Gojek and Tokopedia being an integral part of many people's lives. Despite this clear impact, many challenges still exist for businesses and investors: from dealing with valuation excesses of 2021's zero interest policies to continued monetization challenges and a subdued exit environment for investors.

The future trajectory of digitization in Indonesia will likely deviate from the past pattern of blitzscaling. Instead, the focus will shift toward financially sustainable startups that exhibit clear paths to profitability. This raises questions: Where will this next wave come from? With e-commerce, logistics, and fintech largely built out, where will VCs find value in Indonesia over the next 10 years?

There has never been a better time for global investors to seize one of the world's most significant remaining technology opportunities in emerging markets. Indonesia, with its burgeoning tech sector, is well positioned to provide substantial returns to venture capitalists and limited partners in the coming years.

Google, Bain, and Temasek predict that the country's digital economy will surge to around US$360 billion by 2030. The anticipated growth sectors include relatively untapped domains that gained prominence post-2020, such as agritech and healthtech, along with further sophistication in sectors like finance, AI, and IoT (Internet of Things) tech.

The government's current digital roadmap shows its commitment to expedite the nation's tech evolution. It underscores a recognition that without a sweeping embrace of digital transformation and support for a more robust local talent pipeline, further innovation in highly regulated sectors like healthcare and financial services would remain a pipe dream.[2]

FROM FINANCIAL INCLUSION TO WEALTH TECHNOLOGY

During the pandemic, e-commerce enablers and fintech startups made great strides by aiding MSMEs in digitizing their operations and providing crucial credit support. Traditional banks have, for decades, largely overlooked MSMEs due to factors like size, location, risk profiles, and others. However, as we've shown, innovative digital lenders figured out how to cater to the specific needs of Indonesia's MSMEs.

This trend held firm in recent years, with digital financial services attracting most of the investor funding in Indonesia. As we look ahead, fintech is anticipated to continue serving as the foundation of newly digitized sectors. With this in mind, we expect enhanced growth from more complex financial services such as wealth management.

While the payments vertical is predicted to grow at a CAGR of 17% to US$421 billion in 2025, the less established investment vertical of wealthtech is expected to witness an astounding 74% CAGR to US$10 billion in assets under management in 2025—five times the US$2 billion recorded in 2022.

As Indonesians become more comfortable with fintech, they are likely to explore more advanced financial services such as insurance, projected to increase by 51% in 2025. Similarly, lending books are expected to surge by 51% to US$16 billion by 2025.

Going forward, fintech will need to expand its current scope beyond simply providing loans, savings, and payments solutions for the underbanked in Indonesia. It will need to show that it can deliver additional economic empowerment through sophisticated financial instruments like stock market investments, credit score building, improved mortgage accessibility, and embedded finance.

While companies like Gojek, Tokopedia, and Bukalapak have experimented with offering gold investments, unit trusts, and working capital loans, the future of finance sits in specialized fintech companies with grander visions.

A prime example of a startup empowering locals to take control of their financial future is Stockbit, with its robo-advisory app Bibit launched in 2019.[3] While more than 50% of adults in the United States are stock investors in one way or another, Indonesia's stock market investment penetration is barely at 5%.

Meanwhile, platforms such as Reku have welcomed both new and experienced crypto traders, and wealth management app PINA caters to sophisticated middle-class investors with a suite of comprehensive wealthtech features.[4]

EXPANDING ACCESS TO CAPITAL

Fintech and e-commerce platforms are already collaborating to use data accumulated from people's online transactions. This effort aims to develop a credit history and borrower profile for millions of underbanked Indonesian consumers and MSME owners.

New local fintech startup Skor Technologies, the parent company of SkorLife and Skorcard, takes this a step further. It gives individuals control over their credit data and guidance on how to improve their credit scores.[5]

Meanwhile, affordable housing remains a significant issue for many underbanked Indonesians, particularly those working in informal sectors. As is common in rapidly developing middle-income nations with youthful demographics, the demand for housing in Indonesia is growing.

Multiple startups are streamlining the process by allowing users to compare and apply for mortgage products from multiple banks simultaneously. Indonesia's mortgage industry was valued at US$39 billion in 2021, with an estimated CAGR of 17% through 2026. With that in mind, the nation's mortgage penetration rate is still a mere 3% of GDP, one of the lowest in Southeast Asia. There is clearly a robust opportunity for disruption.

TECH TO SUPPORT A GROWING AND DISPERSED POPULATION

While still nascent, Indonesia's digital health sector demonstrated its potential for growth in 2020 when local healthtech startups swiftly responded to the demand for rapid COVID-19 testing, teleconsultations with doctors, and digital drug purchases. Opportunity remains afoot, as the country's healthcare sector continues to need an upgrade, with some of the lowest doctor-to-patient and hospital bed-to-patient ratios in Southeast Asia.

Further challenges include a scarcity of physicians, subpar service quality, a lack of regulation, and inconsistent tech adoption. That said, the latter two factors notably improved during and after the pandemic, with hospital administrators, doctors, and resource-limited regional governments embracing healthtech that can democratize care while keeping costs low.

Local healthtech startups are already tailoring special services aimed at Indonesia's middle class, offering more than the basic services you get from government health programs. These include things like wellness and fitness apps, but also connecting doctors and health experts with people across the nation.

SwipeRx is the largest network of pharmacies in Southeast Asia, connecting more than 250,000 pharmacy professionals from more than 50,000 pharmacies.[6] The company pioneered a community-driven commerce model that unites the fragmented pharmacy landscape for customers on a single platform, enabling them to access all the information, education, and medicines they need.

Sirka, a digital personal health coaching platform, focuses on weight loss and lifestyle goals. With backing from Sequoia and Y Combinator, it offers subscription-based weight-loss counseling, with plans to supply long-term support medications and supplies for chronic diseases like diabetes.[7]

In Indonesia, one out of every three adults are obese, which is a lot higher than the world's average obesity rate of 13%. Over the last 20 years, the number of obese adults in Indonesia has doubled. Sirka makes it easier for everyone to talk to nutritionists and get personalized help. In this way, the team aims to mitigate health problems caused by obesity, which can also help reduce the money the country spends on healthcare.

CATERING TO THE DIGITAL CONSUMER

In the pre-digital era, venturing into consumer goods and services often demanded significant capital investment, encompassing the establishment of brick-and-mortar stores and promotional endeavors to draw foot traffic. Even with these efforts, there was no assurance of customer loyalty.

Today, however, brand owners are forging their own online communities and go directly to the customer with their products. Rosé All Day Cosmetics (RADC), a local beauty brand tailored for women of all ages, stands as a good example.

The company crafts an array of skin care and treatment products, all proudly bearing certifications for clean beauty, veganism, and halal compliance. With a nimble digital-native approach, RADC saw a 4× revenue growth in 2022 and more than 6× growth in 2023. The company went to market in 2017 on a bootstrapped budget of US$10,000. Now, due to strong performance against incumbents, the profitable startup recently raised a US$5.41 million funding round led by Shunwei Capital subsidiary SWC Global.[8]

A similar approach was adopted by small home appliances brand Simplus. Some of its most popular items include its signature high-speed hair dryers, easy-to-use air fryers, high-quality vacuums, mops, and more. The startup, helmed by e-commerce veteran and former CEO of Lazada Thailand, Jack Zhang, has emerged as a top brand on TikTok, Shopee, and Lazada, tripling its sales in 2023, achieving profitability, and witnessing a record-breaking US$1 million in sales on a single day. Industry insiders are calling it the next "Philips of Southeast Asia."[9]

A GREENER, MORE SUSTAINABLE FUTURE

As detailed in the preceding chapter, companies such as Koltiva, a sustainable farming and supply chain traceability company, play an instrumental role. They are crucial in lifting farmers in emerging markets out of poverty.

As recently as February 2022, agriculture, forestry, and fishery sectors employed 40.6 million people, accounting for 15% of Indonesia's total population. A 2023 report by Boston Consulting Group discovered that agriculture contributes as much as 13% to Indonesia's GDP and 30% of national employment.

The rise of climate change and ESG investing, coupled with increased awareness of food security concerns, strongly supports investment in Indonesia's agritech companies. This is reflected in both the government's policies and VC activity. In recent years, total funding in the sector soared 2.5 times to US$375.9 million, up from US$147.8 million. The backers were the same big foreign entities that invested in e-commerce champions, including Singapore's Temasek, Sequoia Capital, and Japan's SoftBank.[10]

Because farmers in Indonesia frequently lack direct access to end-consumers due to layers of intermediaries, they also struggle to obtain financing at fair interest rates due to inconsistent income. The embrace of digital transformation can augment yields, increase the efficiency of resource utilization, and promote sustainability and resilience across the entire sector.

Agriculture supply chain traceability is already a multibillion-dollar industry that is also now primed to surge. As the EU's Deforestation-Free Products Regulation mandates businesses to prove nondeforestation in their products, more than 50,000 EU-based businesses (and by extension, companies that work closely with them) now require solutions like Koliva's.

With all the improvements in our lives, we naturally want to live on this planet for a long time. Unfortunately, humans have increased the amount of greenhouse gases in the atmosphere, causing changes in the climate that now threaten our future.

The key to addressing this is working together to reduce carbon emissions, cut down on waste, and switch to clean energy sources for making electricity. As the world's fourth largest greenhouse gas emitter, Indonesia is no exception to this.

Waste4Change is a startup that focuses on offering comprehensive, responsible waste management solutions. With local landfills nearing capacity, the company's strategy includes digital integration to enhance waste processing and recovery, aligning with the government's goal of reducing waste by 30% come 2025.[11]

Meanwhile, solar power startup Xurya is helping Indonesian businesses adopt solar energy. By offering a range of services, from feasibility studies to installation and maintenance, it allows building owners to reap the benefits of solar power without a substantial upfront cost.[12]

But we also need to mitigate pollution on the mobility frontier. Founded in 2021 by ride-hailing veterans Raditya Wibowo and Arief Fadillah, MAKA Motors seeks to accelerate the adoption of electric motorcycles in Indonesia.[13] The company's vision is to provide electric motorcycles that offer the perfect blend of driving range, power, usability, and durability at competitive pricing compared to current motorbikes in Indonesia, catering specifically to the needs of local riders.

Indonesia, with more than 127 million motorbikes, is the third-largest market in the world for two-wheeled vehicles. With 6 to 8 million new two-wheelers sold every year, there's a large opportunity to corner the budding market for electric motorbikes.

TOMORROW BELONGS TO TRADITIONAL COMPANIES THAT EMBRACE NEW TECH

There is no denying that at the time of writing, the market for early-stage venture investing in Southeast Asia has undergone a sweeping correction. Recent years (particularly during the pandemic) witnessed an exuberance in VC that quite simply outpaced the underlying fundamentals of emerging markets like Indonesia.

Companies and investors alike were captivated by the allure of building the next super app. However, as reality recalibrates our expectations, as well as valuations and deal volume in the region, it has become clear that the future in Indonesia will belong to enterprises that can adeptly utilize new technology to transform traditional businesses or give them a defensible competitive advantage.

AI is a key component of the new era we are currently entering in Indonesia. The synthesis of predictive and generative AI is poised to transform traditional business sectors in the country significantly.

In agriculture, for example, AI will enable smarter farming techniques, improving yield predictions and pest management. In the manufacturing sector, AI will automate processes, boost efficiency, and enhance quality control and cross-border sales, driving greater productivity across the board.

In the retail sector, AI is already revolutionizing customer service and inventory management, providing tailored shopping experiences, and optimizing supply chains.

This transition phase over the past 12 months has signaled a shift toward a more rational and mature approach in assessing the viability and scalability of local businesses, emphasizing a sustainable integration of digital tools into the core of enduring market sectors.

With the groundwork set, an ocean of economic promise visible on the horizon, and a digital economy set to enter a new transformative age, global financiers have a chance to play a key role in one of the world's biggest investment opportunities.

Through our mission of empowering entrepreneurs with experience, network, and capital, our vision is to be a generational partner for those building the most impactful and disruptive businesses in Indonesia and beyond.

As Indonesia rises to become a top global economy by 2030, investors in this market will be richly rewarded as technological empowerment permeates every industry in the country.

REFERENCES

CHAPTER 1

1. Statistics Indonesia. 28 June 2024. Available from: https://www.bps.go.id/en/statistics-table/2/MTk3NSMy/mid-year-population--thousand-people-.html [Last accessed on 11 November 2024].
2. Google e-Conomy SEA Report (2023). 1 November 2023. Available from: https://economysea.withgoogle.com/report/ [Last accessed on 11 November 2024].
3. Internet Masuk Indonesia dalam Sejarah Hari Ini, 7 Juni 1994. VOI. 7 June 2021. Available from: https://voi.id/memori/57165/internet-masuk-indonesia-dalam-sejarah-hari-ini-7-juni-1994 [Last accessed on 5 November 2024].
4. Wee W. The Story and Future of Kaskus. Tech in Asia. 20 April 2012. Available from: https://www.techinasia.com/story-future-kaskus [Last accessed on 5 November 2024].
5. Tan V. Coffee Chat: A Foreigner Building a Startup in Indonesia. Tech in Asia. 8 June 2012. Available from: https://www.techinasia.com/foreigner-building-startup-in-indonesia [Last accessed on 5 November 2024].
6. Siagian C. Tokobagus repositions itself on speed; shifts focus to C2C market. Yahoo! News. 17 December 2013. Available from: https://sg.news.yahoo.com/tokobagus-repositions-itself-speed-shifts-focus-c2c-market-090704668.html [Last accessed on 5 November 2024].

REFERENCES

7. Wee W. The Story and Future of Kaskus. Tech in Asia. 20 April 2012. Available from: https://www.techinasia.com/story-future-kaskus [Last accessed on 5 November 2024].
8. Wee W. The Story and Future of Kaskus. Tech in Asia. 20 April 2012. Available from: https://www.techinasia.com/story-future-kaskus [Last accessed on 5 November 2024].
9. Kevin J. Remco Lupker, Co-Founder of TokoBagus.com, On E-Commerce in Indonesia. Tech in Asia. 24 September 2011. Available from: https://www.techinasia.com/ecommerce-in-indonesia [Last accessed on 5 November 2024].
10. Adityarani R. Indonesia E-commerce Giant, Tokobagus Launches BlackBerry App. Tech in Asia. 28 May 2011. Available from: https://www.techinasia.com/indonesia-e-commerce-giant-tokobagus-launches-blackberry-app [Last accessed on 5 November 2024].
11. Lukman E. Indonesia's TokoBagus now has 1 billion monthly pageviews. Tech in Asia. 16 December 2013. Available from: https://www.techinasia.com/crazy-indonesias-tokobagus-1-billion-monthly-pageviews [Last accessed on 5 November 2024].
12. Siagian K. Arnold Egg Passionately Speaks about the Future in Digital Industry. DailySocial. 16 April 2021. Available from: https://dailysocial.id/post/arnold-egg-passionately-speaks-about-the-future-in-digital-industry [Last accessed on 5 November 2024].
13. From Tragedy to Techpreneur: William Tanuwijaya. Milestone Magazine. 15 December 2018. Available from: https://milestonemagazine.com/from-tragedy-to-techpreneur-william-tanuwijaya/ [Last accessed on 5 November 2024].
14. Wee W. The Story and Strategy behind Tokopedia. Tech in Asia. 11 February 2011. Available from: https://www.techinasia.com/tokopedia [Last accessed on 5 November 2024].
15. Tokopedia Receives Investment from East Ventures. Tokopedia. 25 March 2010. Available from: https://www.tokopedia.com/blog/press-release-tokopedia-receives-investment-from-east-ventures/ [Last accessed on 6 November 2024].
16. Afifa L. Tokopedia CEO William Tanuwijaya: Large Capital is Necessary. Tempo. 30 January 2019. Available from: https://en.tempo.co/read/1170531/tokopedia-ceo-william-tanuwijaya-large-capital-is-necessary [Last accessed on 5 November 2024].
17. Rakuten Enters Indonesia's E-Commerce Market by Forming a Joint Venture with Global Mediacom, Indonesia's Largest Media Company. Rakuten. 26 May 2010. Available from: https://global.rakuten.com/corp/news/press/2010/0526_01.html [Last accessed on 5 November 2024].

18. Whitney L. Yahoo buys mobile social network provider Koprol. CNET. 25 May 2010. Available from: https://www.cnet.com/tech/services-and-software/yahoo-buys-mobile-social-network-provider-koprol/ [Last accessed on 5 November 2024].
19. Afifa L. Tokopedia CEO William Tanuwijaya: Large Capital is Necessary. Tempo. 30 January 2019. Available from: https://en.tempo.co/read/1170531/tokopedia-ceo-william-tanuwijaya-large-capital-is-necessary [Last accessed on 5 November 2024].
20. 15 key facts about East Ventures. East Ventures. 5 February 2024. Available from: https://east.vc/news/insights/key-facts-east-ventures/ [Last accessed on 6 November 2024].
21. Wee W. The Story and Strategy behind Tokopedia. Tech in Asia. 11 February 2011. Available from: https://www.techinasia.com/tokopedia [Last accessed on 5 November 2024].
22. Wee W. Batavia Incubator Launches, Invests in Bukalapak.com. Tech in Asia. 15 July 2011. Available from: https://www.techinasia.com/batavia-incubator [Last accessed on 5 November 2024].
23. Lukman E. Indonesia's Bukalapak Gets 1 Million Daily Page-Views, Founder Launches Entrepreneurship Blog 'Netpreneur. Tech in Asia. 23 April 2013. Available from: https://www.techinasia.com/indonesias-bukalapak-1-million-daily-pageviews-founder-launches-entrepreneurship-blog-netpreneur [Last accessed on 5 November 2024].
24. Achmad Zaky on the genesis of Bukalapak, Indonesia's C2C marketplace. YourStory. 14 September 2013. Available from: https://yourstory.com/2013/09/bukalapak-indonesia-ecommerce-marketplace [Last accessed on 5 November 2024].
25. Cosseboom L. Rich benefactor supports Indonesian tech startups. Nikkei. 11 June 2016. Available from: https://asia.nikkei.com/Business/Rich-benefactor-supports-Indonesian-tech-startups [Last accessed on 5 November 2024].
26. Yosephine L. Blibli.com acquires Tiket.com, taps into online travel agency market. The Jakarta Post. 16 June 2017. Available from: https://www.thejakartapost.com/life/2017/06/16/blibli-com-acquires-tiket-com-taps-into-online-travel-agency-market.html [Last accessed on 6 November 2024].
27. Lee T. Indonesia's Tiket.com snags top prize of USD25K at international Tech-I competition. Tech in Asia. 28 December 2012. Available from: https://www.techinasia.com/indonesias-tiket-com-snags-top-prize-of-usd25k-at-international-tech-i-competition [Last accessed on 5 November 2024].

REFERENCES

28. Freischlad N. Running on less than $1m in funding, Tiket is Indonesia's bootstrap rockstar. Tech in Asia. 15 December 2015. Available from: https://www.techinasia.com/indonesia-travel-booking-tiket-2015 [Last accessed on 5 November 2024].
29. Anindita A. Ferry Unardi: Dropped Out of Harvard to Create Traveloka. Prestige Indonesia. 12 July 2018. Available from: https://www.prestigeonline.com/id/people-events/ferry-unardi-dropped-harvard-create-traveloka/ [Last accessed on 5 November 2024].
30. Ferry Unardi. Tatler Asia. 5 December 2021. Available from: https://www.tatlerasia.com/people/ferry-unardi [Last accessed on 5 November 2024].
31. Yuliani D. Global Founders Capital makes its first Asia investment in Indonesian travel startup Traveloka. Tech in Asia. 9 September 2013. Available from: https://www.techinasia.com/global-founders-capital-asia-investment-indonesian-travel-startup-traveloka [Last accessed on 5 November 2024].

CHAPTER 2

1. Cowan M. Inside the clone factory: the story of the Samwer brothers and Rocket Internet. Wired. 2 March 2012. Available from: https://www.wired.com/story/inside-the-clone-factory/ [Last accessed on 10 November 2024].
2. Crazy Frog trio back Facebook. This is Money. 17 January 2008. Available from: https://www.thisismoney.co.uk/money/markets/article-1619176/Crazy-Frog-trio-back-Facebook.html [Last accessed on 10 November 2024].
3. Cowan M. Inside the clone factory: the story of the Samwer brothers and Rocket Internet. Wired. 2 March 2012. Available from: https://www.wired.com/story/inside-the-clone-factory/ [Last accessed on 10 November 2024].
4. Arrington M. Groupon Invades Europe with Acquisition of Citydeal. TechCrunch. 16 May 2010. Available from: https://techcrunch.com/2010/05/16/groupon-invades-europe-with-acquisition-of-citydeal/ [Last accessed on 10 November 2024].
5. Cunningham S. Keeping Up With Rocket Internet's Southeast Asian Adventures. Forbes. 31 December 2013. Available from: https://www.forbes.com/sites/susancunningham/2013/12/31/rocket-internets-asian-adventures/ [Last accessed on 10 November 2024].
6. Butcher M. In confidential email Samwer describes online furniture strategy as a 'Blitzkrieg'. TechCrunch. 22 December 2011. Available from:

https://techcrunch.com/2011/12/22/in-confidential-email-samwer-describes-online-furniture-strategy-as-a-blitzkrieg/ [Last accessed on 10 November 2024].

7. Regina G. Groupon Enters Indonesia with Acquisition of East Ventures' Disdus. Tech in Asia. 6 April 2011. Available from: https://www.techinasia.com/groupon-enters-indonesia-with-acquisition-of-east-ventures-disdus [Last accessed on 10 November 2024].

8. Dutt A. An insider account of how Lazada changed the ecommerce game in Indonesia. Tech in Asia. 15 November 2018. Available from: https://www.techinasia.com/insider-view-lazadas-launch-indonesia [Last accessed on 10 November 2024].

9. Leong B. Rocket Internet: Is There a Method to Its Madness or Is It Just Bad for Innovation. TechCrunch. 16 September 2012. Available from: https://techcrunch.com/2012/09/16/rocket-internet-is-there-a-method-to-its-madness-or-is-it-just-bad-for-innovation/ [Last accessed on 10 November 2024].

10. Butcher M. In confidential email Samwer describes online furniture strategy as a 'Blitzkrieg'. TechCrunch. 22 December 2011. Available from: https://techcrunch.com/2011/12/22/in-confidential-email-samwer-describes-online-furniture-strategy-as-a-blitzkrieg/ [Last accessed on 10 November 2024].

11. Ohr T. Berlin-based Airbnb-clone Wimdu raises $90 million to expand further. EU-Startups. Available from: https://www.eu-startups.com/2011/06/wimdu-raises-90m-from-kinnevik-rocket-internet/ [Last accessed on 10 November 2024].

12. Horwitz J. Failure to launch: 5 Rocket Internet misfires. Tech in Asia. 7 November 2013. Available from: https://www.techinasia.com/failure-to-launch-5-rocket-internet-misfires [Last accessed on 10 November 2024].

13. Kevin J. Zalora Rockets to Indonesia and 6 Other Asian Countries. Tech in Asia. 20 March 2012. Available from: https://www.techinasia.com/zalora [Last accessed on 10 November 2024].

14. Kevin J. Rocket Internet's Amazon Clone, Lazada, Hits Indonesia. Tech in Asia. 26 March 2012. Available from: https://www.techinasia.com/lazada-indonesia-launch [Last accessed on 10 November 2024].

15. Wee W. Rocket Internet on Building Companies in Southeast Asia. Tech in Asia. 5 April 2013. Available from: https://www.techinasia.com/rocket-internet-building-companies-southeast-asia [Last accessed on 10 November 2024].

16. Lee T. Rocket Internet's Square clone PayLeven buys domain names in Asia; sets up company in S'pore. Tech in Asia. 15 June 2012. Available from: https://www.techinasia.com/rocket-internets-square-clone-payleven-buys-domain-names-in-southeast-asia-sets-up-company-in-singapore [Last accessed on 10 November 2024].

REFERENCES

17. Lukman E. Rocket Internet's PricePanda to launch in Thailand and open regional office in Southeast Asia. Tech in Asia. 6 November 2013. Available from: https://www.techinasia.com/pricepanda-launch-thailand-regional-office [Last accessed on 10 November 2024].
18. Lukman E. Rocket Internet quietly rolls out e-commerce marketplace Lamido in Indonesia. Tech in Asia. 5 November 2013. Available from: https://www.techinasia.com/lamido-indonesia-marketplace [Last accessed on 10 November 2024].
19. Magdirila P. Rocket Internet drives its vehicle marketplace Carmudi into Indonesia and the Philippines. Tech in Asia. 24 January 2014. Available from: https://www.techinasia.com/rocket-internet-drives-vehicle-marketplace-carmudi-indonesia-philippines [Last accessed on 10 November 2024].
20. Hadi A. Lamudi buys OLX Indonesia's real estate business. Tech in Asia. 11 January 2022. Available from: https://www.techinasia.com/lamudi-indonesia-acquire-olx-group-real-estate-business [Last accessed on 10 November 2024].
21. England L. The insanely successful career of Rocket Internet cofounder Oliver Samwer. Business Insider. 21 August 2015. Available from: https://www.businessinsider.com/rocket-internet-oliver-samwer-2015-8 [Last accessed on 10 November 2024].
22. 2023 financial year: Gothaer outperforms the market in terms of growth. Gothaer Group. 19 April 2024. Available from: https://www.gothaer.de/ueber-uns/investors/corporate-news.htm [Last accessed on 10 November 2024].
23. Bowker J. Samwer brothers buy stake in Facebook. Reuters. 16 January 2008. Available from: https://www.reuters.com/article/facebook-samwer-idUSL1562367720080115/ [Last accessed on 10 November 2024].
24. Vasagar J. Rocket Internet makes case for €3.3bn valuation. Financial Times. 10 August 2014. Available from: https://www.ft.com/content/df748b5e-0919-11e4-8d27-00144feab7de [Last accessed on 10 November 2024].
25. Wauters R. Holtzbrinck Ventures exchanges its stakes in 7 Rocket Internet startups for a direct 2.5% stake in the incubator itself. Tech EU. 22 August 2014. Available from: https://tech.eu/2014/08/22/holtzbrinck-ventures-rocket-internet/ [Last accessed on 10 NovemPber 2024].
26. Schuetze A. Rocket Internet shares slide on stock market debut. Reuters. 2 October 2014. Available from: https://www.reuters.com/article/business/rocket-internet-shares-slide-on-stock-market-debut-idUSKCN0HR0KC/ [Last accessed on 10 November 2024].

27. Shanley M. Stenbeck transforms Swedish family firm into major online investor. Reuters. 22 June 2014. Available from: https://www.reuters.com/article/uk-kinnevik-insight-idUKKBN0EX0GU20140622/ [Last accessed on 10 November 2024].
28. Lunden I. Rocket Internet Raises $500M From Kinnevik And Access, Plans More E-Commerce In Emerging Markets. TechCrunch. 16 July 2013. Available from: https://techcrunch.com/2013/07/16/rocket-internet-raises-500m-from-kinnevik-and-access-plans-more-e-commerce-in-emerging-markets/ [Last accessed on 10 November 2024].
29. Lunden I. Access Industries Leads $112M Round In Rocket Internet Asia-Pacific Fashion Sites Zalora And The Iconic. TechCrunch. 3 December 2013. Available from: https://techcrunch.com/2013/12/03/access-industries-leads-112m-funding-into-rocket-internets-asia-pacific-fashion-sites-zalora-and-the-iconic/ [Last accessed on 10 November 2024].
30. Gould J. United Internet buys stake in Rocket Internet. Reuters. 16 August 2014. Available from: https://www.reuters.com/article/us-united-internet-rocket-internet/united-internet-buys-stake-in-rocket-internet-idUSKBN0GF1XF20140815/ [Last accessed on 10 November 2024].
31. Shu C. PLDT Invests $445M In Rocket Internet to Develop Online Payment Services for Emerging Markets. TechCrunch. 7 August 2014. Available from: https://techcrunch.com/2014/08/07/rocket-pldt/ [Last accessed on 10 November 2024].
32. Lee T. Rocket Internet in Asia: a primer. Tech in Asia. 10 January 2013. Available from: https://www.techinasia.com/rocket-internet-in-asia [Last accessed on 10 November 2024].
33. Dutt A. An insider account of how Lazada changed the ecommerce game in Indonesia. Tech in Asia. 15 November 2018. Available from: https://www.techinasia.com/insider-view-lazadas-launch-indonesia [Last accessed on 10 November 2024].
34. Leong B. Rocket Internet: Is There A Method To Its Madness Or Is It Just Bad For Innovation. TechCrunch. 16 September 2012. Available from: https://techcrunch.com/2012/09/16/rocket-internet-is-there-a-method-to-its-madness-or-is-it-just-bad-for-innovation/ [Last accessed on 10 November 2024].
35. How Lazada Outranked the Rest. Think with Google. 2 July 2015. Available from: https://www.thinkwithgoogle.com/intl/en-apac/marketing-strategies/app-and-mobile/how-lazada-outranked-the-rest/ [Last accessed on 10 November 2024].

REFERENCES

36. Lukman E. Zalora Indonesia Reaches 150,000 Daily Visits Thanks to TV Ad Spot. Tech in Asia. 29 November 2012. Available from: https://www.techinasia.com/zalora-tv-ads-christmas [Last accessed on 10 November 2024].
37. Lukman E. eBay quietly arrives in Indonesia under the name Blanja. Tech in Asia. 11 November 2013. Available from: https://www.techinasia.com/ebay-quietly-arrives-indonesia-blanjacom [Last accessed on 10 November 2024].
38. Lukman E. Elevenia, a joint venture marketplace between XL Axiata and SK Planet opens in Indonesia. Tech in Asia. 13 November 2013. Available from: https://www.techinasia.com/elevenia-joint-venture-marketplace-xl-axiata-sk-planet-opens-indonesia [Last accessed on 10 November 2024].
39. Schwär H. Employees become founders Rocket Internet is the most successful "startup mafia." Get to Text. 12 December 2021. Available from: https://gettotext.com/employees-become-founders-rocket-internet-is-the-most-successful-startup-mafia/ [Last accessed on 10 November 2024].
40. Singh M. Gojek founder and CEO Nadiem Makarim resigns to join Indonesian cabinet; Soelistyo and Aluwi to be new co-CEOs. TechCrunch. 20 October 2019. Available from: https://techcrunch.com/2019/10/20/gojek-founder-and-ceo-nadiem-makarim-resigns-to-join-indonesian-cabinet-soelistyo-and-aluwi-to-be-new-co-ceos/ [Last accessed on 10 November 2024].
41. Cosseboom L. aCommerce CEO Hadi Wenas leaves to join John Riady and MatahariMall. Tech in Asia. 9 April 2015. Available from: https://www.techinasia.com/indonesia-ecommerce-acommerce-hadi-wenas-mataharimall [Last accessed on 10 November 2024].
42. Hadi A. Hadi Kuncoro Mundur dari aCommerce dan Bergabung dengan Komite Peta Jalan E-Commerce. Tech in Asia. 6 September 2017. Available from: https://id.techinasia.com/ceo-acommerce-indonesia-mengundurkan-diri [Last accessed on 10 November 2024].
43. Landmark merger in first PRC education online M&A deal. Asian Legal Business. 10 November 2010. Available from: https://china.legalbusinessonline.com/news/landmark-merger-first-prc-education-online-ma-deal/59281 [Last accessed on 10 November 2024].
44. Punia K. Stanford alumnus co-founds Qraved to satiate Indonesia's food cravings. YourStory. 9 January 2014. Available from: https://yourstory.com/2014/01/qraved-indonesia-stanford [Last accessed on 10 November 2024].
45. Muskita P. How Indonesia's healthtech startups aim to democratize access to healthcare. Tech in Asia. 4 February 2020. Available from: https://www.techinasia.com/indonesias-healthtech-startups-aim-democratize-access-healthcare [Last accessed on 10 November 2024].

46. Wirdana A. Tencent, Jeff Bezos back $87m round of Indonesian B2B ecommerce startup Ula. Tech in Asia. 4 October 2021. Available from: https://www.techinasia.com/tencent-prosus-ventures-87m-indonesian-b2b-ecommerce-startup-ula [Last accessed on 10 November 2024].
47. Lukman E. 5 reasons why Rocket Internet graduates make good entrepreneurs. Tech in Asia. 4 October 2013. Available from: https://www.techinasia.com/5-reasons-rocket-internet-graduates-good-entrepreneurs [Last accessed on 10 November 2024].
48. Lukman E. Rocket Internet Shuts OfficeFab in Southeast Asia, Shifts Focus to India's OfficeYes. Tech in Asia. 1 July 2013. Available from: https://www.techinasia.com/officefab-shuts-officeyes [Last accessed on 10 November 2024].
49. Russell J. Foodpanda is selling its Indonesia business and rethinking the rest of Southeast Asia. TechCrunch. 19 August 2016. Available from: https://techcrunch.com/2016/08/19/foodpanda-is-selling-its-indonesia-business-and-rethinking-the-rest-of-southeast-asia/ [Last accessed on 10 November 2024].
50. Koswaraputra D. Indonesia's foodpanda closes down after being defeated by newcomers. The Jakarta Post. 3 October 2016. Available from: https://www.thejakartapost.com/news/2016/10/03/indonesias-foodpanda-closes-down-after-being-defeated-by-newcomers.html [Last accessed on 10 November 2024].
51. Husain O. Rocket Internet sells Foodpanda. Tech in Asia. 10 December 2016. Available from: https://www.techinasia.com/rocket-internet-sells-foodpanda [Last accessed on 10 November 2024].
52. Lunden I. Wimdu, Rocket Internet's Airbnb clone, to shut down this year 'facing significant business challenges'. TechCrunch. 27 September 2018. Available from: https://techcrunch.com/2018/09/27/wimdu-rocket-internets-airbnb-clone-to-shut-down-this-year-facing-significant-business-challenges/ [Last accessed on 10 November 2024].
53. Cunningham S. Rocket Internet - First Mover In Indonesia? Forbes. 30 August 2015. Available from: https://www.forbes.com/sites/susancunningham/2014/10/23/rocket-internet-first-mover-in-indonesia/ [Last accessed on 10 November 2024].
54. Rosendar Y. Alibaba Invests $378.5 Million Into Its Southeast Asia Arm Lazada. Forbes. 10 May 2022. Available from: https://www.forbes.com/sites/yessarrosendar/2022/05/09/alibaba-invests-3785-million-into-its-southeast-asia-arm-lazada/ [Last accessed on 10 November 2024].
55. Kokalitcheva K. Rocket Internet consolidates 5 of its retailers into a $3.5B global e-commerce giant. VentureBeat. 4 September 2014. Available from: https://venturebeat.com/entrepreneur/rocket-internet-consolidates-5-of-its-retailers-into-a-3-5b-global-e-commerce-giant/ [Last accessed on 10 November 2024].

REFERENCES

56. Sri D. Rocket Internet-backed coffee startup bags $15m funding, to hire 2,000 employees. Tech in Asia. 7 April 2021. Available from: https://www.techinasia.com/rocket-internetbacked-flash-coffee-lands-15m-hire-2000-employees [Last accessed on 10 November 2024].

CHAPTER 3

1. e-Conomy SEA 2016. Google. 26 May 2016. Available from: https://www.thinkwithgoogle.com/intl/en-apac/future-of-marketing/digital-transformation/e-conomy-sea-unlocking-200b-digital-opportunity/ [Last accessed on 10 November 2024].
2. Shu C. Indonesian Marketplace Tokopedia Raises $100M From SoftBank and Sequoia. TechCrunch. 22 October 2014. Available from: https://techcrunch.com/2014/10/22/indonesian-marketplace-tokopedia-raises-100m-from-softbank-and-sequoia/ [Last accessed on 10 November 2024].
3. Wee W. Indonesian marketplace Tokopedia raises $147m. Tech in Asia. 8 April 2016. Available from: https://www.techinasia.com/indonesia-tokopedia-raises-147m [Last accessed on 10 November 2024].
4. Priatna K. The One who Developed Tokopedia Android App for the First Time. Tokopedia. 10 January 2020. Available from: https://medium.com/life-at-tokopedia/the-one-who-developed-tokopedia-android-app-for-the-first-time-f6d36d3e0726 [Last accessed on 10 November 2024].
5. Gojek and Tokopedia combine to form GoTo, the largest technology group in Indonesia and the "go to" ecosystem for daily life. Gojek. 24 February 2024. Available from: https://www.gojek.com/blog/gojek/goto [Last accessed on 10 November 2024].
6. Yusra Y. Tokopedia Rambah Layanan Fintech Tahun Ini. DailySocial. 9 January 2017. Available from: https://dailysocial.id/post/tokopedia-fintech [Last accessed on 10 November 2024].
7. Maulia E. Indonesia's top e-tailer switches to Lippo-backed payment app. Nikkei. 31 October 2018. Available from: https://asia.nikkei.com/Business/Companies/Indonesia-s-top-e-tailer-switches-to-Lippo-backed-payment-app [Last accessed on 10 November 2024].
8. Russell J. Alibaba leads $1.1B investment in Indonesia-based e-commerce firm Tokopedia. TechCrunch. 17 August 2017. Available from: https://techcrunch.com/2017/08/17/alibaba-tokopedia/ [Last accessed on 10 November 2024].

9. Balea J. Alibaba seeks to conquer Southeast Asia, takes $1b stake in Rocket Internet's Lazada. Tech in Asia. 12 April 2016. Available from: https://www.techinasia.com/alibaba-buys-controlling-stake-lazada [Last accessed on 10 November 2024].
10. Muskita P. Tokopedia raises $1.1b from SoftBank, Alibaba to evolve into infrastructure-as-a-service. Tech in Asia. 12 December 2018. Available from: https://www.techinasia.com/tokopedia-raises-11b-softbank-alibaba [Last accessed on 10 November 2024].
11. Mulia K. Indonesian Tokopedia launches service to bridge online and offline retailing. KrAsia. 16 November 2018. Available from: https://kr-asia.com/indonesian-tokopedia-launches-service-to-bridge-online-and-offline-retailing [Last accessed on 11 November 2024].
12. Mulia K. Tokopedia projects to contribute USD 12 billion to the Indonesian economy this year. KrAsia. 11 October 2019. Available from: https://kr-asia.com/tokopedia-projects-to-contribute-usd-12-billion-to-the-indonesian-economy-this-year [Last accessed on 11 November 2024].
13. Cosseboom L. Indonesian marketplace BukaLapak receives series B funding from local media group Emtek. Tech in Asia. 4 February 2015. Available from: https://www.techinasia.com/indonesia-emtek-bukalapak-funding-news [Last accessed on 11 November 2024].
14. Gani H. How Mitra Bukalapak Helped Indonesia's Warung Move to a 21st Century Business Model. Bukalapak. 17 March 2022. Available from: https://medium.com/inside-bukalapak/how-mitra-bukalapak-helped-indonesias-warung-move-to-a-21st-century-business-model-6a993302446d [Last accessed on 11 November 2024].
15. Nabila M. Bukalapak Aims to Dominate E-Procurement Market through BukaPengadaan. DailySocial. 5 February 2020. Available from: https://dailysocial.id/post/bukalapak-aims-to-dominate-e-procurement-market-through-bukapengadaan [Last accessed on 11 November 2024].
16. Mulia K. Bukalapak launches new fintech subsidiary Buka Investasi Bersama. KrAsia. 5 October 2020. Available from: https://kr-asia.com/bukalapak-launches-new-fintech-subsidiary-buka-investasi-bersama [Last accessed on 11 November 2024].
17. Tang W. Bukalapak launches sharia mutual fund product. The Jakarta Post. 11 April 2017. Available from: https://www.thejakartapost.com/news/2017/04/11/bukalapak-launches-sharia-mutual-fund-product.html [Last accessed on 11 November 2024].

REFERENCES

18. Maulani A. Bukalapak to launch gold transaction feature on its platform, expanding fintech vertical. E27. 1 June 2017. Available from: https://e27.co/bukalapak-to-launch-gold-transaction-feature-on-its-platform-20170601/ [Last accessed on 11 November 2024].
19. Nabila M. Bukalapak Team Up with BRI to Extend Banking Facility. DailySocial. 7 December 2017. Available from: https://dailysocial.id/post/bukalapak-team-up-with-bri-to-extend-banking-facility [Last accessed on 11 November 2024].
20. Ellis J. Bukalapak launches digital wallet. Tech in Asia. 27 September 2018. Available from: https://www.techinasia.com/brief-bukalapak-digital-wallet-bukadana [Last accessed on 11 November 2024].
21. Maulani A. Indonesian e-commerce startup Bukalapak raises funding, claims to be a unicorn. E27. 17 November 2017. Available from: https://e27.co/indonesian-e-commerce-startup-bukalapak-raises-funding-claims-unicorn-20171117/ [Last accessed on 11 November 2024].
22. Wirdana A. Bukalapak acquihires second-hand goods marketplace Prelo. DealStreetAsia. 16 October 2018. Available from: https://www.dealstreetasia.com/stories/indonesia-bukalapak-prelo-108897 [Last accessed on 11 November 2024].
23. Marzuki Y. Indonesia's Bukalapak turns eight. Digital News Asia. 15 January 2018. Available from: https://www.digitalnewsasia.com/startups/indonesias-bukalapak-turns-eight [Last accessed on 11 November 2024].
24. Arief I. From 100 to 1100 Tech Talents: How Bukalapak Became the Largest Product Development Company in Indonesia. LinkedIn. 28 January 2019. Available from: https://www.linkedin.com/pulse/from-100-1100-tech-talents-how-bukalapak-became-largest-ibrahim-arief/ [Last accessed on 11 November 2024].
25. Freischlad N. How Indonesia's richest families run the ecommerce industry. Tech in Asia. 9 March 2016. Available from: https://www.techinasia.com/indonesias-richest-families-run-indonesias-ecommerce-industry [Last accessed on 11 November 2024].
26. Sutrisno G. How Indonesia's Blibli stood up to giants via a niche strategy. Tech in Asia. 21 October 2021. Available from: https://www.techinasia.com/indonesia-blibli-giants-niche [Last accessed on 11 November 2024].
27. HaloDoc Raises $13m Series A. HaloDoc. 9 September 2016. Available from: https://www.halodoc.com/media/indonesia-halodoc-raises-13m-series-a [Last accessed on 11 November 2024].
28. Ellis J. Blibli makes another online travel agent play with Indonesia Flight acquisition. Tech in Asia. 28 November 2017. Available from: https://www.techinasia.com/blibli-buys-indonesia-flight [Last accessed on 11 November 2024].

29. Putra J. BliBli: A New Player in Indonesian E-Commerce. Tech in Asia. 10 May 2011. Available from: https://www.techinasia.com/indonesian-ecommerce-blibli [Last accessed on 11 November 2024].
30. Nabila M. BCA Introduces "OneKlik," New Payment Solution for E-Commerce. DailySocial. 6 February 2018. Available from: https://dailysocial.id/post/bca-introduces-oneklik-new-payment-solution-for-e-commerce [Last accessed on 11 November 2024].
31. Prakoso J. Blibli.com Tempatkan Kiosk Blibli Instore di Kantor Pos Indonesia. Bisnis.com. 1 February 2018. Available from: https://ekonomi.bisnis.com/read/20180201/98/733276/blibli.com-tempatkan-kiosk-blibli-instore-di-kantor-pos-indonesia [Last accessed on 11 November 2024].
32. Nabila M. Blibli Partners with Pos Indonesia, Targeting Consumers in Rural Areas. DailySocial. 5 February 2018. Available from: https://en.dailysocial.id/post/blibli-partners-with-pos-indonesia-targeting-consumers-in-rural-areas [Last accessed on 11 November 2024].
33. Millward S. Shoppers on Lazada last year spent $350 million as ecommerce booms in Southeast Asia. Tech in Asia. 20 March 2015. Available from: https://www.techinasia.com/shoppers-lazada-spent-350-million-2014-ecommerce-booms-southeast-asia [Last accessed on 11 November 2024].
34. Nguyen J. Lazada at 10: Milestones, Innovations and Key Achievements. Lazada. 16 March 2022. Available from: https://www.lazbeat.net/business/lazada-at-10-milestones-innovations-and-key-achievements/ [Last accessed on 11 November 2024].
35. Shu C. PLDT Invests $445M In Rocket Internet To Develop Online Payment Services For Emerging Markets. TechCrunch. 7 August 2014. Available from: https://techcrunch.com/2014/08/07/rocket-pldt/ [Last accessed on 11 November 2024].
36. Freischlad N. How Indonesia's richest families run the ecommerce industry. Tech in Asia. 9 March 2016. Available from: https://www.techinasia.com/indonesias-richest-families-run-indonesias-ecommerce-industry [Last accessed on 11 November 2024].
37. Russell J. Lazada, Rocket Internet's Amazon Clone In Southeast Asia, Raises $250M Led By Temasek. TechCrunch. 29 November 2014. Available from: https://techcrunch.com/2014/11/29/lazada-rocket-internets-amazon-clone-in-southeast-asia-raises-250m-led-by-temasek/ [Last accessed on 11 November 2024].
38. Russell J. Spiralling losses show Lazada desperately needed Alibaba investment. TechCrunch. 14 April 2016. Available from: https://techcrunch.com/2016/04/14/spiralling-losses-show-lazada-desperately-needed-alibaba-investment/ [Last accessed on 11 November 2024].

39. Russell J. Alibaba ups its stake in Southeast Asia's Lazada with $1 billion investment. TechCrunch. 28 June 2017. Available from: https://techcrunch.com/2017/06/28/alibaba-ups-its-stake-in-southeast-asias-lazada-with-1-billion-investment/ [Last accessed on 11 November 2024].
40. Lazada launches regional trade with DFTZ. Digital News Asia. 20 April 2018. Available from: https://www.digitalnewsasia.com/digital-economy/lazada-launches-regional-trade-dftz [Last accessed on 11 November 2024].
41. Lazada officially launches LazMall and 9.9 sales event. RetailAsia. 6 September 2018. Available from: https://retailasia.com/stores/more-news/lazada-officially-launches-lazmall-and-99-sales-event [Last accessed on 11 November 2024].
42. Karimuddin A. Matahari Mall Appointed Credit Suisse and Bank of America Merrill Lynch to Spearhead Their Fundraising Campaign. Daily Social. 21 April 2015. Available from: https://dailysocial.id/post/mataharimall-appointed-credit-suisse-and-bank-of-america-merrill-lynch-to-spearhead-their-fundraising-campaign [Last accessed on 11 November 2024].
43. Matahari Mall banks on localization to lure shoppers. The Jakarta Post. 29 June 2016. Available from: https://www.thejakartapost.com/news/2016/06/29/matahari-mall-banks-localization-lure-shoppers.html [Last accessed on 11 November 2024].
44. Freischlad N. Indonesian Matahari Mall pivoting from everything-store to focus on fashion e-tailing. KrAsia. 21 November 2018. Available from: https://kr-asia.com/indonesian-matahari-mall-pivoting-from-everything-store-vision-to-focus-on-fashion-e-tailing [Last accessed on 11 November 2024].
45. Nugrahani N. C2C marketplace Shopee officially launches in Indonesia. The Jakarta Post. 1 December 2015. Available from: https://www.thejakartapost.com/news/2015/12/01/c2c-marketplace-shopee-officially-launches-indonesia.html [Last accessed on 11 November 2024].
46. Peh C. Khazanah leads new US$170 million round of investment in Garena. The Edge Malaysia. 31 March 2016. Available from: https://theedgemalaysia.com/article/khazanah-leads-new-us170-million-round-investment-garena [Last accessed on 11 November 2024].
47. Chia J. A Look At Shopee's Key Milestones As It Rose To Become SEA's Top E-Commerce Player. Vulcan Post. 17 March 2021. Available from: https://vulcanpost.com/737433/shopee-key-milestones-singapore/ [Last accessed on 11 November 2024].
48. Syarizka D. Kekuatan K-Pop: Dongkrak Traffic hingga Eksposur Global buat E-commerce Lokal. Tech in Asia. 26 February 2021. Available from: https://

References

id.techinasia.com/k-pop-dongkrak-traffic-eksposur-globale-commerce [Last accessed on 11 November 2024].

49. Sea Limited Reports Fourth Quarter and Full Year 2018 Results. Sea Limited. 26 February 2019. Available from: https://www.businesswire.com/news/home/20190226006240/en/Sea-Limited-Reports-Fourth-Quarter-and-Full-Year-2018-Results [Last accessed on 11 November 2024].
50. Inilah Road Map E-Commerce Indonesia 2017–2019. The Communications and Informatics Ministry. 11 August 2017. Available from: https://www.komdigi.go.id/berita/berita-pemerintahan/detail/inilah-road-map-e-commerce-indonesia-2017-2019 [Last accessed on 11 November 2024].
51. OJK Issues Umbrella Regulation for Fintech Development, Establishes Regulatory Sandbox Regime. ABNR Counsellors at Law. 20 September 2018. Available from: https://www.abnrlaw.com/news/ojk-issues-umbrella-regulation-for-fintech-development-establishes-regulatory-sandbox-regime [Last accessed on 11 November 2024].

CHAPTER 4

1. DOKU di 2023: Lebih dari Sekadar Angka, Ini Kisah Keberhasilan Nyata. Doku. 24 November 2023. Available from: https://www.doku.com/blog/doku-di-2023-lebih-dari-sekadar-angka-ini-kisah-keberhasilan-nyata/ [Last accessed on 11 November 2024].
2. Cosseboom L. Nabilah Alsagoff and the story behind Doku, Indonesia's epayments pioneer. Tech in Asia. 23 July 2014. Available from: https://www.techinasia.com/nabilah-alsagoff-doku-payment-gateway-founder-story-indonesia [Last accessed on 11 November 2024].
3. Masna A. Doku Launches MyShortCart, a Shopping Cart for Social Media Merchants. DailySocial. 5 July 2013. Available from: https://dailysocial.id/post/doku-launches-myshortcart-a-shopping-cart-for-social-media-merchants [Last accessed on 11 November 2024].
4. Perez S. PayPal Launches PayPal.Me, A Simpler Way To Request Money Using Your Own Personalized URL. TechCrunch. 1 September 2015. Available from: https://techcrunch.com/2015/09/01/paypal-launches-paypal-me-a-simpler-way-to-request-money-using-your-own-personalized-url/ [Last accessed on 11 November 2024].
5. Stripe launches Payment Links to enable online sales in minutes without any code. Stripe. 25 May 2021. Available from: https://stripe.com/

REFERENCES

en-my/newsroom/news/stripe-launches-payment-links [Last accessed on 11 November 2024].

6. PayPal enters partnership with Doku. The Paypers. 6 December 2012. Available from: https://thepaypers.com/online-payments/paypal-enters-partnership-with-doku--749446# [Last accessed on 11 November 2024].

7. Shu C. Alibaba's AliExpress Sets Its Sights On Indonesia's Promising E-Commerce Market. TechCrunch. 11 February 2015. Available from: https://techcrunch.com/2015/02/11/aliexpress-to-indonesia/ [Last accessed on 11 November 2024].

8. Mamuaya R. IPaymu Officially Launches, Announced Partnership with Paypal, Pos Indonesia, CIMB Niaga. DailySocial. 13 December 2012. Available from: https://dailysocial.id/post/ipaymu-officially-launches-announced-partnership-with-paypal-pos-indonesia-cimb-niaga [Last accessed on 11 November 2024].

9. Nabila M. iPaymu Luncurkan Bayar Disini. DailySocial. 20 September 2016. Available from: https://dailysocial.id/post/ipaymu-luncurkan-bayar-disini [Last accessed on 11 November 2024].

10. Kevin J. Veritrans Indonesia Officially Launches, Aspires to be the Nation's Payment System. Tech in Asia. 3 October 2012. Available from: https://www.techinasia.com/veritrans-indonesia-launch [Last accessed on 11 November 2024].

11. Wee W. Rakuten Remains Committed to Indonesia with Payment Gateway Upgrade and Global Marketplace Launch. Tech in Asia. 29 May 2013. Available from: https://www.techinasia.com/rakuten-belanja-online-veritrans [Last accessed on 11 November 2024].

12. Veritrans is now Midtrans. Midtrans. 20 October 2016. Available from: https://midtrans.com/id/blog/veritrans-is-now-midtrans [Last accessed on 11 November 2024].

13. Lynley M. P2P Payments App Xendit Launches In Indonesia. TechCrunch. 17 August 2015. Available from: https://techcrunch.com/2015/08/17/p2p-payments-app-xendit-launches-in-indonesia/ [Last accessed on 11 November 2024].

14. Ohanian A. Xendit (YC S15) Is Bringing Peer-To-Peer Mobile Money Transfers To Indonesia. Y Combinator. 18 August 2015. Available from: https://www.ycombinator.com/blog/xendit-yc-s15-is-bringing-peer-to-peer-mobile-money-transfers-to-indonesia [Last accessed on 11 November 2024].

15. Lo M. Two Cofounders of Xendit on Pioneering Fintech in Southeast Asia. Harvard Business Review. 1 July 2022. Available from: https://hbr.org/2022/07/

two-cofounders-of-xendit-on-pioneering-fintech-in-southeast-asia [Last accessed on 11 November 2024].
16. Suhartanto C. Profil Xendit, Unicorn Fintech yang Reorganisasi untuk Keberlanjutan Bisnis. Bisnis. 22 January 2024. Available from: https://teknologi.bisnis.com/read/20240122/266/1734410/profil-xendit-unicorn-fintech-yang-reorganisasi-untuk-keberlanjutan-bisnis [Last accessed on 11 November 2024].
17. Wen T. How Xendit rose quickly in Southeast Asia's crowded fintech space. Tech in Asia. 14 April 2021. Available from: https://www.techinasia.com/xendit-rose-quickly-southeast-asias-crowded-fintech-space [Last accessed on 11 November 2024].
18. Kunjana G. Persaingan Meningkat, Logistik Indonesia Tertinggi di Asean. Investor. 16 May 2017. Available from: https://investor.id/industry-trade/160196/persaingan-meningkat-logistik-indonesia-tertinggi-di-asean [Last accessed on 11 November 2024].
19. Cakti A. Pos Indonesia's assets can become e-commerce distribution centers. Antara. 12 September 2021. Available from: https://en.antaranews.com/news/188761/pos-indonesias-assets-can-become-e-commerce-distribution-centers [Last accessed on 11 November 2024].
20. Inilah Road Map E-Commerce Indonesia 2017–2019. The Communications and Informatics Ministry. 11 August 2017. Available from: https://www.komdigi.go.id/berita/berita-pemerintahan/detail/inilah-road-map-e-commerce-indonesia-2017-2019 [Last accessed on 11 November 2024].
21. Pos Indonesia eyes role as logistical backbone for e-commerce. The Jakarta Post. 11 November 2016. Available from: https://www.thejakartapost.com/news/2016/11/11/pos-indonesia-eyes-role-as-logistical-backbone-for-e-commerce--.html [Last accessed on 11 November 2024].
22. Maulani A. Anchanto announces partnership with Pos Logistik Indonesia. E27. 19 January 2016. Available from: https://e27.co/anchanto-announces-partnership-pos-logistik-indonesia-20160119/ [Last accessed 11 November 2024].
23. Maulani A. MatahariMall partners with Pos Indonesia on O2O services. E27. 8 December 2015. Available from: https://e27.co/mataharimall-partners-pos-indonesia-o2o-services-20151208/ [Last accessed on 11 November 2024].
24. Maulani A. Kioson launches a new partnership that enables kiosk owners to serve as postal service agents. E27. 13 February 2018. Available from: https://e27.co/kioson-new-partnership-allow-kiosk-owners-serve-postal-service-agents-20180213/ [Last accessed on 11 November 2024].

REFERENCES

25. Sudrajat A. Pos Indonesia jalin kerja sama dengan Bhinneka. Antara. 16 December 2021. Available from: https://www.antaranews.com/berita/2590457/pos-indonesia-jalin-kerja-sama-dengan-bhinneka [Last accessed on 11 November 2024].
26. Pendiri TIKI dan JNE, Sejarah, beserta Jenis Layanannya. Kumparan. 20 December 2022. Available from: https://kumparan.com/berita-bisnis/pendiri-tiki-dan-jne-sejarah-beserta-jenis-layanannya-1zTBV8Srxqb/full [Last accessed on 11 November 2024].
27. Freischlad N. Southeast Asia's ecommerce surge is a blessing for logistics. Tech in Asia. 10 April 2015. Available from: https://www.techinasia.com/rocket-execs-set-solve-southeast-asian-logistics-built-operational-backbone-ecommerce-empire [Last accessed on 11 November 2024].
28. JNE riding on wave of Indonesia's e-commerce boom. The Jakarta Post. 26 November 2015. Available from: https://www.thejakartapost.com/news/2015/11/26/jne-riding-wave-indonesia-s-e-commerce-boom.html [Last accessed on 11 November 2024].
29. Molasiarani K. JNE akan menjalin kerja sama dengan mitra baru untuk mendongkrak kinerja. Kontan. 11 February 2018. Available from: https://industri.kontan.co.id/news/jne-akan-menjalin-kerja-sama-dengan-mitra-baru-untuk-mendongkrak-kinerja [Last accessed on 11 November 2024].
30. Tang W. TIKI sees growth potential in e-commerce. The Jakarta Post. 9 June 2017. Available from: https://www.thejakartapost.com/news/2017/06/09/tiki-sees-growth-potential-e-commerce.html [Last accessed on 11 November 2024].
31. Sutrisno G. Former Lazada Logistics Indonesia CEO joins SiCepat. Tech in Asia. 21 June 2024. Available from: https://www.techinasia.com/exceo-lazada-logistics-indonesia-joins-sicepat [Last accessed on 11 November 2024].
32. Yu D. Indonesia's SiCepat raises $170m in series B round from Falcon House, others. Tech in Asia. 5 March 2021. Available from: https://www.techinasia.com/indonesia-logistics-startup-sicepat-closes-170-series [Last accessed on 11 November 2024].
33. Wang Y. Chinese Logistics Entrepreneur Becomes A Billionaire As His J&T Express Gears Up For Hong Kong IPO. Forbes. 20 June 2023. Available from: https://www.forbes.com/sites/ywang/2023/06/20/chinese-logistics-entrepreneur-becomes-a-billionaire-as-his-jt-express-gears-up-for-hong-kong-ipo/ [Last accessed on 11 November 2024].
34. Rosendar Y. J&T Express Raises $2 Billion In Latest Funding From Temasek, Other Investors Ahead of Hong Kong IPO. Forbes. 21 February 2022. Available

from: https://www.forbes.com/sites/yessarrosendar/2022/02/18/jt-express-raises-2-billion-in-latest-funding-from-temasek-other-investors-ahead-of-hong-kong-ipo/ [Last accessed on 11 November 2024].

35. Chiang S. Shares of Tencent-backed J&T Express fall in lackluster Hong Kong debut. CNBC. 27 October 2023. Available from: https://www.cnbc.com/2023/10/27/tencent-backed-jt-express-fell-in-hong-kong-ipo-debut.html [Last accessed on 11 November 2024].

36. Shu C. Shipper, a platform for e-commerce logistics in Indonesia, raises $5 million. TechCrunch. 18 September 2019. Available from: https://techcrunch.com/2019/09/18/shipper-a-platform-for-e-commerce-logistics-in-indonesia-raises-5-million/ [Last accessed on 11 November 2024].

37. Yu D. Logistics startup Shipper bags series A money to double down on Indonesia. Tech in Asia. 19 June 2020. Available from: https://www.techinasia.com/shipper-bags-series-money-double-down-indonesia [Last accessed on 11 November 2024].

38. Cordon M. Y Combinator-backed Shipper secures $63m in series B funding. Tech in Asia. 15 April 2021. Available from: https://www.techinasia.com/combinatorbacked-shipper-secures-63m-series-funding [Last accessed on 11 November 2024].

39. Lukman E. Here are 17 emoney options Indonesians can use for shopping, travel, and ecommerce. Tech in Asia. 25 June 2014. Available from: https://www.techinasia.com/17-emoney-options-indonesia [Last accessed on 11 November 2024].

40. International Migrants Day 2010: A stronger commitment for the protection of Indonesian migrant workers. International Labour Organization. 17 December 2010. Available from: https://www.ilo.org/resource/news/international-migrants-day-2010-stronger-commitment-protection-indonesian [Last accessed on 11 November 2024].

41. Major changes to electronic money regulation, including new foreign ownership limit and restriction of holding multiple licenses in two different categories. Walalangi & Partners. 11 June 2018. Available from: https://www.wplaws.com/major-changes-electronic-money-regulation-including-new-foreign-ownership-limit-restriction-holding-multiple-licenses-two-different-categories/ [Last accessed on 11 November 2024].

42. Retail Payments in Indonesia. KPMG. 24 January 2017. Available from: https://assets.kpmg.com/content/dam/kpmg/id/pdf/2017/01/id-retail-payments-in-indonesia.pdf [Last accessed on 11 November 2024].

REFERENCES

CHAPTER 5

1. Rondonuwu O. Jakarta traffic chaos peaks in Indonesia's mass exodus. Reuters. 7 September 2010. Available from: https://www.reuters.com/article/us-indonesia-exodus/jakarta-traffic-chaos-peaks-in-indonesias-mass-exodus-idUKTRE68612Q20100907/ [Last accessed on 12 November 2024].
2. Jumlah Kendaraan Bermotor Menurut Jenis Kendaraan (unit) di Provinsi DKI Jakarta. Statistics Indonesia. 17 October 2023. Available from: https://jakarta.bps.go.id/id/statistics-table/2/Nzg2IzI=/jumlah-kendaraan-bermotor-menurut-jenis-kendaraan-unit-di-provinsi-dki-jakarta.html [Last accessed on 12 November 2024].
3. How many cars are there in London and who owns them? Transport for London. July 2013. Available from: https://content.tfl.gov.uk/technical-note-12-how-many-cars-are-there-in-london.pdf [Last accessed on 12 November 2024].
4. Pramudya S. H. Online Transportation Price War: Indonesian Style. CORE. 3 December 2019. Available from: https://core.ac.uk/works/75542204/ [Last accessed on 12 November 2024].
5. Hutton J. The Taxi Wars of Jakarta. Harvard Business School. 1 September 2016. Available from: https://www.alumni.hbs.edu/stories/Pages/story-impact.aspx?num=5779 [Last accessed on 12 November 2024].
6. Cosseboom L. This guy turned Go-Jek from a zombie into Indonesia's hottest startup. Tech in Asia. 27 August 2015. Available from: https://www.techinasia.com/indonesia-go-jek-nadiem-makarim-profile [Last accessed on 12 November 2024].
7. Kevin J. Nadiem Makarim Talks About Zalora Indonesia and Go-jek. Tech in Asia. 1 May 2012. Available from: https://www.techinasia.com/nadiem-makarim-zalora [Last accessed on 12 November 2024].
8. Lukman E. Uber's first celebrity passengers chauffeured around Jakarta. Tech in Asia. 10 June 2014. Available from: https://www.techinasia.com/ubers-celebrity-passengers-chauffeured-jakarta [Last accessed on 12 November 2024].
9. Panji A. Aplikasi Pesan Taksi GrabTaxi Masuk Indonesia. Kompas. 7 June 2014. Available from: https://tekno.kompas.com/read/2014/06/07/1159117/Aplikasi.Pesan.Taksi.GrabTaxi.Masuk.Indonesia [Last accessed on 12 November 2024].
10. Lukman E. This smartphone app lets you call motorcycle taxis in Indonesia. Tech in Asia. 8 January 2015. Available from: https://www.techinasia.com/go-jek-uber-motorcycle-jakarta-apps [Last accessed on 12 November 2024].

11. GrabTaxi launches GrabBike for safer on-demand "Ojek" rides. Grab. 20 May 2015. Available from: https://www.grab.com/id/en/press/consumers-drivers/grabtaxi-launches-grabbike-for-safer-on-demand-ojek-rides/ [Last accessed on 12 November 2024].
12. Freischlad N. Uber brings motorbike service to Jakarta to compete with Go-Jek, Grab. Tech in Asia. 13 April 2016. Available from: https://www.techinasia.com/uber-launches-ubermotor-in-indonesia [Last accessed on 12 November 2024].
13. The Great Ojek Price War continues: Rp 15k flat for Go-Jek rides, Rp 5k flat for GrabBike. Coconuts. 11 August 2015. Available from: https://coconuts.co/jakarta/news/great-ojek-price-war-continues-rp-15k-flat-go-jek-rides-rp-5k-flat-grabbike/ [Last accessed on 12 November 2024].
14. Uber introduces uberMOTOR for Jakartans. The Jakarta Post. 13 April 2016. Available from: https://www.thejakartapost.com/news/2016/04/13/uber-introduces-ubermotor-for-jakartans.html [Last accessed on 12 November 2024].
15. Velayanikal M. Sequoia plays matchmaker: Go-Jek acquires 2 Indian startups for tech muscle. Tech in Asia. 19 February 2016. Available from: https://www.techinasia.com/sequoia-plays-matchmaker-go-jek-acquires-2-indian-start-ups [Last accessed on 12 November 2024].
16. Priambada A. Go-Jek Acquires Indian Healthcare Marketplace Pianta. DailySocial. 27 September 2016. Available from: https://en.dailysocial.id/post/go-jek-akuisisi-pianta [Last accessed on 12 November 2024].
17. Chathurvedula S. Indonesian bike-hailing app Go-Jek buys LeftShift Technologies. Mint. 8 November 2016. Available from: https://www.livemint.com/Companies/m5QBrhaa7NgiyVqef7uSnK/Indonesian-bikehailing-app-GoJek-buys-LeftShift-Technologi.html [Last accessed on 12 November 2024].
18. Cosseboom L. Confirmed: Sequoia Capital invested in Indonesia's Go-Jek. Tech in Asia. 15 October 2015. Available from: https://www.techinasia.com/indonesia-sequoia-go-jek [Last accessed on 12 November 2024].
19. Lee Y. Go-Jek Raises Over $550 Million in KKR, Warburg-Led Round. Bloomberg. 4 August 2016. Available from: https://www.bloomberg.com/news/articles/2016-08-04/go-jek-said-to-raise-over-550-million-in-kkr-warburg-led-round [Last accessed on 12 November 2024].
20. Russell J. SoftBank Invests $250M In GrabTaxi, Uber's Archrival In Southeast Asia. TechCrunch. 3 December 2014. Available from: https://techcrunch.com/2014/12/03/softbank-invests-250m-in-grabtaxi-ubers-archrival-in-southeast-asia/ [Last accessed on 12 November 2024].

REFERENCES

21. Lee T. Didi Kuaidi and China's sovereign wealth fund invests in GrabTaxi's $350M round. Tech in Asia. 19 August 2015. Available from: https://www.techinasia.com/grabtaxi-raises-400m-led-china-sovereign-wealth-fund [Last accessed on 12 November 2024].
22. Pham S. Uber quits 8 countries in Southeast Asia, selling out to rival Grab. CNN. 26 March 2018. Available from: https://money.cnn.com/2018/03/25/technology/uber-grab-deal-southeast-asia/index.html [Last accessed on 12 November 2024].
23. GO-JEK to Launch International Expansion Into Four New Markets. Gojek. 24 May 2018. Available from: https://www.gojek.com/blog/gojek/go-jek-to-launch-international-expansion-into-four-new-markets [Last accessed on 12 November 2024].
24. Balea J. Go-Jek buys 3 fintech firms to conquer Indonesia payments. Tech in Asia. 15 December 2017. Available from: https://www.techinasia.com/go-jek-acquisition-kartuku-mapan-midtrans [Last accessed on 12 November 2024].
25. Yu D. Gojek rolls out insurance service GoSure with PasarPolis. Tech in Asia. 5 February 2020. Available from: https://www.techinasia.com/gojek-launches-gosure [Last accessed on 12 November 2024].
26. Cordon M. Go-Ventures leads $3m series A round for Indonesian fintech firm Pluang. Tech in Asia. 11 September 2019. Available from: https://www.techinasia.com/gojek-leads-3m-indonesian-fintech-firm-pluang [Last accessed on 12 November 2024].
27. Sri D. Gojek now owns nearly a quarter of Indonesia's Bank Jago in $159m deal. Tech in Asia. 18 December 2020. Available from: https://www.techinasia.com/gojek-pay-159m-acquire-22-stake-bank-jago [Last accessed on 12 November 2024].
28. Mulia K. Grab launches Grab Defence anti-fraud technology suite. KrAsia. 14 March 2019. Available from: https://kr-asia.com/grab-launches-grab-defence-anti-fraud-technology-suite [Last accessed on 12 November 2024].
29. Silviana C. Grab enhances its Grab for Business suite with gift vouchers to target enterprises. KrAsia. 10 October 2019. Available from: https://kr-asia.com/grab-enhances-its-grab-for-business-suite-to-target-enterprises [Last accessed on 12 November 2024].
30. Grab Launches GrabAds Online-to-Offline Advertising Platform for Brands. Grab. 21 August 2018. Available from: https://www.grab.com/my/press/business/grab-launches-grabads-online-to-offline-advertising-platform-for-brands/ [Last accessed on 12 November 2024].

31. Grab announces acquisition of Bangalore-based payments startup iKaaz. Grab. 17 January 2018. Available from: https://www.grab.com/sg/press/others/grab-announces-acquisition-of-bangalore-based-payments-startup-ikaaz/ [Last accessed on 12 November 2024].
32. Grab acquires wealth tech start-up Bento to bring retail wealth solutions to millions across Southeast Asia. Grab. 4 February 2020. Available from: https://www.grab.com/sg/press/business/grab-acquires-wealth-tech-start-up-bento-to-to-bring-retail-wealth-solutions-to-millions-across-southeast-asia/ [Last accessed on 12 November 2024].
33. Freischlad N. Grab confirms it will acquire Kudo to boost digital payments. Tech in Asia. 3 April 2017. Available from: https://www.techinasia.com/grab-kudo-confirm-deal-boost-digital-payments [Last accessed on 12 November 2024].
34. Yu D. Grab leads series B round of up to $100m in Indonesian fintech LinkAja. Tech in Asia. 10 November 2020. Available from: https://www.techinasia.com/grab-leads-seriesb-round-100m-indonesias-fintech-linkaja [Last accessed on 12 November 2024].
35. Cordon M. Thai bank Krungsri to take part in MUFG's investment deal with Grab. Tech in Asia. 24 February 2020. Available from: https://www.techinasia.com/krungsri-part-mufg-investment-grab [Last accessed on 12 November 2024].
36. Setboonsarng C. Thailand's Kasikornbank invests $50 million in ride-hailing firm Grab. Reuters. 8 November 2018. Available from: https://www.reuters.com/article/business/thailand-s-kasikornbank-invests-50-million-in-ride-hailing-firm-grab-idUSKCN1ND0JP/ [Last accessed on 12 November 2024].
37. Iwamoto K. Grab taps Ping An, Naver in fresh $1bn funding. Nikkei. 2 August 2018. Available from: https://asia.nikkei.com/Spotlight/Sharing-Economy/Grab-taps-Ping-An-Naver-in-fresh-1bn-funding [Last accessed on 12 November 2024].
38. Experian invests in Grab to improve access to financial products and services for consumers across Southeast Asia. Experian. 5 July 2019. Available from: https://www.experianplc.com/newsroom/press-releases/2019/investment-in-grab [Last accessed on 12 November 2024].
39. Toh M. Grab plunges 21% in biggest Wall Street debut by a Southeast Asian company. CNN. 2 December 2021. Available from: https://edition.cnn.com/2021/12/02/investing/grab-ipo-spac-nasdaq-intl-hnk/index.html [Last accessed on 12 November 2024].
40. Poh O. GoTo Shares Jump After Raising $1.1 Billion in One of 2022's Biggest IPOs. Bloomberg. 11 April 2022. Available from: https://www.bloomberg.com/news/articles/2022-04-11/goto-shares-jump-on-first-day-in-boon-for-indonesia-tech-giant [Last accessed on 12 November 2024].

REFERENCES

41. Sutrisno G. B. Gojek to add $17.6b to Indonesian economy: report. Tech in Asia. 27 October 2021. Available from: https://www.techinasia.com/gojek-contribute-176-billion-indonesian-economy-2021 [Last accessed on 12 November 2024].
42. Mufti R. R. Grab contributes Rp 77.4 trillion to Indonesian economy: Research. The Jakarta Post. 25 June 2020. Available from: https://www.thejakartapost.com/news/2020/06/25/grab-contributes-rp-77-4-trillion-to-indonesian-economy-research.html [Last accessed on 12 November 2024].
43. Ellis J. The race to become Southeast Asia's super app. Tech in Asia. 10 November 2018. Available from: https://www.techinasia.com/grab-gojek-super-app-race [Last accessed on 12 November 2024].

CHAPTER 6

1. Regina G. New Technology Incubation Scheme To Fill 6-digit Funding Gap. Tech in Asia. 30 August 2009. Available from: https://www.techinasia.com/new-technology-incubation-scheme-to-fill-6-digit-funding-gap [Last accessed on 12 November 2024].
2. Lukman E. Show me the money! Here are 30 funding rounds and acquisitions from Indonesia this year. Tech in Asia. 31 December 2013. Available from: https://www.techinasia.com/30-fundings-acquisitions-indonesias-tech-scene-2013 [Last accessed on 12 November 2024].
3. Pratama A. H. Go-Jek: A unicorn's journey. Tech in Asia. 13 August 2016. Available from: https://www.techinasia.com/how-go-jek-became-unicorn [Last accessed on 12 November 2024].
4. Yu D. Gojek to close several GoLife services. Tech in Asia. 17 December 2019. Available from: https://www.techinasia.com/gojek-close-golife-services [Last accessed on 12 November 2024].
5. Go-Jek praises Jokowi for withdrawing ban. The Jakarta Post. 18 December 2015. Available from: https://www.thejakartapost.com/news/2015/12/18/go-jek-praises-jokowi-withdrawing-ban.html [Last accessed on 12 November 2024].
6. Lee Y. Go-Jek Raises Over $550 Million in KKR, Warburg-Led Round. Bloomberg. 4 August 2016. Available from: https://www.bloomberg.com/news/articles/2016-08-04/go-jek-said-to-raise-over-550-million-in-kkr-warburg-led-round [Last accessed on 12 November 2024].
7. Russell J. Alibaba leads $1.1B investment in Indonesia-based e-commerce firm Tokopedia. TechCrunch. 17 August 2017. Available from: https://techcrunch.com/2017/08/17/alibaba-tokopedia/ [Last accessed on 12 November 2024].

8. Balea J. Go-Jek reveals first close of new funding round, crucial stats. Tech in Asia. 1 February 2019. Available from: https://www.techinasia.com/confirmed-google-jd-tencent-lead-close-gojeks-series [Last accessed on 12 November 2024].
9. Russell J. Insurance giant Allianz confirms $35M investment in Asian ride-sharing unicorn Go-Jek. TechCrunch. 11 April 2018. Available from: https://techcrunch.com/2018/04/11/allianz-35m-investment-go-jek/ [Last accessed on 12 November 2024].
10. Uranaka T. Japanese banks to invest in $3 billion CVC Asia private equity fund. Reuters. 24 March 2014. Available from: https://www.reuters.com/article/us-japan-investment-idUKBREA2N07E20140324/ [Last accessed on 12 November 2024].
11. Mamuaya R. AliExpress Launches Its Indonesian Site. DailySocial. 24 October 2014. Available from: https://dailysocial.id/post/aliexpress-indonesia [Last accessed on 12 November 2024].
12. China's Tencent to delve deeper into Indonesia social media market. Reuters. 28 February 2013. Available from: https://www.reuters.com/article/us-tencent-indonesia-idUSBRE91R0AE20130228/ [Last accessed on 12 November 2024].
13. China's Tencent invests in Indonesia's Go-Jek amid SE Asia push. Reuters. 4 July 2017. Available from: https://www.reuters.com/article/gojek-ma-tencent-idUKL3N1JV32O/ [Last accessed on 12 November 2024].
14. Cosseboom L. China's ecommerce giant JD sets up shop in Indonesia. Tech in Asia. 27 October 2015. Available from: https://www.techinasia.com/indonesia-ecommerce-news-jd [Last accessed on 12 November 2024].
15. Nearly US $500 Million Investment by Expedia, East Ventures, Hillhouse Capital Group, JD.com and Sequoia Capital Highlight Confidence in Traveloka and Potential of Southeast Asia Travel Market. Traveloka. 31 July 2017. Available from: https://www.traveloka.com/en-id/explore/news/nearly-us-500-million-investment-expedia-east-ventures-hillhouse-capital-group-jd-com-sequoia-capital-highlight-confidence-traveloka-potential-southeast-asia-travel-market/63411 [Last accessed on 12 November 2024].
16. KKR seals first Indonesia deal with food company investment. Reuters. 22 July 2013. Available from: https://www.reuters.com/article/us-kkr-indonesia-idUSBRE96L03X20130722/ [Last accessed on 12 November 2024].
17. Lee T. 500 Startups' first investment in Indonesia is restaurant booking site Qraved. Tech in Asia. 5 September 2013. Available from: https://www.techinasia.com/500-startups-first-investment-in-indonesia-is-restaurant-booking-site-qraved [Last accessed on 12 November 2024].

REFERENCES

18. PT. Nirvana Development Gandeng Warburg Pincus Kembangkan Platform Ritel Inovatif di Indonesia. Antara. 16 February 2015. Available from: https://www.antaranews.com/berita/480312/pt-nirvana-development-gandeng-warburg-pincus-kembangkan-platform-ritel-inovatif-di-indonesia [Last accessed on 12 November 2024].
19. Maheshwari A. Indonesian fintech Payfazz raises over $21m from Tiger Global, others. DealStreetAsia. 21 November 2018. Available from: https://www.dealstreetasia.com/stories/indonesia-payfazz-tiger-global-111525 [Last accessed on 12 November 2024].
20. Yu D. Facebook, PayPal back Gojek to boost digital payments in Asia. Tech in Asia. 3 June 2020. Available from: https://www.techinasia.com/gojek-bags-funds-facebook-paypal-google-tencent [Last accessed on 12 November 2024].
21. Jusuf R. Celebrating 10 years of Google Indonesia. Google. 30 March 2022. Available from: https://blog.google/around-the-globe/google-asia/10-years-google-indonesia/ [Last accessed on 12 November 2024].
22. Putera A. D. Bertemu Jokowi, Amazon Bakal Investasi 1 Miliar Dollar AS di Indonesia. Kompas. 21 September 2018. Available from: https://ekonomi.kompas.com/read/2018/09/21/200818526/bertemu-jokowi-amazon-bakal-investasi-1-miliar-dollar-as-di-indonesia [Last accessed on 12 November 2024].
23. Wirdana A. Tencent, Jeff Bezos back $87m round of Indonesian B2B ecommerce startup Ula. Tech in Asia. 4 October 2021. Available from: https://www.techinasia.com/tencent-prosus-ventures-87m-indonesian-b2b-ecommerce-startup-ula [Last accessed on 12 November 2024].
24. Visa Investasi di GOJEK, Berkolaborasi dalam Memajukan Sistem Pembayaran Digital di Asia Tenggara. Gojek. 17 July 2019. Available from: https://www.gojek.com/blog/gojek/visa-investasi-di-gojek [Last accessed on 12 November 2024].
25. Eka R. Qoala Bukukan "Seed Round Investment" Lebih dari 21,6 Miliar Rupiah, Siap Hadirkan Produk Asuransi Digital di Berbagai Sektor. DailySocial. 13 May 2019. Available from: https://dailysocial.id/post/pendanaan-seed-round-qoala [Last accessed on 12 November 2024].
26. Facebook opens Indonesia's office. The Jakarta Post. 15 August 2017. Available from: https://www.thejakartapost.com/news/2017/08/15/facebook-opens-indonesias-office.html [Last accessed on 12 November 2024].
27. Cahyafitri R. Toba Bara to raise up to Rp 763b from IPO. The Jakarta Post. 12 June 2012. Available from: https://www.thejakartapost.com/news/2012/06/12/toba-bara-raise-rp-763b-ipo.html [Last accessed on 12 November 2024].

28. Pratama A. H. An influential new Indonesian VC could open doors for startups. Tech in Asia. 7 April 2020. Available from: https://www.techinasia.com/ac-ventures-influential-pandu-sjahrir [Last accessed on 12 November 2024].
29. Karimuddin A. Jakarta-Based Convergence Accel Setups $25 Million Fund for Startup Investment in Indonesia. DailySocial. 24 November 2014. Available from: https://dailysocial.id/post/convergence-accel-setups-25-million-fund-for-startup-investment-in-indonesia [Last accessed on 12 November 2024].
30. Agaeti Ventures and Convergence Ventures announce merger forming AC Ventures. AC Ventures. 5 April 2020. Available from: https://acv.vc/insights/acv-portfolio-news/agaeti-ventures-and-convergence-ventures-announce-merger-forming-ac-ventures/ [Last accessed on 12 November 2024].
31. Indonesia Venture Capital Outlook 2017. Google. September 2017. Available from: https://www.thinkwithgoogle.com/_qs/documents/4881/TWG-APAC-Indonesia-VC-Outlook-2017-Report.pdf [Last accessed on 12 November 2024].
32. Wijaya K. K. Here we go! 36 Indonesian startups who got funding in 2014. Tech in Asia. 7 January 2015. Available from: https://www.techinasia.com/36-indonesian-startups-funding-2014-infographic [Last accessed on 12 November 2024].
33. Eka R. Tren Pendanaan Startup Indonesia Sepanjang 2021. DailySocial. 17 January 2022. Available from: https://dailysocial.id/post/tren-pendanaan-startup-indonesia-2021 [Last accessed on 12 November 2024].
34. Mulia K. Indonesia's AC Ventures closes third fund at USD 205 million. KrAsia. 1 December 2021. Available from: https://kr-asia.com/indonesias-ac-ventures-closes-third-fund-at-usd-205-million [Last accessed on 12 November 2024].

CHAPTER 7

1. Summary of Indonesia's Finance Sector Assessment. Asian Development Bank. December 2015. Available from: https://www.adb.org/publications/summary-indonesias-finance-sector-assessment [Last accessed on 13 November 2024].
2. Mobile Banking in Indonesia: Assessing the Market Potential for Mobile Technology to Extend Banking to the Unbanked and Underbanked. Access Partnership. 1 October 2010. Available from: https://accesspartnership.com/mobile-banking-in-indonesia-assessing-the-market-potential-for-mobile-technology-to-extend-banking-to-the-unbanked-and-underbanked-final-report/ [Last accessed on 13 November 2024].

REFERENCES

3. The Future of Southeast Asia's Digital Financial Services. Bain & Company. 30 October 2019. Available from: https://www.bain.com/insights/fufilling-its-promise/ [Last accessed on 13 November 2024].
4. Li A. Indonesia's Fintech Industry Is Ready to Rise. BCG. 29 March 2023. Available from: https://www.bcg.com/publications/2023/fintech-industry-indonesia-growth [Last accessed on 13 November 2024].
5. Yeo S. How Ovo aims to drive financial inclusion in Indonesia. Tech in Asia. 17 September 2021. Available from: https://www.techinasia.com/ovo-aims-drive-financial-inclusion-indonesia [Last accessed on 13 November 2024].
6. Shofa J. N. OVO Claims It's Now Indonesia's Largest Fintech Ecosystem. Jakarta Globe. 1 August 2020. Available from: https://jakartaglobe.id/business/ovo-claims-its-now-indonesias-largest-fintech-ecosystem [Last accessed on 13 November 2024].
7. Sri D. Grab buys majority stake in Ovo from Tokopedia, Lippo Group. Tech in Asia. 4 October 2021. Available from: https://www.techinasia.com/grab-ups-stake-indonesias-ovo-90 [Last accessed on 13 November 2024].
8. Shu C. Southeast Asian payments infrastructure unicorn Xendit banks $300M. TechCrunch. 19 May 2022. Available from: https://techcrunch.com/2022/05/19/southeast-asian-payments-infrastructure-unicorn-xendit-banks-300m/ [Last accessed on 13 November 2024].
9. Modalku Bekerja Sama dengan Bank DBS untuk Mendukung UMKM di Tengah Pandemi. Modalku. 2 June 2022. Available from: https://blog.modalku.co.id/apa-kabar-modalku/kabar-media/modalku-bekerja-sama-dengan-bank-dbs-untuk-mendukung-umkm-di-tengah-pandemi/ [Last accessed on 13 November 2024].
10. Freischlad N. 500 Startups funds Stockbit, a social network for stock trading. Tech in Asia. 25 April 2017. Available from: https://www.techinasia.com/trading-platform-stockbit-gets-funding-from-500-startups [Last accessed on 13 November 2024].
11. Indonesian insurtech firm PasarPolis sees significant growth potential in Indonesia. TechNode. 10 April 2023. Available from: https://technode.global/2023/04/10/indonesian-insurtech-firm-pasarpolis-sees-significant-growth-potential-in-indonesia/ [Last accessed on 13 November 2024].
12. Indonesia insurtech PasarPolis partners Shopee for SEA expansion. TechNode. 14 September 2022. Available from: https://technode.global/2022/09/14/indonesia-insurtech-pasarpolis-partners-shopee-for-sea-expansion/ [Last accessed on 13 November 2024].

13. Amirio D. Peer-to-peer lender Modalku raises Rp 110b. The Jakarta Post. 5 August 2016. Available from: https://www.thejakartapost.com/news/2016/08/05/peer-peer-lender-modalku-raises-rp-110b.html [Last accessed on 13 November 2024].
14. Cordon M. P2P lender Koinworks banks $12m from EV Growth, Quona, others. Tech in Asia. 25 June 2019. Available from: https://www.techinasia.com/koinworks-banks-12m-ev-growth-quona [Last accessed on 13 November 2024].
15. Maulani A. M. JULO raises US$80M from Credit Saison to further expand in Indonesia. E27. 13 April 2022. Available from: https://e27.co/julo-raises-us80m-from-credit-saison-to-further-expand-in-indonesia-20220413/ [Last accessed on 13 November 2024].
16. Penyelenggara Fintech Lending Terdaftar dan Berizin di OJK per 28 Desember 2020. The Financial Services Authority (OJK). 6 January 2021. Available from: https://ojk.go.id/id/kanal/iknb/financial-technology/Pages/Penyelenggara-Fintech-Lending-Terdaftar-dan-Berizin-di-OJK-per-28-Desember-2020.aspx [Last accessed on 13 November 2024].
17. Nugroho A. A. A Deep Dive Into Indonesia's Digital Payments Transformation. 2C2P. 17 February 2022. Available from: https://2c2p.com/blog/indonesia-digital-payments-transformation [Last accessed on 13 November 2024].
18. Freischlad N. Kredivo confirms new funding from Jungle Ventures and early Go-Jek backer NSI. Tech in Asia. 4 October 2017. Available from: https://www.techinasia.com/confirming-funding-nsi-jungle-ventures [Last accessed on 13 November 2024].
19. Akulaku Introduces New Features to Buy Now Pay Later Market in Indonesia. Akulaku. 6 July 2022. Available from: https://www.akulaku.com/artikel/akulaku-introduces-new-features-to-buy-now-pay-later-market-in-indonesia/ [Last accessed on 13 November 2024].
20. Indonesian fintech startup Akulaku invests $35m in local bank. Tech in Asia. 22 March 2019. Available from: https://www.techinasia.com/akulaku-invests-35m-local-bank [Last accessed on 13 November 2024].
21. Freischlad N. Payfazz is the first Indonesian startup to make it into Y Combinator. Tech in Asia. 4 August 2017. Available from: https://www.techinasia.com/first-indonesian-startup-makes-yc [Last accessed on 13 November 2024].
22. Shu C. Payfazz gets $53 million to give more Indonesians access to financial services. TechCrunch. 6 July 2020. Available from: https://techcrunch.com/2020/07/06/payfazz-gets-53-million-to-give-more-indonesians-access-to-financial-services/ [Last accessed on 13 November 2024].

REFERENCES

23. Suzuki W. Indonesia's BRI embraces banking by satellite. Financial Times. 25 July 2016. Available from: https://www.ft.com/content/503d9044-4f4d-11e6-8172-e39ecd3b86fc [Last accessed on 13 November 2024].
24. Yusra Y. OVO Confirms Partnership with Bank Mandiri, Grab, Alfamart, and MOKA. DailySocial. 11 July 2018. Available from: https://dailysocial.id/post/ovo-confirms-partnership-with-bank-mandiri-grab-alfamart-and-moka#google_vignette [Last accessed on 13 November 2024].
25. Muskita P. Bukalapak partners three P2P lenders to provide loans for offline businesses. Tech in Asia. 27 March 2019. Available from: https://www.techinasia.com/bukalapak-partners-3-p2p-lenders-provide-loans-offline-vendors [Last accessed on 13 November 2024].
26. Allianz Indonesia Bekerja Sama dengan Gojek dan PasarPolis Sediakan Akses Perlindungan Asuransi Kesehatan Mudah, Terjangkau, Cepat dan Aman. Allianz. 7 October 2020. Available from: https://www.allianz.co.id/tentang-kami/berita-perusahaan/rilis-media/2020/2020-oktober/allianz-indonesia-bekerja-sama-dengan-gojek-dan-pasarpolis-sediakan-akses-perlindungan-asuransi-kesehatan--mudah-terjangkau-cepat-dan-aman.html [Last accessed on 13 November 2024].
27. Muskita P. Tokopedia's next 10 years. Tech in Asia. 23 October 2019. Available from: https://www.techinasia.com/tokopedias-10-years [Last accessed on 13 November 2024].
28. Lifestyle superapp Traveloka expands its Financial Services offering and partners with Bank Negara Indonesia for Southeast Asia's first PayLater 'Virtual Card Number'. Traveloka. 14 September 2021. Available from: https://www.traveloka.com/en-id/explore/news/lifestyle-superapp-traveloka-expands-its-financial-services-offering-and-partners-with-bank-negara-indonesia-for-southeast-asias-first-paylater-virtual-card-number/94581 [Last accessed on 13 November 2024].
29. Hastuti R. K. BRI Agro & PAYFAZZ Kerja Sama Agen & Layanan Perbankan. CNBC Indonesia. 8 December 2020. Available from: https://www.cnbcindonesia.com/tech/20201208152156-37-207681/bri-agro-payfazz-kerja-sama-agen-layanan-perbankan [Last accessed on 13 November 2024].
30. Wirdana A. A new digital bank could instill VC faith in Indonesia's Shariah fintech. Tech in Asia. 18 August 2021. Available from: https://www.techinasia.com/digital-bank-instill-vc-faith-indonesias-sharia-fintech [Last accessed on 13 November 2024].
31. Akulaku Establishes Partnership with Alipay+ To Make Cross-Border Shopping More Accessible for Consumers. Akulaku. 7 September 2022. Available from:

https://www.akulaku.com/artikel/akulaku-establishes-partnership-with-alipay-to-make-cross-border-shopping-more-accessible-for-consumers/ [Last accessed on 13 November 2024].

32. Pratama A. H. Fintech unicorn Xendit buys minority stake in local bank. Tech in Asia. 21 April 2022. Available from: https://www.techinasia.com/xendit-strategic-investment-local-bank [Last accessed on 13 November 2024].

33. Hadi A. Fintech firm launches youth-focused digital bank Krom. The Jakarta Post. 27 February 2024. Available from: https://www.thejakartapost.com/business/2024/02/27/fintech-firm-kredivo-launches-youth-focused-digital-bank-krom.html [Last accessed on 13 November 2024].

34. Rahadian L. Ajaib Beli 16% Saham Bank Bumi Arta (BNBA) Rp 596,53 M. CNBC Indonesia. 12 April 2022. Available from: https://www.cnbcindonesia.com/market/20220412105444-17-330892/ajaib-beli-16-saham-bank-bumi-arta-bnba-rp-59653-m [Last accessed on 13 November 2024].

35. Li A. Indonesia's Fintech Industry Is Ready to Rise. BCG. 29 March 2023. Available from: https://www.bcg.com/publications/2023/fintech-industry-indonesia-growth [Last accessed on 13 November 2024].

CHAPTER 8

1. Widiadana R. Explore4Action to discover what youths really want. The Jakarta Post. 17 January 2019. Available from: https://www.thejakartapost.com/youth/2019/01/17/explore4action-to-discover-what-youths-really-want.html [Last accessed on 13 November 2024].

2. Aspiring Indonesia: Expanding the Middle Class. World Bank. 30 January 2020. Available from: https://www.worldbank.org/en/country/indonesia/publication/aspiring-indonesia-expanding-the-middle-class [Last accessed on 13 November 2024].

3. Lee Y. Ride-Hailing Giant Gojek Raises $1.2 Billion for Clash With Grab. Bloomberg. 17 March 2020. Available from: https://www.bloomberg.com/news/articles/2020-03-17/ride-hailing-giant-gojek-raises-1-2-billion-for-clash-with-grab [Last accessed on 13 November 2024].

4. Lee Y. Traveloka Nears Fundraising at Lower Valuation. Bloomberg. 7 July 2020. Available from: https://www.bloomberg.com/news/articles/2020-07-07/traveloka-is-said-near-fundraising-at-sharply-lower-valuation [Last accessed on 13 November 2024].

REFERENCES

5. Potkin F. SE Asia's biggest travel app Traveloka raises $250 million as lockdowns ease. Reuters. 28 July 2020. Available from: https://www.reuters.com/article/technology/se-asias-biggest-travel-app-traveloka-raises-250-million-as-lockdowns-ease-idUSKCN24T0OG/ [Last accessed on 13 November 2024].
6. Maheshwari A. Indonesia's Traveloka in talks to raise over $200m. Nikkei. 6 June 2022. Available from: https://asia.nikkei.com/Spotlight/DealStreet Asia/Indonesia-s-Traveloka-in-talks-to-raise-over-200m [Last accessed on 13 November 2024].
7. Cordon M. Microsoft strikes a $100m investment deal with Bukalapak. Tech in Asia. 3 November 2020. Available from: https://www.techinasia.com/microsoft-strikes-100m-investment-deal-bukalapak [Last accessed on 13 November 2024].
8. Lee Y. Google, Temasek Agree to Invest $350 Million in Tokopedia. Bloomberg. 26 October 2020. Available from: https://www.bloomberg.com/news/articles/2020-10-26/google-temasek-are-said-to-invest-350-million-in-tokopedia [Last accessed on 13 November 2024].
9. Muskita P. Co-working spaces see a surge in demand – but it may not last. Tech in Asia. 1 April 2020. Available from: https://www.techinasia.com/age-social-distancing-demand-coworking-spaces-soars-southeast-asia [Last accessed on 13 November 2024].
10. Nabila M. CoHive Receives Series B Funding of Over 192 Billion Rupiah, Aiming to Close at 285 Billion Rupiah. DailySocial. 20 June 2019. Available from: https://en.dailysocial.id/post/pendanaan-seri-b-cohive-192-miliar [Last accessed on 13 November 2024].
11. Sutrisno G. B. Indonesia's CoHive officially bankrupt. Tech in Asia. 3 February 2023. Available from: https://www.techinasia.com/indonesias-cohive-is-officially-collapsed [Last accessed on 13 November 2024].
12. Muskita P. A closer look at Indonesia's furniture and home living startups. Tech in Asia. 29 November 2019. Available from: https://www.techinasia.com/closer-indonesias-furniture-home-living-startups [Last accessed on 13 November 2024].
13. Akhaya P. Fabelio makes US$9M first close of ongoing Series C funding round. E27. 17 June 2020. Available from: https://e27.co/fabelio-makes-us9m-first-close-of-ongoing-series-c-funding-round-20200617/ [Last accessed on 13 November 2024].
14. Fitri A. N. Bangkit dari pandemi Covid-19, Fabelio ekspansi ke tiga kota tahun ini. Kontan. 18 August 2020. Available from: https://industri.kontan.co.id/news/bangkit-dari-pandemi-covid-19-fabelio-ekspansi-ke-tiga-kota-tahun-ini [Last accessed on 13 November 2024].

15. Former employees, employees and customers of Fabelio speak up. TFR. 13 December 2021. Available from: https://tfr.news/articles/2021/12/6/former-employees-employees-and-customers-of-fabelio-speak-up [Last accessed on 13 November 2024].
16. Taufik S. Indonesia-based Fabelio declares bankruptcy. Tech in Asia. 12 October 2022. Available from: https://www.techinasia.com/fabelio-declares-bankruptcy-settle-debt [Last accessed on 13 November 2024].
17. Muskita P. Behind Sorabel's shutdown: could it have been avoided? Tech in Asia. 29 July 2020. Available from: https://www.techinasia.com/sorabels-shutdown-could-it-have-been-avoided [Last accessed on 13 November 2024].
18. Silviana C. Indonesian fashion e-commerce site Sorabel files for liquidation. KrAsia. 24 July 2020. Available from: https://kr-asia.com/indonesian-fashion-e-commerce-site-sorabel-files-for-liquidation [Last accessed on 13 November 2024].
19. Yu D. Indonesian fashion startup Sorabel to close down as Covid-19 wipes out cash. Tech in Asia. 24 July 2020. Available from: https://www.techinasia.com/sorabel-close-down-covid-wipes-cash [Last accessed on 13 November 2024].
20. Yu D. Indonesian hospitality startup Airy to permanently shut down amid pandemic. Tech in Asia. 7 May 2020. Available from: https://www.techinasia.com/airy-cease-operations [Last accessed on 13 November 2024].
21. Surviving the Valley of Death in Southeast Asia. Deloitte. 25 August 2022. Available from: https://kr-asia.com/surviving-the-valley-of-death-in-southeast-asia [Last accessed on 13 November 2024].
22. Maheshwari A. Indonesia's Stoqo raises Series A round from Monk's Hill, Accel Partners. DealStreetAsia. 19 December 2018. Available from: https://www.dealstreetasia.com/stories/stoqo-monks-hill-accel-114393 [Last accessed on 13 November 2024].
23. Muskita P. Inside Stoqo's sudden demise. Tech in Asia. 6 May 2020. Available from: https://www.techinasia.com/real-reasons-stoqos-sudden-demise [Last accessed on 13 November 2024].
24. Pratama A. H. Traveloka closes food, logistics services as travel takes off again. Tech in Asia. 30 September 2022. Available from: https://www.techinasia.com/traveloka-close-eats-send [Last accessed on 13 November 2024].
25. Furtado C. East Ventures leads funding in biotech startup that develops Covid-19 test kits. Tech in Asia. 7 January 2021. Available from: https://www.techinasia.com/east-ventures-leads-series-a-round-in-biotech-startup-that-develops-covid-19-test-kits [Last accessed on 13 November 2024].

REFERENCES

26. Williamson L. How This Indonesian Startup Pivoted Within Days To Produce Covid-19 Testing Kits. Tatler Asia. 8 February 2021. Available from: https://www.tatlerasia.com/gen-t/leadership/how-this-indonesian-startup-pivoted-within-days-to-produce-covid-19-testing-kits [Last accessed on 13 November 2024].
27. Achiko AG Announces Successful Integration of its Teman Sehat Digital Ecosystem and AptameX Covid-19 Diagnostic Testing Platform for Launch in Indonesia. Achiko. 3 June 2021. Available from: https://finance.yahoo.com/news/achiko-ag-announces-successful-integration-044500447.html [Last accessed on 13 November 2024].
28. Shu C. How SOSV-backed Achiko pivoted from financial services to health tech during the COVID-19 pandemic. TechCrunch. 1 April 2021. Available from: https://techcrunch.com/2021/04/01/how-sosv-backed-achiko-pivoted-from-financial-services-to-health-tech-during-the-covid-19-pandemic/ [Last accessed on 13 November 2024].
29. Yu D. Indonesia's Social Bella bags $58m in series E money. Tech in Asia. 6 July 2020. Available from: https://www.techinasia.com/social-bella-bags-58m [Last accessed on 13 November 2024].
30. Goh C. T. Youth was no barrier to success for this founder of a multimillion-dollar startup. CNBC. 1 November 2022. Available from: https://www.cnbc.com/2022/11/02/sociolla-she-built-a-startup-that-raised-millions-shares-3-tips.html [Last accessed on 13 November 2024].
31. Rayda N. 'Pushing the boundaries of innovation': How 9 Indonesia start-ups become unicorns during the pandemic. CNA. 4 June 2022. Available from: https://www.channelnewsasia.com/asia/indonesia-new-unicorns-during-pandemic-jd-id-xendit-akulaku-2724756 [Last accessed on 13 November 2024].
32. Putera I. Indonesia's Akulaku raises US$100 million Series D from Alibaba's Ant Financial, others. Finch Capital. 20 January 2019. Available from: https://news.finchcapital.com/post/102fdcd/indonesias-akulaku-raises-us100-million-series-d-from-alibabas-ant-financial [Last accessed on 13 November 2024].
33. Nabila M. Halodoc Raises Series B+ Investment from Bill & Melinda Gates Foundation, Prudential, and Allianz X. DailySocial. 25 July 2019. Available from: https://dailysocial.id/post/halodoc-raises-series-b-investment-from-bill-melinda-gates-foundation-prudential-and-allianz-x [Last accessed on 13 November 2024].
34. Nur A. Gojek, Halodoc launch telemedicine service "Check COVID-19." Antara. 23 March 2020. Available from: https://en.antaranews.com/news/144362/gojek-halodoc-launch-telemedicine-service-check-covid-19 [Last accessed on 13 November 2024].

35. Nabila M. Aplikasi PeduliLindungi Tambah Layanan Telemedicine dari Halodoc. DailySocial. 25 June 2020. Available from: https://dailysocial.id/post/aplikasi-pedulilindungi-tambah-layanan-telemedicine-dari-halodoc [Last accessed on 13 November 2024].
36. Wirdana A. Indonesia's CoLearn bags more funding to wrap up $27m series A. Tech in Asia. 26 January 2022. Available from: https://www.techinasia.com/exclusive-indonesias-colearn-bags-funding-wrap-27m-series [Last accessed on 13 November 2024].
37. Shu C. Indonesian edtech CoLearn gets $10M Series A led by Alpha Wave Incubation and GSV Ventures. TechCrunch. 20 April 2021. Available from: https://techcrunch.com/2021/04/19/indonesian-edtech-colearn-gets-10m-series-a-led-by-alpha-wave-incubation-and-gsv-ventures/ [Last accessed on 13 November 2024].
38. Indonesian quick-commerce startup Astro grabs US$4.5M seed round. AC Ventures. 26 November 2021. Available from: https://acv.vc/insights/acv-portfolio-news/astro-a-15-minute-quick-commerce-startup-raised-us4-5m-in-seed-round/ [Last accessed on 13 November 2024].
39. Pratama A. H. Tiger Global, Accel co-lead $60m round of Indonesian quick commerce firm. Tech in Asia. 30 May 2022. Available from: https://www.techinasia.com/astro-series-b-funding [Last accessed on 13 November 2024].
40. Cosseboom L. How Astro is thinking about profitability in a post-Covid era. AC Ventures. 18 April 2023. Available from: https://acv.vc/insights/podcast/astro-profitability-post-covid-era/ [Last accessed on 13 November 2024].
41. Liao R. Indonesia's Astro raises $60M to work on 15-minute grocery delivery. TechCrunch. 29 May 2022. Available from: https://techcrunch.com/2022/05/29/astro-indonesia-grocery-delivery-60-million-funding/ [Last accessed on 13 November 2024].
42. Maheshwari A. AC Ventures leads seed round of Indonesian restaurant ERP startup ESB. DealStreetAsia. 5 May 2020. Available from: https://www.dealstreetasia.com/stories/ac-ventures-esb-187109 [Last accessed on 13 November 2024].
43. Yu D. Logistics startup Shipper bags series A money to double down on Indonesia. Tech in Asia. 19 June 2020. Available from: https://www.techinasia.com/shipper-bags-series-money-double-down-indonesia [Last accessed on 13 November 2024].
44. Maheshwari A. Indonesian logistics startup Shipper said to have raised up to $20m from Naspers, others. DealStreetAsia. Available from: https://www.dealstreetasia.com/stories/shipper-naspers-others-189184 [Last accessed on 13 November 2024].

REFERENCES

45. Mulia K. Shipper connects SMEs with reliable logistics services: Startup Stories. KrAsia. 7 November 2020. Available from: https://kr-asia.com/shipper-connects-smes-with-reliable-logistics-services-startup-stories [Last accessed on 13 November 2024].
46. Desideria B. Rasio Dokter RI Hanya 0,47 per 1.000 Penduduk, Lebih Rendah dari Timor Leste dan Filipina. Liputan6. 9 February 2023. Available from: https://www.liputan6.com/health/read/5195130/rasio-dokter-ri-hanya-047-per-1000-penduduk-lebih-rendah-dari-timor-leste-dan-filipina [Last accessed on 13 November 2024].
47. Freischlad N. Go-Jek spins out medicine delivery to separate app, continues unbundling. Tech in Asia. 18 May 2017. Available from: https://www.techinasia.com/go-jek-spins-out-medicine-delivery [Last accessed on 13 November 2024].
48. Zhafira A. N. Gojek dan Halodoc luncurkan layanan "Check COVID-19." Antara. 22 March 2020. Available from: https://www.antaranews.com/berita/1373986/gojek-dan-halodoc-luncurkan-layanan-check-covid-19 [Last accessed on 13 November 2024].
49. Yasmin N. Ruangguru Offers Free Live Classes During School Shutdown. Jakarta Globe. 16 March 2020. Available from: https://jakartaglobe.id/tech/ruangguru-offers-free-live-classes-during-school-shutdown [Last accessed on 13 November 2024].
50. All-in-one restaurant operations platform ESB raises US$ 7.6mn in Series A+ round led by Alpha JWC Ventures. AC Ventures. 13 October 2021. Available from: https://acv.vc/insights/acv-portfolio-news/all-in-one-restaurant-operations-platform-esb-raises-us-7-6mn-in-series-a-round-led-by-alpha-jwc-ventures/ [Last accessed on 13 November 2024].
51. Cordon M. Indonesian logistics startup Shipper bags $5m from Y Combinator, Insignia, others. Tech in Asia. 23 September 2019. Available from: https://www.techinasia.com/shipper-bags-5m-seed [Last accessed on 13 November 2024].
52. Cosseboom L. Covid-19 unlocked new capital for ASEAN's tech investors. AC Ventures. 27 July 2022. Available from: https://acv.vc/insights/acv-portfolio-news/adrian-li-avcj-new-capital/ [Last accessed on 13 November 2024].
53. Kurmala A. Contribution of MSMEs to GDP at Rp8,574 trillion: minister. Antara. 3 October 2022. Available from: https://en.antaranews.com/news/252977/contribution-of-msmes-to-gdp-at-rp8574-trillion-minister [Last accessed on 13 November 2024].

CHAPTER 9

1. Digitalization: A Safe Path to a More Inclusive Recovery in Indonesia? IMF. 2 March 2021. Available from: https://www.elibrary.imf.org/view/journals/002/2021/047/article-A006-en.xml [Last accessed on 14 November 2024].
2. Rahman D. F. Bank Indonesia expands regulation on minimum lending for MSMEs. The Jakarta Post. 6 September 2021. Available from: https://www.thejakartapost.com/news/2021/09/06/bank-indonesia-expands-regulation-on-minimum-lending-for-msmes.html [Last accessed on 14 November 2024].
3. Statistik Fintech Lending Periode Desember 2020. OJK. 28 January 2021. Available from: https://www.ojk.go.id/id/kanal/iknb/data-dan-statistik/fintech/Pages/-Statistik-Fintech-Lending-Periode-Desember-2020.aspx [Last accessed on 14 November 2024].
4. Cosseboom L. How KoinWorks boosts financial inclusion for Indonesia's MSMEs. AC Ventures. 23 February 2023. Available from: https://acv.vc/insights/podcast/koinworks-financial-inclusion-msmes-indonesia/ [Last accessed on 14 November 2024].
5. Pratama A. H. SoftBank backs Indonesian social commerce firm's $70m round. Tech in Asia. 2 June 2022. Available from: https://www.techinasia.com/super-series-c-funding [Last accessed on 14 November 2024].
6. Pratama A. H. Warung Pintar grows user base 20× following evolution and strategic shake-up. Tech in Asia. 4 August 2021. Available from: https://www.techinasia.com/warung-pintar-evolution-supply-chain [Last accessed on 14 November 2024].
7. Poverty Data: Indonesia. Asian Development Bank. 18 August 2022. Available from: https://www.adb.org/where-we-work/indonesia/poverty [Last accessed on 14 November 2024].
8. Cosseboom L. Ula and Bukalapak on inventory and digitalization for MSMEs. AC Ventures. 20 April 2023. Available from: https://acv.vc/insights/podcast/ula-bukalapak-inventory-digitalization-msmes/ [Last accessed on 14 November 2024].
9. Cosseboom L. How Majoo made an e-commerce stack for Indonesia's MSMEs. AC Ventures. 9 September 2022. Available from: https://acv.vc/insights/podcast/majoo-indonesias-msme-ecommerce/ [Last accessed on 14 November 2024].
10. Cosseboom L. Indonesia's fisheries leapfrog supply chain gaps with Aruna. AC Ventures. 29 September 2022. Available from: https://acv.vc/insights/podcast/aruna-fisheries-indonesia/ [Last accessed 14 November 2024].

REFERENCES

11. Cosseboom L. Koltiva: Beyond traceability in the US$75.6B global supply chain management game. AC Ventures. 7 August 2023. Available from: https://acv.vc/insights/podcast/koltiva-supply-chains/ [Last accessed on 14 November 2024].
12. Cosseboom L. RAENA's founder on the outsized impact of micro-influencers. AC Ventures. 26 January 2023. Available from: https://acv.vc/insights/podcast/raena-founder-micro-influencers-indonesia/ [Last accessed on 14 November 2024].

CHAPTER 10

1. Eka R. 2019 Indonesian Startups Book More Than 40 Trillion Rupiah Funding, Local Venture Investors "Exit" 14 Times. DailySocial. 20 December 2019. Available from: https://en.dailysocial.id/post/pendanaan-startup-indonesia-2019 [Last accessed on 14 November 2024].
2. Indonesia: Digital Economy Opportunities. International Trade Administration. 12 September 2021. Available from: https://www.trade.gov/market-intelligence/indonesia-digital-economy-opportunities [Last accessed on 14 November 2024].
3. Shu C. Bibit raises another growth round led by Sequoia Capital India, this time for $65M. TechCrunch. 2 May 2021. Available from: https://techcrunch.com/2021/05/02/bibit-raises-another-growth-round-led-by-sequoia-capital-india-this-time-for-65m/ [Last accessed on 14 November 2024].
4. Shu C. PINA offers wealth management for Indonesia's growing middle- to upper-class. TechCrunch. 4 July 2022. Available from: https://techcrunch.com/2022/07/03/pina-offers-wealth-management-for-indonesias-growing-middle-to-upper-class/ [Last accessed on 14 November 2024].
5. Shu C. Indonesia's Skorlife gets funding to give Indonesians power over their credit scores. TechCrunch. 23 May 2023. Available from: https://techcrunch.com/2023/05/23/skorlife-seed/ [Last accessed on 14 November 2024].
6. Ahmad S. J&J, Sanofi back SG pharma platform's $10m round. Tech in Asia. 9 February 2023. Available from: https://www.techinasia.com/singapores-swiperx-10m-booster-shot-series-topup [Last accessed on 14 November 2024].
7. Cordon M. YC, Sequoia back ID healthtech platform's $2.6m round. Tech in Asia. 7 February 2022. Available from: https://www.techinasia.com/yc-sequoia-backs-indonesian-healthtech-platforms-26m [Last accessed on 14 November 2024].

8. Yow D. Beauty startup Rose All Day Cosmetics raises US$5.41 million Series A round. The Business Times. 15 December 2023. Available from: https://www.businesstimes.com.sg/startups-tech/startups/beauty-startup-rose-all-day-cosmetics-raises-us541-million-series-round [Last accessed on 14 November 2024].
9. Cordon M. Lazada alum's D2C home appliance brand tripled sales, hit profitability in 2023. Tech in Asia. 7 February 2024. Available from: https://www.techinasia.com/simplus-triples-yearly-sales-hits-profitability-2023 [Last accessed on 14 November 2024].
10. Pratama A. H. Mapping Indonesia's key agritech players. Tech in Asia. 20 December 2022. Available from: https://www.techinasia.com/key-players-indonesias-promising-agritech-space [Last accessed on 14 November 2024].
11. Shu C. Waste4Change is building a circular economy in Indonesia. TechCrunch. 13 October 2022. Available from: https://techcrunch.com/2022/10/13/waste4change-is-building-a-circular-economy-in-indonesia/ [Last accessed on 14 November 2024].
12. Lempp M. Series A funding for Indonesia's solar start-up Xurya upped to $33 million. The Jakarta Post. 24 October 2022. Available from: https://www.thejakartapost.com/business/2022/10/24/series-a-funding-for-indonesias-solar-start-up-xurya-upped-to-us33-million.html [Last accessed on 14 November 2024].
13. Park K. With $37M seed round, Maka Motors begins EV pilot on Indonesia's streets. TechCrunch. 19 July 2023. Available from: https://techcrunch.com/2023/07/19/with-37m-seed-round-maka-motors-begins-ev-pilot-on-indonesias-streets/ [Last accessed on 14 November 2024].

INDEX

A

AC Ventures, 30, 35, 36, 61, 70, 92, 100, 101, 129, 135
Accel, 35, 96, 97
Access Industries, 25
Accion Venture Lab, 33
Achiko, 125, 127
aCommerce Indonesia, 29
Advance Intelligence Group, 36
advertising, 4, 16, 27–28. *See also* marketing
Aegis, 60
Agaeti Venture Capital, 30, 61, 100
Agoda, 81, 88
agriculture, 145, 155–156, 158
Agusetiawan, Wenas, 11
AI (artificial intelligence), 132, 158
Airbnb, 23, 31
AirCTO, 88
Airizu, 17, 29
Airy, 123, 124
Ajaib, 115
Akulaku, 112, 113, 115, 126, 127
Alami, 115
Alando, 18, 20
Alfa Group, 115
Alfamart, 115
Alibaba, 32, 42, 43, 48, 51, 57, 95, 96, 101
AliExpress, 57–58, 96
Alipay, 115
Allianz, 95, 115, 128
Alodokter, 30, 131
Alpha JWC Ventures, 36, 92, 101
Alsagoff, Nabilah, 56–57
Alto Partners, 34, 35, 36
Aluwi, Kevin, 29
Aman, 35
Amand Ventures, 33
Amartha, 115
Amazon, 21, 23, 96, 97
"America's Most Successful Startups," 18
Anchanto, 65

INDEX

apartment rentals, 46
APIs (application programming interfaces), 62, 66, 114, 134
apps, 42, 43, 50, 77
Appworks, 35
Ardianto, Natali, 11
Aruna, 144, 145, 147
Asetku, 113
Asian Development Bank, 35, 142
Astra International, 88
Astro, 35, 129
Atlas Global Kapital, 36
Atma, 35
automobiles, 74

B

B Capital Group, 34
Bain, 150
BaliCamp, 3
Bank Bisnis Internasional, 115
Bank Bumi Arta, 115
Bank Indonesia, 70–71, 139–140
Bank Jago, 80, 89
Bank Mandiri, 104, 114, 115
Bank Neo Commerce, 115
Bank of Ayudhya, 81, 89
Bank Sahabat Sampoerna, 115
Bank Yudha Bhakti, 113, 115
banks, 103–104, 106–107, 113–116
Bareksa, 44, 115
Batavia Incubator, 9
BayarDisini products, 59
BCA (Bank Central Asia), 45, 57, 104

Beacon VC, 87
"Belajar dari Rumah," 131
Bento, 81, 89
Bezos, Jeff, 97
Bhinneka, 66
BI, 57
Bibit, 110, 152
BI-FAST, 117
Binus University, 7–8
Blackpink, 50
Blanja, 28, 51
Blauwpark Partners, 35
Blavatnik, Len, 25
Bleckwenn, Arne, 23
Blibli, 39, 40, 45–47, 51, 60, 87, 88, 128
"blitzkrieg" strategy, 18, 20–21
Blue Bird, 86, 89
Blue7, 33
BNI (Bank Negara Indonesia), 87, 115
BNPL (buy-now-pay-later) sector, 66, 112–113
Booking.com, 81, 87, 88
Borer, Manfred, 145
Boyu Capital, 69
BRI (Bank Rakyat Indonesia), 44, 58, 104, 113, 114, 115
Bridestory, 33
Brunier, David, 36
B2B (business-to-business) platform, 44, 61, 109
B2B2C (business-to-business-to-consumer) platform, 45

B2C (business-to-consumer) platform, 10, 45, 50
Budi Setiadharma, 33
BukaDana, 44
Bukalapak, 5, 9, 10, 15, 39, 40, 43–45, 60, 114, 122, 131, 138, 142–143
BukaPengadaan, 44
BukaReksa, 44
Bukuwarung, 36

C

Cainiao, 69
Cakra Ventures, 35
Capital Group Private Markets, 79
Carmudi, 24
cars, 74
Carsome, 99–100
Carstens, Karl, 24
Cempaka Al Amin, 115
Central Group, 88
C42, 78, 85
Chelbat, Jonas, 23
Chen, Bo, 62
Chen, Tony, 68
China Investment Corporation, 79, 84
Chinese investors, 42–43, 95–96
CIMB Niaga, 58
Cinemaxx theaters, 48
Citius, 35
CityDeal, 17
climate solutions. *See* ESG values
CodeIgnition, 78, 85
CoHive, 124

Coins.ph, 88
CoLearn, 129, 132
Conny & Co., 37
Convergence Ventures, 30, 61, 99–100
Corfina Group, 9
COVID-19 pandemic, 118, 119–136
Crazy Frog, 16
Creative Gorilla Capital, 36
credit cards, 42, 58, 71
Credit Saison, 112
Crewdible, 33
C2C (consumer-to-consumer) platform, 4, 6, 9, 43, 44, 49, 60–61
Cu, Brian, 83
Cuaca, Willson, 8
CyberAgent, 8

D

Dafiti, 32
Darmawan, Budi, 3
Darwis, Andrew, 3
DBS, 104
Deals, 42
Deb, Sreejita, 147
delivery, 10, 40, 42, 46–49, 59, 67. *See also* logistics
DeliveryHero, 31, 36
Detik, 3
Dian Ping, 99
Didi Kuaidi, 79, 84, 86
digital banks, 116

Digital Indonesia: Connectivity and Divergence, 19
Disdus, 18
Djarum Group, 10, 45
Doku, 56–58, 61, 97
Dreiling, Hinrich, 23
DST Global, 35, 70, 79, 84, 95
Dutch investors, 3–5

E
Earlsfield Capital, 33
East Ventures, 8, 12, 33, 34, 35, 92, 101
eBay, 18, 28
Ebihara, Takeshi, 9
E-Commerce Road Map, 52, 64–65
Edion, Leontinus Alpha, 6, 7, 9
education, 129, 131–132, 134
Egg, Arnold, 3–5
electric motorbikes, 157
Eleutian Technology, 29
Elevenia, 28, 51
Emtek Group, 43–44, 86, 122
ESB, 129, 133
Escapex, 87
escrow system, 6, 41, 59
ESG (environmental, social, and governance) values, 81, 138, 147, 156–157
Eto, Batara, 8
Eurazeo Smart City, 34
e-wallet, 42, 44, 57, 105, 113, 143
Experian, 81, 88

F
Fabelio, 124, 130
Facebook, 24, 96, 97, 122
Fadillah, Arief, 157
Faibis, Nathaniel, 30
Farallon Capital, 79
Faspay, 61
Fazz, 113
FedEx, 67
Fenox VC, 33
Ficari, Giacomo, 24
Finantier, 34
Finch Capital, 33
Finger, Max, 18
Finku, 34
Finpay, 61
fintech (financial technology) sector, 42, 44, 104–118, 151–153
fishing industry, 144, 147, 155
Fituh, 36
500 Global, 34, 83, 99
500 Startups, 97, 99
FJ Labs, 35
Flash Coffee, 36–37
Floodgate, 70
food security, 132–133, 144–145
Foodpanda, 23, 26, 30, 31
Forbes, 32
foreign currencies, 57
Fox Ventures, 33
fraud, 40, 41
    prevention of, 60, 62
French Partners, 88

FundedHere, 33
Funding Societies, 111
Fungkong, Victor, 7
Future Shape, 34

G
Garena Interactive Holding, 40–41, 49–50
Gates Foundation, 128
GDP Venture, 4, 45
gender equality, 146–147
General Atlantic, 50
Genesia Ventures, 34
German investors, 12, 15–37
Get, 87
GFG (Global Fashion Group), 32
GFC (Global Founders Capital), 12, 16, 36
GGV Capital, 84, 86
GIC, 122
Global Mediacom, 8, 96
GMO VenturePartners, 34
Go suite, 80
Gogo print, 30
Gojek, 28–29, 31, 32, 42, 46, 47, 60, 74–89, 94–97, 100, 101, 115, 122, 128, 131, 134, 135, 150
Golden Gate Ventures, 34, 93
GoMed, 131
Gonzalez, Juan, 62
Goodwater Capital, 34, 35, 36
Google, 27, 40, 87, 95, 96, 97, 121, 122, 150

GoSend, 59
GoSure, 115
Gothaer Group, 24
GoTo Group, 32, 36
Grab, 74–89, 94, 109, 115
GrabBike, 77, 78
GrabFood, 79, 87
greenhouse gases. *See* ESG values
Groupon, 17, 18
GudangAda, 133

H
Hai, The Kim, 68
Halodoc, 46, 85, 128, 131, 134
Handoko, Budi, 69, 70
Hangry, 36
HappyFresh, 81, 87
Hartono family, 4, 10, 45
Haryono, Benedicto, 36
Haubold, Stefan, 24
healthcare, 130–131, 153–154
Heritas Capital, 33
Herucahyono, Nugroho, 9
Hijra Bank, 115
Hillhouse Capital, 84
Hipcar, 33
hiring, 7–8, 19–20, 27, 45
Hitijahubessy, Adrianus, 111
Hi2 Global Venture Fund, 34
Holtzbrinck Ventures, 25, 26
Home24, 30
Honda, 85
HSBC, 86

INDEX

Hypermart, 48
Hyundai, 87

I
Idapted, 29, 99
Ideosource, 33
IFC (International Finance
    Corporation), 146
iKaaz, 81, 87
Impack Ventures, 36
Indies Capital Partners, 100
Indonesia
    beginnings of digital economy
        in, 2–3, 40
    financial sector in, 103–118
    forecasts for, 1, 150–151
    logistics issues in, 63–64, 73–75
    pandemic in, 118, 119–136
    role of MSMEs in, 138–147
    VC landscape in, 101
IndonesiaFlight, 46
Indonesian Fintech Association, 111
Indonesian Payment System Blueprint
    2025, 116
Indonusa Dwitama, 7
Insignia Ventures Partners, 34, 70
instant delivery, 42
InStore kiosks, 46
insurance, 108, 110, 115, 152
Integra Partners, 35
International Labour
    Organization, 146
International Monetary Fund, 139

Intudo Ventures, 34
Invesco, 88
investments, online, 44, 110,
    115, 151–152
iPayMu, 58–59, 61

J
Jabong, 32
Jakarta, 8, 73–74, 78
Jamba!, 16, 18
J&T Express, 68–69
Japanese investors, 8–9, 15
JD.com, 87, 88, 95, 96, 101
JD.ID, 51, 88, 96
Jempol, 67
Jendela360, 46
Jeneration Capital, 89
JNE, 64, 66–67
JPMorgan, 26
Julo, 100, 111, 112
Jungle Ventures, 93
Juwara, 44

K
Kaizenvest, 33
Kartuku, 76, 80, 83, 84, 86
Kasikornbank, 81, 87
Kaskus, 2–4, 10, 45
Keystone Ventures, 50
keywords, targeting, 27
Khazanah Nasional Bhd, 50
Kim, Steven, 23, 29
Kinnevik AB, 25, 26

204

Kioson, 66
Kitabisa, 88
KKR, 79, 85, 95, 96, 97
Kleiner Perkins, 62
Klikdaily, 33
KoinWorks, 36, 100, 111, 136, 140, 142, 146
Koltiva, 145, 155
Kopi Kenangan, 36
Koprol, 8
Kredit Usaha Rakyat program, 52
Kredivo, 112–113, 115
Krom Bank Indonesia, 115
Krungsri Finnovate, 89
K3 Ventures, 35, 86
Kube VC, 33
Kudo, 81, 86
Kumparan, 87, 88
Kuncoro, Hadi, 29
Kusuma, Derianto, 12

L
Lalamove, 134
Lamido, 24
Lamoda, 25
Lamudi, 24
Lawadinata, Ken Dean, 4
Lazada, 23, 24, 26, 27, 30, 32, 40, 42, 47–48, 51, 78, 83, 96
LazMall, 48
Lee, Jet, 68
Leftshift, 78, 85
Lemonilo, 36

lending
  to consumers, 10, 106, 108, 109–118, 152–153
  to MSMEs, 107, 139–140, 142
Liao, Sean, 29
Lightspeed Venture Partners, 35, 70
LinkAja, 81, 89
Lippo Group, 33, 41, 48, 49, 51, 109
Lo, Moses, 61, 62
logistics, 47, 63–70, 130, 133–134. *See also* delivery
Loket, 86
Longbang Express, 69
Lummo, 36
Lupker, Remco, 3–5
Lyft, 84

M
Ma, Jack, 48
Macquaries, 86
Madura, 141
Majoo, 136, 143
MAKA Motors, 157
Makarim, Nadiem, 23, 28–29, 75–76, 80, 83, 84
Mandiri Clickpay, 58
Mapan, 86
MAPeMall, 60
marketing, 143. *See also* advertising
Matahari Mall, 29, 41, 48–49, 51, 60
Matahari.com, 49
Mazza, Antonio, 36
McKinsey, 69, 75, 83

INDEX

MDI Ventures, 99
MDS, 49
Meituan, 87, 95, 96
Meta, 89
Microsoft, 87, 122
MidPlaza, 60
Midtrans, 59–60, 61, 86
mitra, 105
Mitra Bukalapak, 44, 115, 138, 142
Mitra Tokopedia, 43, 44
Mitsubishi, 81, 89, 122
Mixi, 8
MMS Group, 36
mobile devices, 42
Modalku, 111, 115
Moini, Kian, 24
Moka, 89, 100, 115
Moladin, 35
mortgage market, 153
motorbikes, 28, 47, 74–78, 157
MSMEs (micro, small, and medium enterprises), 6, 9
  loans to, 107
  and pandemic, 118, 133, 136
  relevance of, 137–148
MUFG Innovation Partners, 88
Multi-Family Office, 34, 35, 36
MVCommerce, 85
MyShortCart, 57
MyTeksi, 76, 83

N
Nagel, Lukas, 23
Namshi, 32
Naspers, 5
National Research Foundation of Singapore, 92
Nebeng, 85
Netprice, 8, 59–60
New Oriental Group, 99
1982 Ventures, 35, 36
Ninja Van, 88
Nirvana, 97
NOBI, 35
Northstar Group, 35, 77
NSI Ventures, 84
Nusa Satu Inti Artha, 57
Nusantics, 126

O
oBike, 81, 86, 87
Oetomo, Teddy, 143
OfficeFab, 23, 29, 31
Offmeat, 35
ojek, 28, 47, 74–78, 83, 84, 157
OJK (Otoritas Jasa Keuangan), 52–53, 112
Ola, 84
OLX Indonesia, 3
one-day shopping festivals, 27, 48, 51
OneKlik, 46
online marketplace, first, 6
Ontario Teachers Pension Plan, 50
Opamuratawongse, Phil, 69
Openspace, 84, 85
OPPO, 68
O2O (online-to-offline) services, 43, 46, 48–49, 52, 66

OVO, 109, 115
OYO, 81, 87

P
P&G, 50
Partech, 34
PasarPolis, 80, 87, 89, 110, 115
Pathao, 86
Payfazz, 97, 100, 113, 114, 115
PayLater, 80, 87
Payleven, 23, 30
payments market, 6–7, 9, 41, 42, 46, 47, 49, 57–63, 108, 115
PayPal, 57, 58, 61, 89, 96, 97, 122
PayPal Mafia, 28
Peak XV Partners, 79
Peddisetty, Abhinay, 36
Pegasus Tech Ventures, 33
pharmacies, 154
Phenomen Ventures, 26
Pianta, 78, 85
pickup points, 49
PINA, 152
Pinang, 115
Ping, Xu Xiao, 99
Ping An, 81, 87
Pinhome, 34
Pinspire, 23, 25, 30, 31
Pintek, 33
Pinterest, 23
PLDT (Philippine Long Distance Telephone Company), 25, 47
Pluang, 80, 88, 89
PohonDana, 115

Pos Indonesia, 46, 58, 59, 64–66
Poslong (Pos Logistik Indonesia), 65
Prasetia Dwidharma, 33
Prelo, 44
Pricepanda, 24
Prinzio, 30
Prism, 60
Promogo, 87
Prosus Ventures, 70
Prudential, 128

Q
Qatar Investment Authority, 122
Qlapa, 33
Qoala, 97
Qraved, 29, 97, 99

R
RADC (Rosé All Day Cosmetics), 155
RAENA, 146, 147
Rahadi, Adi Wahyu, 143
Rakuten, 8, 60, 85
R&D (research and development), 45, 56, 78, 79, 82
Rasyid, Fajrin, 9
Rebel Foods, 88
Rebright Partners, 9
refunds, 50
regional trade, 48
regulation
 of banking, 116–117, 139–140
 of e-money instruments, 70–71
 of fintech development, 52–53
Reku, 152

INDEX

restaurants, 133
Rheingau Founders, 83
Riady family, 48
Ribbit Capital, 34
ride-hailing. *See ojek*
Rocket Internet, 12, 13, 16–37, 39–40, 47, 78, 80, 83
Rocket Mafia, 28, 39, 93
RPX, 67
Ruangguru, 132
Rudiantara, Minister, 65

S

Safeboda, 88
Saison Capital, 34
Salim, Anthony, 47
Salim Group, 47
Sampoerna Group, 36, 115
Samwer, Karl, 24
Samwer brothers, 12, 16–37, 47, 76, 94
scalability, 6
Schiller, Christian, 24
Sea Indonesia, 100
Sea Limited, 40–41, 50, 98
search engine results, 27
SeedPlus, 97
Segari, 146–147
Seilern, Karl Josef, 23
Sequoia Capital, 35, 41, 69, 70, 78–79, 84, 94, 95, 97, 154, 156
Shipper, 69–70, 130, 133–134
Shopee, 40–41, 45, 49–51, 98, 100
shopping festival, online, 27, 48, 51

SiCepat Express, 68, 69
Simplus, 155
Sinbad, 133, 141
Singaporean investors, 92–93
Sirka, 154
Sjahrir, Pandu, 30, 98, 100
SK Planet, 51
Skor Technologies, 153
Skystar Capital, 33, 35
SNAP national standard, 116
Social Bella, 125–126, 127
social media, 3, 59
Soelistyo, Andrea, 29
Soerijadji, Michael, 30, 100
SoftBank, 41, 43, 79, 84, 85, 86, 88, 94, 155
solar power, 157
Sorabel, 124, 130
Sovereign's Capital, 33
SPAC, 81
Splyt Technologies, 88
Sprout Digital Labs, 5
Square, 23
Statistics Indonesia, 74
Stenbeck family, 25
Stephanus, Ronald, 3
STIC Investment, 89
StickEarn, 88
Stockbit, 110, 152
Stoqo, 125
Stripe, 57, 62
STRIVE, 33
StudiVZ, 25

sukuk, 110
Summit Partners, 26
Suparno, Soeprapto, 66–67
Super, 36, 133, 141
Super Cintaku program, 48
SuperSakti program, 48
SWC Global, 155
Swigo, Rudy Darwin, 68
SwipeRx, 154

T
Tan, Anthony, 75, 76, 80, 83
Tan, Hooi Ling, 75, 76, 80, 83
Tan, Jurist, 83
Tan, Robin, 36
Tan Chong Group, 83
Tanuwijaya, William, 5–9, 15, 41
Tao, Zhang, 99
Taurus Ventures, 34
taxis, 74–76. *See also ojek*
TBS (Toba Bara Sejahtra), 98, 99
Technology Incubation Scheme, 92–93
Teja Ventures, 33
telemedicine, 128, 131, 134
Telkom Indonesia, 28, 51, 99
Telkomsel, 89
Teman Sehat app, 127
Temasek, 47, 69, 87, 122, 150, 156
Tencent, 50, 87, 95, 96, 101
Tengelmann Group, 26
Tenggara, Riky, 30
Tesco Plc, 26
Third Point Ventures, 86

Tiga Pilar Sejahtera Food, 97
Tiger Global, 35, 79, 84, 96, 97
Tiket, 10–11
Tiket.com, 46, 88
TIKI (Citra Van Titipan Kilat), 64, 66–67
TIKI JNE (Tiki Jalur Nugraha Ekakurir), 67
Timmer, Angelique, 140, 142, 146
TIS, 89
Tjipto, Phillip, 36
Tokobagus, 3–5
TokoCash, 42
Tokopedia, 5–9, 15, 32, 39, 40–45, 60, 81, 94–97, 101, 109, 115, 122, 135, 150
Tokyo Century, 81, 85, 88
TotalEnergies, 88
Toyota, 87
traffic, 73–74
transportation, 28, 47, 63–64, 73–78, 83, 84, 157
travel sector, 10–11, 123
Traveloka, 12, 15, 33, 60, 96, 101, 115, 121–123, 125, 126, 135
Trihill Capital, 34, 35, 36
Trip Planner, 81
truck utilization, 63–64
Two Culture Capital, 34

U
Uber, 76, 77, 82, 87
Uber Eats, 79, 87

INDEX

UberMotor, 77, 78
Ula, 30, 36, 97, 133
Unardi, Ferry, 11–12
Undarsa, Mikhael Gaery, 11
Unit Desa village banking network, 113–114
United Family Capital, 36
United Internet, 25
Universitas Indonesia, 88
U.S. investors, 95, 96–97
Ustadiyanto, Riyeke, 59

V

VC (venture capital)
    early, 12, 15–37
    from local firms, 92–93, 98–101
    and pandemic, 121–122, 135
Venmo, 61
Venturra, 33
Verisign, 18
Veritrans Indonesia, 59–60
Verlinvest, 26
Vertex Ventures, 83, 84
Visa, 89, 96, 97, 122

W

Wagely, 35
Walujo, Patrick, 77
Warburg Pincus, 79, 85, 95, 97
warung operators, 43–44, 113, 132, 141, 142
WarungPintar, 141

waste management, 156–157
Waste4Change, 156–157
Wavemaker, 93
wealth tech, 108, 115. *See also* investments
#WeAreNotAfraid, 8
WeChat, 61, 96
Wenas, Hadi, 29
WePay, 89
Westwing, 25
WhatsApp, 61
Wibowo, Raditua, 157
Wihardja, Donald, 99
Wijaya, Tessa, 62
Wimdu, 23, 31–32
women in labor force, 146–147
Wongsoredjo, Steven, 36
World Bank, 146
Wright Partners, 5
Wyder, Rico, 23

X

Xendit, 60–63, 99, 109, 115
Xiaomi, 36
XL Axiata, 28, 51
Xurya, 157

Y

Y Combinator program, 34, 61, 70, 113, 154
Yahoo!, 8
Yamaha, 87

Yaputra, Dimas Surya, 11
Youche, 83

Z
Zaky, Achmad, 9
Zalora, 23, 25, 26, 28, 30, 32, 76, 83
Zappos, 23
Zein, Johari, 66–67
Zhang, Albert, 11–12
Zhang, Jack, 155
Zhen Fund, 99
Zulu, 89